RACHEL AND HER CHILDREN

Books by Jonathan Kozol
Death at an Early Age
Free Schools
The Night Is Dark and I Am Far From Home
Children of the Revolution
On Being a Teacher
Illiterate America

RACHEL AND HER CHILDREN

HOMELESS FAMILIES IN AMERICA

JONATHAN KOZOL

Crown Publishers, Inc.
New York

Publisher's Note: The case histories in this book are taken from actual interviews and research. The relevant facts are real, but names and other identifying details have been changed to protect the privacy of the individuals.

Copyright © 1988 by Jonathan Kozol

Published by Crown Publishers, Inc., 225 Park Avenue South, New York, New York, 10003 and represented in Canada by the Canadian MANDA Group

CROWN is a trademark of Crown Publishers, Inc.
Manufactured in the United States of America

Library of Congress Cataloging-in-Publication Data
Kozol, Jonathan.
    Rachel and her children.
    1. Homeless persons—United States.   2. Poor—United
States.   I. Title.
HV4505.K69   1988   362.5'0973   87-22273
ISBN 0-517-56730-X

10 9 8 7 6 5 4 3 2 1

For Yvonne Ruelas
Beverly Curtis
Michael Stoops

Contents

To The Reader:

Homeless people in this book are not identified by their real names. This decision is dictated in part by the wishes of the people interviewed. It is commonly believed by residents of homeless shelters, including hotels, that they render themselves subject to retaliation or eviction by authorities if they speak with candor to a writer or reporter. For this and other reasons, many have asked me to disguise sufficient details (time, date, place of interview, hotel room, floor number, physical features, exact ages of children in a family, and other identifying details) to assure their anonymity.

In some instances, conversations are condensed and events told to me out of order are resequenced. Dialogue is reconstructed from notes or edited from tapes. Apparent inconsistencies or contradictions that occur from time to time, especially in stories told by children, are allowed to stand. Corrective information is provided in the notes.

All events described to me within this book took place in the locations indicated. All events that I describe firsthand took place in my presence. All words spoken by shelter residents of New York City in this book were spoken by residents of the shelters I describe.

Ordinary People

He was a carpenter. She was a woman many people nowadays would call old-fashioned. She kept house and cared for their five children while he did construction work in New York City housing projects. Their home was an apartment in a row of neat brick buildings. She was very pretty then, and even now, worn down by months of suffering, she has a lovely, wistful look. She wears blue jeans, a yellow jersey, and a bright red ribbon in her hair—"for luck," she says. But luck has not been with this family for some time.

They were a happy and chaotic family then. He was proud of his acquired skills. "I did carpentry. I painted. I could do wallpapering. I earned a living. We spent Sundays walking with our children at the beach." They lived near Coney Island. That is where this story will begin.

"We were at the boardwalk. We were up some. We had been at Nathan's. We were eating hot dogs."

He's cheerful when he recollects that afternoon. The children have long, unruly hair. They range in age from two to ten. They crawl all over him—exuberant and wild.

Peter says that they were wearing summer clothes: "Shorts and sneakers. Everybody was in shorts."

When they were told about the fire, they grabbed the children and ran home. Everything they owned had been destroyed.

"My grandmother's china," she says. "Everything." She adds: "I had that book of gourmet cooking . . ."

What did the children lose?

"My doggy," says one child. Her kitten, born three days before, had also died.

Peter has not had a real job since. "Not since the fire. I had tools. I can't replace those tools. It took me years of work." He explains he had accumulated tools for different jobs, one tool at a time. Each job would enable him to add another tool to his collection. "Everything I had was in that fire."

They had never turned to welfare in the twelve years since they'd met and married. A social worker helped to place them in a homeless shelter called the Martinique Hotel. When we meet, Peter is thirty. Megan is twenty-eight. They have been in this hotel two years.

She explains why they cannot get out: "Welfare tells you how much you can spend for an apartment. The limit for our family is $366. You're from Boston. Try to find a place for seven people for $366 in New York City. You can't do it. I've been looking for two years."

The city pays $3,000 monthly for the two connected rooms in which they live. She shows me the bathroom. Crumbling walls. Broken tiles. The toilet doesn't work. There is a pan to catch something that's dripping from the plaster. The smell is overpowering.

"I don't see any way out," he says. "I want to go home. Where can I go?"

A year later I'm in New York. In front of a Park Avenue hotel I'm facing two panhandlers. It takes a moment before I can recall their names.

They look quite different now. The panic I saw in them a year ago is gone. All five children have been taken from them. Having nothing left to lose has drained them of their desperation.

The children have been scattered—placed in various foster homes. "White children," Peter says, "are in demand by the adoption agencies."

Standing here before a beautiful hotel as evening settles in over New York, I'm reminded of the time before the fire when they had their children and she had her cookbooks and their children had a dog and cat. I remember the words that Peter used: "We were up some. We had been at Nathan's." Although I am not a New Yorker, I know by now what Nathan's is: a glorified hot-dog stand. The other phrase has never left my mind.

Peter laughs. "Up some?"

The laughter stops. Beneath his street-wise manner he is not a hardened man at all. "It means," he says, "that we were happy."

By the time these words are printed there will be at least 500,000 homeless children in America. If all of them were gathered in one city, they would represent a larger population than that of Atlanta, Denver, or St. Louis. Because they are scattered in a thousand cities, they are easily unseen. And because so many die in infancy or lose the strength to struggle and prevail in early years, some will never live to tell their stories.

Not all homeless children will be lost to early death or taken from their parents by the state. Some of their parents will do better than Peter and Megan. Some will be able to keep their children, their stability, their sense of worth. Some will get back their vanished dreams. A few will find jobs again and some may even find a home they can afford. Many will not.

Why are so many people homeless in our nation? What has driven them to the streets? What hope have they to reconstruct their former lives?

The answers will be told in their own words.

Overview:
A Captive State

Since 1980 homelessness has changed its character. What was once a theater of the grotesque (bag ladies in Grand Central Station, winos sleeping in the dusty sun outside the Greyhound station in El Paso) has grown into the common misery of millions.

"This is a new population," said a homeless advocate in Massachusetts. "Many are people who were working all their lives. When they lose their jobs they lose their homes. When they lose their homes they start to lose their families too."

Even in New York City, with its permanent population of the long-term unemployed, 50 percent of individuals served at city shelters during 1984 were there for the first time. The same percentage holds throughout the nation.

The chilling fact, from any point of view, is that small children have become the fastest-growing sector of the homeless. At the time of writing there are 28,000 homeless people in emergency shelters in the city of New York. (An additional 40,000 are believed to be unsheltered citywide.) Of those who are sheltered, about 10,000 are homeless individuals. The remaining 18,000 are parents and children in almost 5,000 families. The average homeless family includes a parent with two or three children. The average child is six years old, the average parent twenty-seven.

In Massachusetts, three fourths of all homeless people are now children and their parents. In certain parts of Massachusetts (Plymouth, Attleboro, and Northampton) 90 to 95 percent of those who have no homes are families with children.

Homeless people are poor people. Four out of ten poor people in America are children, though children make up only one fourth of our population. The number of children living in poverty has grown to 14 million—an increase of 3 million over 1968—while welfare benefits to families with children have declined one third.

Seven hundred thousand poor children, of whom 100,000 have no health insurance, live in New York City. Approximately 20 percent of New York City's children lived in poverty in 1970, 33 percent in 1980, over 40 percent by 1982.

Where are these people?

We have seen that they are in midtown Manhattan. They are also in the streets of Phoenix, Salt Lake City, Philadelphia, San Antonio, Miami, and St. Paul. They are in The Steel Belt. They are in the Sun Belt. They are in Kansas City and Seattle. They are in the heartland of America.

In Denver, where evictions rose 800 percent in 1982, hundreds of families were locked on waiting lists for public housing. Many were forced to live in shelters or the streets. In Cleveland, in one classic situation, the loss of a home precipitated by the layoffs in a nearby plant led to the dissolution of a family: the adolescent daughter put in foster care, the wife and younger children ending up on welfare, the husband landing in a public shelter when he wasn't sleeping underneath a bridge. Cleveland was obliged to open shelters and soup kitchens in blue-collar neighborhoods that housed traditional white ethnic populations.

The *Milwaukee Journal* wrote: "The homeless in our midst are no longer mainly urban hobos and bag ladies. In recent months, joblessness has pushed heretofore self-reliant families into this subculture." In Michigan, in 1982, the loss of jobs in heavy industry forced Governor Milliken to declare "a state of human emergency"—a declaration other governors may be forced to contemplate by 1988.

As an easterner, I had at first assumed that most of these

families must be urban, nonwhite, unemployable—perhaps a great deal like the ghetto families I have worked with for much of my life. In 1985, however, I was given an opportunity to visit in over 50 cities and in almost every region of the nation. My hosts were governors and other local politicians, leaders of industry, organizers of the working poor, leaders and advocates of those who recently had joined the unemployed, teachers, school-board members, farmers, bankers, owners of local stores. Often they were people who had never met each other and had never even been in the same room with one another, even though they lived in the same towns and cities. They had come together now out of their shared concern over the growth of poverty, the transformation of the labor market, and the rising numbers of those people who no longer could find work at all.

I was invited, in most cases, to address the problems of the public schools. Often, however, education issues became overshadowed by more pressing matters. For many poorly educated people, literacy problems proved of little urgency when they were threatened with the loss of work and loss of home. In a depressed industrial town in Pennsylvania, Lutheran church leaders spoke of the loss of several hundred jobs as truck and auto manufacture left the area and families saw their savings dwindle and their unemployment benefits and pensions disappear while rents rose, food prices climbed, and federal benefits declined.

"Yes, there are new jobs," a minister said. "There's a new McDonald's and a Burger King. You can take home $450 in a month from jobs like that. That might barely pay the rent. What do you do if somebody gets sick? What do you do for food and clothes? These may be good jobs for a teenager. Can you ask a thirty-year-old man who's worked for G.M. since he was eighteen to keep his wife and kids alive on jobs like that? There are jobs cleaning rooms in the hotel you're staying at. Can you expect a single mother with three kids to hold her life together with that kind of work? All you hear about these days are so-called service jobs—it makes me wonder where America is going. If we aren't producing anything of value, will we keep our nation going on hamburger stands? Who is all this 'service' for, if no one's got a real job making something of real worth?"

In Oklahoma, Arkansas and Texas I met heads of families who had been, only a year or two before, owners of farms, employees of petroleum firms, shopkeepers who supplied the farmers and the oil workers. They had lost their farms, their jobs, their stores. Bankers in Oklahoma City spoke about the rising number of foreclosures. "Oil and agriculture—those are everything for people here. Both are dying. Where will these people go after their farms are boarded and their restaurants and barbershops and hardware stores have been shut down?"

The answers were seen in Phoenix and Los Angeles, where the shelters overflowed and people slept in huge encampments on the edges of the seamy areas of town. In one city homeless families lived in caves. I went out to visit. I had never seen a family living in a cave before.

In Portland, Oregon, the governor told me of some counties in which unemployment caused by the declining lumber industry had climbed above 30 percent. Where did the lumber workers go? I met some of them the same night in a homeless shelter by the Burnside Bridge. A pregnant woman and her husband spoke to me while waiting for the soup line to be formed. "We had good work until last year. Since then we've had no home. Our kids were put in foster care." They had been sleeping on a plywood plank supported by the girders of the bridge. The traffic was two feet above their heads.

"The sound of the trucks puts me to sleep at night," she said. I learned that even makeshift housing space under the bridge was growing scarce.

In San Antonio I met a father with two boys who had been sleeping for four months next to the highway not far from the Hyatt Regency Hotel. He sold blood plasma twice a week to buy food for his kids. "They draw my blood, put it in a centrifuge, take the white cells, and inject the red cells back into my arm." If he showed up four weeks straight he got a bonus. In a good month he made $100. "The blood places," he told me, "poor people call them 'stab labs.' They're all over." He showed me a card he carried listing stab labs, with phone numbers and addresses, in a dozen cities. He had been an auto worker in Detroit. When he lost his job his wife became depressed and since was hospitalized. He had developed crippling asthma—"from the panic and the tension, I believe." He had thought mistakenly that San Antonio might offer health and labor and cheap housing that were not available in Michigan.

In Miami I met a woman, thirty-five years old, from Boston. She had attended Girls' Latin, the same high school that my mother had attended. After graduation she had gone to college and had worked for many years until she was the victim of a throat disease that led to complications that wiped out her savings, forced her to lose her home, ended her marriage, and at last compelled her to give up her kids. She'd moved to Miami hoping it would help her health but couldn't cope with illness, loss of family, loss of home—and now was sleeping on Miami Beach.

She had a tube in her stomach to bypass her damaged throat. At a shelter run by Catholic brothers she would pulverize the food, mix it with water, and inject the liquid mix into her tube.

In New York I spoke with Robert Hayes, counsel to the National Coalition for the Homeless. Hayes and his co-workers said that three fourths of the newly homeless in America are families with children.

In Washington, D.C., in late September 1986, I spent an afternoon with the director of a shelter, Sandy Brawders, one of those saints and martyrs of whom Robert Hayes has said, only half-jokingly, the homeless movement is primarily composed. ("There are the saints," he says, "and then there are the martyrs who have to put up with the saints.") Sandy told me that the homeless population was exploding in the District; the largest growth in numbers was among young children and their parents.

Four months later, the *Washington Post* reported that the number of homeless families in the District had increased 500 percent in just one year and that there were 12,000 people on a waiting list for public housing, with a waiting period of more than seven years.

Home in New England in a small town north of Boston, I shared some of these stories with a woman who works at the counter of the cleaner's where I take my shirts. "You didn't have to go to San Antonio and Florida," she said. "There's hundreds of homeless families just a couple miles from here." When I asked her where, she said: "In Ipswich, Gloucester, Haverhill

. . . There are families who are living in the basement of my church." After a moment's pause she told me this: "After my husband lost his job—we had some troubles then, I was divorced . . . I had to bring my family to the church . . . Well, we're still there."

How many are homeless in America?

The U.S. Department of Health and Human Services (HHS), relying on groups that represent the homeless, suggested a figure of 2 million people in late 1983. Diminished numbers of low-income dwelling units and diminished welfare grants during the four years since may give credence to a current estimate, accepted by the Coalition for the Homeless, of 3 to 4 million people.

There is much debate about the numbers; the debate has a dreamlike quality for me because it parallels exactly the debates about the numbers of illiterate Americans. Government agencies again appear to contradict each other and attempt to peg the numbers low enough to justify inaction—or, in this case, negative action in the form of federal cuts.

Officials in the U.S. Department of Housing and Urban Development (HUD) puzzled congressional leaders during hearings held in 1984 by proposing a low estimate of 250,000 to 350,000 homeless people nationwide. The study from which HUD's estimate was drawn had contemplated as many as 586,000 people, but this number was discredited in its report.

A House subcommittee revealed serious flaws in the HUD study. Subsequent investigations indicated HUD had "pressured its consultants to keep the estimates low." HUD's researchers, for example, suggested a "reliable" low estimate of 12,000 homeless persons in New York City on a given night in January 1984. Yet, on the night in question, over 16,000 people had been given shelter in New York; and this, of course, does not include the larger number in the streets who had received no shelter. U.S. Representative Henry Gonzalez termed HUD's study intentionally deceptive.

Estimates made by shelter operators in twenty-one selected cities in October 1986 total about 230,000 people. This sampling does not include Chicago, San Francisco, Houston, Cleveland, Philadelphia, Baltimore, Atlanta, Pittsburgh, St. Paul, San Diego, or Detroit. With estimates from these and other major cities added, the total would exceed 400,000.

Even this excludes the metropolitan areas around these cities and excludes those middle-sized cities—Lawrence, Lowell, Worcester, Brockton, Attleboro, for example, all in Massachusetts—in which the loss of industrial jobs has marginalized hundreds of thousands of the working poor. Though technically not unemployed, most of these families live in economic situations so precarious that they cannot meet the basic costs of life, particularly rent, which in all these cities has skyrocketed. Nor does this include the rural areas of the Midwest and the Plains states, the oiltowns of the Southwest, the southern states from which assembly plants and textile industries have fled, lumber counties such as those in Oregon and their New England counterparts in northern Maine. The homeless in these areas alone, if added to the major-city totals, would bring a cautious national count above 1.5 million.

We would be wise, however, to avoid the numbers game. Any search for the "right number" carries the assumption that we may at last arrive at an acceptable number. There is no acceptable number. Whether the number is 1 million or 4 million or the administration's estimate of less than a million, there are too many homeless people in America.*

Homeless people are, of course, impossible to count because they are so difficult to find. That is intrinsic to their plight. They have no address beyond a shelter bed, room number, tent or cave. In this book I follow my own sense that the number is between 2 and 3 million. If we include those people housing organizers call the "hidden homeless"—families doubled up illegally with other families, with the consequent danger that both families may be arbitrarily evicted—we are speaking of much larger numbers.

---

* One reason for discrepancies in estimates derives from various ways of counting. Homeless advocates believe that all who ask for shelter during any extended period of time ought to be termed homeless. The government asks: "How many seek shelter on a given day?" If the HUD study, cited above, had considered those who asked for shelter in the course of one full year, its upper estimate would have exceeded 1.7 million.

In 1983, 17,000 families were doubled up illegally in public housing in New York City. The number jumped to 35,000 by spring of 1986. Including private as well as public housing, the number had risen above 100,000 by November 1986. If we accept the New York City estimate of three to four family members in each low-income household, the total number of people (as opposed to families) doubled up in public and private housing in New York is now above 300,000.

The line from "doubling up" to homelessness is made explicit in a study by Manhattan's borough president: At least 50 percent of families entering New York City shelters (1986) were previously doubled up. Nationwide, more than 3 million families now are living doubled up.

It is, however, not only families doubled up or tripled up who are in danger of eviction. Any poor family paying rent or mortgage that exceeds one half of monthly income is in serious danger. Over 6 million American households pay half or more of income for their rent. Of these, 4.7 million pay 60 percent or more. Of mortgaged homeowners, 2 million pay half or more of income for their housing. Combining these households with those who are doubled up, it appears that well above 10 million families may be living near the edge of homelessness in the United States.

Why are they without homes?

Unreflective answers might retreat to explanations with which readers are familiar: "family breakdown," "drugs," "culture of poverty," "teen pregnancies," "the underclass," etc. While these are precipitating factors for some people, they are not the cause of homelessness. *The cause of homelessness is lack of housing.*

Half a million units of low-income housing are lost every year to condominium conversion, abandonment, arson, demolition. Between 1978 and 1980, median rents climbed 30 percent for those in the lowest income sector. Half these people paid nearly three quarters of their income for their housing. Forced to choose between housing and food, many of these families soon were driven to the streets. That was only a beginning. After

1980, rents rose at even faster rates. In Boston, between 1982 and 1984, over 80 percent of housing units renting below $300 disappeared, while the number of units renting above $600 more than doubled.

Hard numbers, in this instance, may be of more help than social theory in explaining why so many of our neighbors end up in the streets. By the end of 1983, vacancies averaged 1 to 2 percent in San Francisco, Boston and New York. Vacancies in *low-income* rental units averaged less than 1 percent in New York City by 1987. In Boston they averaged .5 percent. Landlords saw this seller's market as an invitation to raise rents. Evictions grew. In New York City, with a total of nearly 2 million rental units, there were half a million legal actions for eviction during 1983.* Half of these actions were against people on welfare, four fifths of whom were paying rents above the maximum allowed by welfare. Rent ceilings established by welfare in New York were frozen for a decade at the levels set in 1975. They were increased by 25 percent in 1984; but rents meanwhile had nearly doubled.

During these years the White House cut virtually all federal funds to build or rehabilitate low-income housing. Federal support for low-income housing dropped from $28 billion to $9 billion between 1981 and 1986. "We're getting out of the housing business. Period," said a HUD deputy assistant secretary in 1985.

The consequences now are seen in every city of America.

What distinguishes housing from other basic needs of life? Why, of many essentials, it is the first to go?

Housing has some unique characteristics, as urban planning specialist Chester Hartman has observed. One pays for housing well in advance. The entire month's rent must be paid on the first day of any rental period. One pays for food only a few days before it is consumed, and one always has the option

---

* Half a million families, of course, were not evicted in one year. Many of these legal actions are "repeats." Others are unsuccessful. Still others are settled with payment of back rent.

of delaying food expenditures until just prior to eating. Housing is a nondivisible and not easily adjustable expenditure. "One cannot pay less rent for the next few months by not using the living room," Hartman observes. By contrast, one can rapidly and drastically adjust one's food consumption: for example, by buying less expensive food, eating less, or skipping meals. "At least in the short run," Hartman notes, "the consequences of doing so are not severe." The cost of losing housing and then paying for re-entry to the housing system, on the other hand, is very high, involving utility and rent deposits equal sometimes to twice or three times the cost of one month's rent. For these reasons, one may make a seemingly "rational" decision to allocate scarce funds to food, clothing, health care, transportation, or the search for jobs—only to discover that one cannot pay the rent. "Some two and a half million people are displaced annually from their homes," writes Hartman. While some find other homes and others move in with their friends or relatives, the genesis of epidemic and increasing homelessness is there.

Is this a temporary crisis?

As families are compelled to choose between feeding their children or paying their rent, homelessness has taken on the characteristics of a captive state. Economic recovery has not relieved this crisis. Adults whose skills are obsolete have no role in a revived free market. "The new poor," according to the U.S. Conference of Mayors, "are not being recalled to their former jobs, because their formers plants are not being reopened. . . . Their temporary layoffs are from dying industries."

Two million jobs in steel, textiles, and other industries, according to the AFL-CIO, have disappeared each year since 1979. Nearly half of all new jobs created from 1979 to 1985 pay poverty-level wages.

Increased prosperity among the affluent, meanwhile, raises the profit motive for conversion of low-income properties to upscale dwellings. The Conference of Mayors reported in January 1986 that central-city renewal has accelerated homelessness by dispossession of the poor. The illusion of recovery, therefore, has the ironic consequence of worsening the status of the homeless and near-homeless, while diluting explanations for their presence and removing explanations for their indigence.

But it is not enough to say that this is not a "temporary" crisis: Congressional research indicates that it is likely to grow worse. The House Committee on Government Operations noted in April 1985 that, due to the long advance-time needed for a federally assisted housing program to be terminated, the United States has yet to experience the full impact of federal cuts in housing aid. "The committee believes that current federal housing policies, combined with the continuing erosion of the private inventory of low-income housing, will add to the growth of homelessness. . . ." The "harshest consequences," the committee said, are "yet to come."

Why focus on New York?

New York does more than any other city I have visited to serve the homeless. But what it does is almost imperceptible in context of the need.

New York is spending, in 1987, $274 million to provide emergency shelter to its homeless population. Of this sum, about $150 million is assigned to homeless families with children. Nonetheless, the growth in numbers of the dispossessed far outpaces city allocations. Nine hundred families were given shelter in New York on any given night in 1978; 2,900 by 1984; 4,000 by the end of 1985; 5,000 by the spring of 1987. The city believes the number will exceed 6,000 by the summer of 1988. With an average of 2.3 children in each homeless family in New York, and with a significant number of two-parent families in this group (many men, not being included on a woman's welfare budget, have not been recorded), these estimates suggest that over 20,000 family members will be homeless in New York by 1988: nearly the number of residents of Laramie, Wyoming, or Key West. This does not include the estimated increase in those homeless *individuals* (12,000 or more) who will be given shelter by the end of 1988; nor does it include at least another 40,000 people who will be refused or will no longer try to locate shelter. Nor does it include the hidden homeless (over 300,000). By 1990, the actual homeless, added to the swelling numbers of the hidden homeless, will exceed 400,000 in New York. The population of New York is 7 million.

There is another reason to examine New York City. New York is unique in many ways but, in homelessness as in high fashion, it gives Americans a preview of the future. Millions of Americans, secure at home on New Year's Eve with relatives or friends, watch the celebration in Times Square on television as they face the promises or dangers of the year ahead. Almost half the homeless families sheltered in hotels in New York City now are living within twenty blocks of Forty-second Street and Broadway.

The Martinique Hotel at Herald Square and the Prince George Hotel on Twenty-eigth Street near Fifth Avenue, both under the same management, are the largest family shelters in New York—and, very likely, in America.

What is the route a family takes when it is dispossessed in New York City?

The first step brings a family to its Income Maintenance (welfare) center. If the center cannot offer shelter before evening, the family goes to one of a number of Emergency Assistance Units (EAUs), which are open all night and on weekends. The EAU assigns the family either to a barracks shelter (these large, sometimes undivided buildings are called "congregate" shelters by the city) or to a hotel. For several years, city policy has been to send such families to a barracks shelter first, on the assumption that the publicized discomforts of these places—inability of residents to sleep or dress in privacy, for instance—will discourage families doubled up or living in substandard buildings from requesting shelter.*

Once families are placed in such a shelter, many are obliged

---

* For many years, the best known and most feared of these barracks was the Robert Clemente shelter in the Bronx. The Clemente, housing over 200 people in a large gymnasium, was ordered closed in early 1986 by state officials. The city resisted the state's order. After a suit brought by the Coalition for the Homeless, the Clemente was closed in September 1986. Several other barracks shelters continued to operate. The city's policy on congregate shelters may be changing somewhat at the present time. See Appendix.

to go back to their welfare center in the morning in the effort to restore lost welfare benefits. (Families are frequently cut off by sudden changes of address.) Many end up at an EAU at night hoping for assignment to a safer shelter. After the barracks, the next stopping place is likely to be one of a large number of "short-term" hotels, where a family may spend a night, a weekend, or part of a week, after which they go back to the EAU in the hope of being given a less temporary placement. This hope is generally disappointed. "Instead," according to a study by the New York City Council, "the homeless family often must stay at another short-term hotel for a few days before returning to the EAU. This cycle can continue for months, even years."

The luckier families are sometimes placed at this point in a "twenty-eight day hotel." The time limit is established by a number of hotels in order to deny the family occupancy rights, which take effect after a residence of thirty days. After this interval the family goes back to an EAU in the hope of being placed in one of the long-term hotels.

There are hundreds of families, however, who for various reasons get no placement and spend weeks commuting between the daytime welfare center and the evening EAU. According to the New York Human Resources Administration (HRA), families are not to be forced to sleep all night at EAUs. As we will see, this has happened frequently. Because the HRA is "able to place a family anywhere in New York City," the city council has observed, "this seemingly endless shuttling between hotels and shelters can come to resemble a game of 'human pinball.' " Two thirds of these pinballs are dependent children.

The next stage, one that many families do not reach for months, is to be placed in one of the long-term hotels. There were fifty-five of these hotels when I first visited New York in 1985. There now are over sixty. Approximately 3,400 families had been placed in these hotels by 1986. The rest remained in congregate shelters, in short-term hotels, or (those who were very fortunate) in model shelters operated by nonprofit groups.

Of the hotels, eleven house more than 100 families each. Of these, all but three are in Manhattan. Six hotels, all in Manhattan, house a total of approximately 1,500 families. Although populations in particular hotels rise and fall somewhat inexplicably, the three largest (Prince George, Martinique, and Holland) together housed over 1,000 families at the start of 1986. While the Prince George housed 444 families and the Martinique 389, family size in the Martinique was larger than the norm, so more children may have been living in this building than in any other shelter in New York.*

The average length of stay in these hotels in 1986 was thirteen months. In the Martinique it was longer: sixteen months. In one hotel, the Carter, near Times Square, length of stay had grown to nearly four years at the time of writing.

The city council notes that families living in two model shelters have a shorter length of stay: eight months and four months respectively. These are also the facilities that charge the city least for rental and provide the most effective social services, including help in finding housing. The city council believes this represents a strong rebuttal to the arguments in favor of "deterrence." Comfortable and healthy shelter does not seem to foster lethargy or to induce dependence. We will return to this.

The next step for homeless families in long-term hotels is to begin the search for housing. For a number of reasons which we will learn directly from the residents of these hotels, getting out to search for housing is a difficult task. Because of the shortage of low-income housing, which has brought these people here to start with, the search they are obliged to undertake is almost always self-defeating. Even for public housing in New York, the waiting list contains 200,000 names. There are only 175,000 public-housing units in New York. Manhattan Borough President David Dinkins calculates the waiting time at eighteen years.

After eighteen months of residence in a hotel, a family is allowed to use a city van to look for housing. At the Martinique, however, the waiting time is thirty months. Only thirty-five families in the Martinique have lived here long enough to meet this stipulation. Pregnant women in their third trimester and

---

* At the time of my first visit (December 1985) there were over 1,400 children in 389 families in the Martinique. By June of 1987, according to the city, there were 438 families in the Martinique.

mothers with infants are now given first priority.

What is the breakdown of the costs in New York City?

The small but excellent shelters operated by nonprofit groups charge the city $34 to $41 nightly to give housing to a family of four. Hotels like the Martinique charge $63 nightly for a family of this size. Rents in the Martinique Hotel are said to be determined by the number of people in a room or by the number of rooms a family is assigned. Families of five or more are generally given two rooms. Average monthly rents may range from $1,900 (family of four) to about $3,000 (family of six). A barracks shelter costs $65 a night to house a family of four people; but additional costs for social services and administration, according to the *New York Times*, bring the actual cost of barracks shelters to about $200 nightly for a family of four— $70,000 if projected for a year. Cost and quality bear no relation to each other.

Several mothers of large families in the Martinique have observed that rental costs alone over the course of three years would be equal to the purchase price of a nice home. The city pays only one quarter of these hotel costs. The state pays an additional quarter. The remaining half is paid from federal funds.

What forms of support do homeless families regularly receive?

If unsheltered, virtually none. If sheltered, and enrolled on all the proper lists, they receive some combination of the following: a twice-monthly AFDC allocation (Aid to Families with Dependent Children) to meet basic costs of life; a monthly food-stamp allocation; a "restaurant allowance," calculated by Robert Hayes in 1986 at seventy-one cents per meal per person; a very small sum of money to pay transportation costs to aid in search of housing; Medicaid; an allocation for nutrition supplements to pregnant women and to children under five. This assistance—a major weapon in preventing infant death—is know as WIC (Women, Infants, Children). More than half the women and children eligible for WIC in New York City don't receive it.*

In addition to these benefits, a family in the Martinique receives a rental check for the hotel. This is a two-party check and must be obtained by going to a welfare center. The city requires families to travel, often considerable distances, to obtain these checks at welfare centers in the neighborhoods from which they were displaced. A woman living in the Martinique almost two years travels three hours by bus and subway twice a month, and waits an average of four hours, to receive the check she then hands over at the desk in the hotel.

What are the chances of getting out of the hotel and into a real home?

We have seen the waiting period for public housing. For private housing a number of programs, both federal and local, offer subsidies to bridge the gap between the family's income and prevailing rents. Chief among these is Section Eight, a federally supported plan that offers a "certificate" to an eligible family, which is then presented to a landlord as a guarantee that government will pay a certain portion of the rent. Federal cuts in Section Eight make these certificates quite scarce. The reluctance of landlords to accept them often renders their possession worthless. Once a certificate has been assigned, it must be used in a fixed period of time. In one familiar instance, a woman who has lived in several places like the Martinique has been "recertified" for seven years but cannot find a landlord to accept her.

Without subsidies, the maximum rent a family on welfare is allowed to pay in New York City is $244 for a family of three, $270 for a family of four. If the government were to raise these limits by $100, sufficient to approach the lowest rents in New York City, the cost would still be less than one-fifth what is spent for hotel rentals.*

---

* The WIC program—reduced by the Reagan administration by $5 billion from 1982 to 1985—reaches about one-third of those who need it nationwide.

* Rent allowances in New York City will rise an average of $35 in 1988.

Who are the people in these buildings? Are they alcoholics, mentally ill people, prostitutes, drug addicts, or drug dealers?

Some of them are; and some of this group were probably as tortured and disordered long before they came here as they are right now. Most, if those I've come to know are a fair sample, certainly were not—not before the sledgehammer of dispossession knocked them flat. Many people in these buildings do need medical help; some need psychiatric care, which they are not receiving. But the focus of this book is not on ancillary apsects of the fact of homelessness. It is on the *meaning* of that fact. The emphasis, again, is not on individuals, though individual homeless people will be seen and heard from in these pages; the focus is on families and children. The focus, again, is not on "the urban underclass," though some of the families we will meet are products of an underclass existence; the focus, rather, is on the way that homelessness *creates* an underclass, enhances the underclass that may already have existed, and, combining newly poor and always-poor together in one common form of penury, assigns the children of them all to an imperiled life. Black families represent the largest single group in New York City's shelters; but many who are white, Hispanic, and of multiracial parentage are homeless too. All participate in one desegregating fact: absolute destitution which, unlike most other aspects of life in America, is blind to color, race or place of birth.

It is worth adding also that this book is not about the "lifestyle homeless"—young people, for example, who leave home out of the wish to drift and wander for a time, much as children of the counterculture might have done in the late 1960s. Such people, if they are in danger, need protection. They are not the subject of this work.

Finally, the emphasis is not on those who were confined in mental hospitals and were deinstitutionalized ten years ago. The emphasis, if anything, is the reverse: It is the *creation* of an institution that makes healthy people ill, normal people clinically depressed, and those who may already be unwell a great deal worse. Few of the people in the Martinique were inates of those institutions that were emptied prior to the 1980s; but all are inmates of an institution now. And it is this institution, one of our own invention, which will mass-produce pathologies, addictions, violence, dependencies, perhaps even a longing for retaliation, for self-vindication, on a scale that will transcend, by far, whatever deviant behaviors we may try to write into their pasts. It is the present we must deal with, and the future we must fear. These, then, are the subjects of this book.

PART ONE

Christmas at the Martinique Hotel

For nine months the infant grows and grows in the womb. . . . At the end an x-ray shows the small but developed body quite bent over on itself and cramped; yet so very much has happened—indeed, a whole new life has come into being. For some hundreds of thousands of American children that stretch of time, those months, represent the longest rest ever to be had, the longest stay in any one place.

—Robert Coles, Uprooted Children

1

A Mood of Resignation

It is possible to picture what a cheerful place this might have been at Christmas in the years when Woodrow Wilson was alive and Edward was the king of England and there was a tsar in Russia and fashionable musicians entertained the patrons in the ballroom of the Martinique Hotel.

A faded brochure from 1910 contains this information: "The Hotel Martinique is located at the intersection of Broadway, Sixth Avenue and 32nd Street, and the plaza thus formed is termed Herald or Greeley Square. . . . One block east is Fifth Avenue, the great residential street of New York. Within a radius of three blocks are to be found the greatest of the city's retail stores, making it an ideal headquarters for shoppers. The best theaters are centered in this vicinity, and the two great Opera Houses are within easy walking distance."

Of the hotel's less formal restaurant, the brochure says this: "The Gentlemen's Broadway Cafe is a veritable architectural gem." The walls and columns of Italian marble "give to this room a richness which is completed by Pompeiian panels of unquestioned merit."

More elegant, it seems, was the Louis XVI dining room: "The wainscoting and pillars are of Circassian walnut, enclosing panels of gold silk tapestry, producing a result described as the most refined public dining room in the city. No better evidence as to the quality of the cuisine can be given than that the restaurants are filled daily with a patronage of the very highest order.

25

The food is invariably good, the wines of exceptional excellence, and the attendance unobtrusive."

The building is said to tower over all adjacent structures, "furnishing views and a degree of light seldom secured in a city hotel. The sanitary precautions, plumbing, etc., are the most complete." Prices for rooms, according to the brochure, were $3.50 a day for room and bath, $6.00 and up for bedroom, bath and parlor.

Prices are higher now. The patronage has changed. The Louis XVI dining room with its Circassian walnut and silk tapestry is gone. The Italian marble, however, is still there. The attendance remains unobtrusive.

December 20, 1985: Heavy chains secure the doorway of the former ballroom. They are removed to let a dozen people enter at a time. The line of people waiting for their lunch goes back about 200 feet. In the semidarkness I see adults trying to keep children at their sides. Some of the kids are acting up, yelling, racing back and forth. A few are sitting on the floor.

This is the lunch program of the Coalition for the Homeless. Meals are served to residents five days a week. The program is organized by a young man named Tom Styron. He has enlisted the help of several women living in the building. Because I have come with him today, he has enlisted my help too.

One of the women sits by the door and checks the names of those who enter. Another woman helps to serve the food. The room is so cold that both keep on their coats. One has a heavy coat. The other has an unlined army jacket. She is very thin, a Puerto Rican woman, and is trembling.

I watch the people coming to the table. The children don't avert their eyes; nor do the women. It is the men who seem most scared: grown men in shabby clothes with nervous hands. They keep their eyes fixed on the floor.

The meal is good: turkey, potatoes, raisins, milk, an orange. It would be enough if it were one of three meals to be eaten in one day. For many, however, this will be the only meal. For an adult who has had no breakfast, this is at best a pacifier to fend off the hunger pangs until late afternoon.

Many of the children have on coats and sweaters. After they

eat, some of them come back to the table, timidly. They ask if there are seconds.

There are no seconds. Several families at the back of the line have to be turned away. In my pocket I have one enormous apple that I bought in Herald Square for fifty cents. I give it to a tall Italian man. He doesn't eat the apple. He polishes it against his shirt. He turns it in his hand, rubs it some more. I watch him bring it back to where he's sitting with his children: one boy, two little girls.

The coalition buys the lunches from the New York Board of Education. The program therefore does not operate when school is not in session. Christmas, for this and other reasons, may be one of the most perilous and isolated times for families in the Martinique Hotel. Christmas is a difficult time for homeless families everywhere in the United States.

It will be 1986 before these people are assembled here again. As they get up to drift into the corridors and cubicles in which they will remain during the last week of the year, some of them stop to thank the people at the table.

The Martinique is not the worst of the hotels for homeless families in New York. Because its tenants have refrigerators (a very precious item for the mother of a newborn), it is considered by some residents to be one of the better shelters in the city. In visiting the Martinique, one tries to keep this point in mind; but it is, at first, not easy to imagine something worse.

Members of the New York City Council who visited the building in July of 1986 were clearly shaken: "People passing by the hotel have no sense of the tragic dimensions of life inside. Upon entering the hotel, one is greeted by a rush of noise, made in large part by the many small children living there. These children share accommodations with a considerable cockroach and rodent population. The nearly 400 families housed at the Martinique are assisted by just seven HRA caseworkers, whose efforts to keep in touch with each family—at least once each month—often amount to no more than a note slipped under a door."

The report made by the city council offers this additional information: The average family is a mother with three children. Thirty-four percent of families became homeless after eviction by a landlord; 47 percent after being doubled up with other families; 19 percent after living in substandard housing. Fifty percent of heads of households report that they have once held full-time jobs. Seventy percent have seen at least five vacant units they could not afford or from which they have been turned away by landlords who did not want children or welfare recipients.

The city council describes a family living here more than one year: The family was originally forced to leave a city-owned apartment when one child, a daughter, became ill from lead-paint poison. In their next apartment the family's son became ill from lead poison. "After six months of shuttling back and forth between hotels and EAUs," the city council writes, "the family found itself at the Martinique, where lead paint peels from the ceiling of their room."

The city council makes this final observation: "On the day of the committee's visit, just two elevators were operating. . . . The elevator on which the committee rode did not operate properly." At the time of my first visit, six months earlier, one elevator was in operation.

It is difficult to do full justice to the sense of hopelessness one feels on entering the building. It is a haunting experience and leaves an imprint on one's memory that is not easily erased by time or cheerful company. Even the light seems dimmer here, the details harder to make out, the mere geography of twisting corridors and winding stairs and circular passageways a maze that I found indecipherable at first and still find difficult to figure out. After fifty or sixty nights within this building, I have tried but cannot make a floor plan of the place.

Something of Dickens's halls of chancery comes to my mind whenever I am wandering those floors. It is the knowledge of sorrow, I suppose, and of unbroken dreariness that dulls the vision and impairs one's faculties of self-location and discernment. If it does this to a visitor, what does it do to those for whom this chancery is home?

The city council tells us that the owners of the building are Bernard and Robert Sillins. The apparent manager (he is described as a consultant) is a gentleman, Mr. Tucelli, whom some of the tenants view with fear. Mr. Tucelli is consultant also to the nearby Prince George, but he maintains his office here.

The lobby is long, high-ceilinged, vast. On the right side, as one enters, is a sort of "guard post," where a visitor must either be signed in by residents or else present good reason to be in the building. Even the best reason (meeting with the social workers) does not guarantee admission. Residents must be notified of waiting guests by guards. There are fifteen occupied floors above the lobby. There is no bell system.

In a recess on the left side of the lobby are two elevators and a winding flight of stairs. Again on the left, but farther back, is an alcove that contains a row of public phones. On the right side of the lobby, opposite the phones, there is a registration area—part of it original marble, part composed of plastic sheets and wooden slats. Though the wood and plastic give it the appearance of a temporary structure, it has been like this for several years. In this, it is suggestive of the total situation: a temporary shelter that has now been home to many children for two years and in some cases three. At the end of the lobby, on the left side, there are two more elevators and another flight of stairs. On the right side is a laundry room for use by residents.

On the first floor above the lobby there are two connected rooms, once used for banquets, one of which is used for the lunch program. A year from now, this room will have been painted and it will be heated. Two years from now, it will be divided to create a space for preschool. For now, it is a ghost of 1910. The other room is sometimes used for gift distribution (Christmas and Thanksgiving), tutoring, women's groups, and other similar activities run by the city or by volunteers.

Next to these is a third room in which crisis workers and a nurse have desks and phones. This room feels like a safe haven in a number of respects (emergencies of every kind are handled here) but chiefly because the people in this room include some of the most hard-working and devoted souls whom I have ever known. Two of the men who work here have become my friends. They are, I have no doubt, two of the most overburdened people in New York; but they dispense good cheer and absolutely unrestricted love to people in despair with a reserve of energy that I have rarely seen in twenty years of work among poor people.

I go out of my way to mention this because the general experience of homeless people with the city workers they confront is anything but benign. Harsh words will be heard within this book; I have no doubt that they are frequently deserved. But no one in the Martinique Hotel has spoken without gratitude of these extraordinary men. Robert Hayes spoke of the saints and martyrs in the homeless cause. Not all of them are radical activists or volunteers; some of them work for the city of New York and two at least are here.

If "Crisis," as the families call this center, puts a visitor in mind of a safe haven, it is nearly the last haven one will find. Above and beyond are all those rooms, some as small as ten feet square, in which the residents do what they can to make it through the hours and the years. Although I have spent a great deal of time in recent years in some of the most desolate, diseased, and isolated areas of Haiti, I find the Martinique Hotel the saddest place that I have been in my entire life. Why it should seem worse than Haiti I cannot explain.

What is life like for children in this building?

For many the question may be answered briefly, as their lives will be extremely short. The infant mortality rate in the hotel is twenty-five per thousand, over twice the national rate and higher even than the rate in New York's housing projects.* The term used by health professionals for the endangered status of an infant—a child of low birth weight, for example, or a child who does not gain weight after birth—is "failure to thrive." We will learn more of the implications of this term in speaking with the residents of the hotel. There is one nurse present (daytime hours only) to meet all the health needs of the people in the building.

What of the children who manage to survive? Those who do not fail to thrive in their first hours of life will be released from the obstetric wards to rooms devoid of light, fresh air, or educative opportunities in early years. Play is a part of education

---

* Infant mortality is 9.4 per 1,000 for white Americans, 10.8 per 1,000 for the nation as a whole, 16.6 per 1,000 in New York's low-income projects, 24.9 per 1,000 in New York's welfare hotels.

too; they will not have much opportunity for play. Their front doors will give out upon a narrow corridor; their windows on a courtyard strewn with glass, or on the street, or on the wall of an adjacent wing of the hotel. The Empire State Building is two blocks away; if they are well situated they may have a lot of time to gaze at that. They are children who will often have no opportunity for Head Start. Many will wait for months before they are assigned to public school. Those who do get into school may find themselves embarrassed by the stigma that attaches to the "dirty baby," as the children of the homeless are described by hospitals and sometimes perceived by their schoolteachers. Whether so perceived or not, they will *feel* dirty. Many, because of overflowing sewage in their bathrooms, will be dirty and will bring the smell of destitution with them into class.

They are children who write letters each December to a Santa Claus who sometimes has no opportunity to answer. If their mothers or social workers are attentive, they may get a Christmas present from the fire department or the *New York Daily News.* They are children who receive used clothes from volunteers, emergency food from crisis workers, quarters sometimes from pedestrians in Herald Square.

If the children are awake at night they may hear their mothers pray. Some of these women pray a great deal more than other people I have met. There are Bibles in most of their rooms. Many, however, cannot read.

By December 22, two nights after I arrive in New York City, I have met about a dozen families living in the Martinique. I've been told that people here would be reluctant to confide in someone they don't know. Perhaps they ought to be reluctant. But this doesn't prove to be the case. I ask some questions to begin each conversation. How did you end up here? How do you manage? What do you long for? What may happen next? The mechanical matters are answered quickly. People in pain move to the heart of things more rapidly than I expect.

In a small room on the ninth floor there is a mood of resignation and a smell of unwashed clothes. There is no place to sit except the floor or beds. Gwen sits with her children on one of the beds. The baby is two. The older child is eight. I sit on the floor. There is another bed next to the window.

"I was the youngest child in my family. My father was a seaman, so he was away from home for many years. He died when I was a young girl. I was a serious student and I graduated from Jamaica High. I had worked since I was seventeen. I did private-duty nursing: taking care of chronically ill people. When I graduated I received a scholarship to Stony Brook. I wanted to become a surgical nurse.

"What I would have wanted, to be honest, was to be a surgeon. I have dreamed of this for many years. I dream about it still. In my dream I see myself as I had hoped to be: wearing the green robe. But I did not think that I could go so far; it would have taken many years."

She speaks in a beautiful voice about her interrupted dreams. "I had already had one child. I had done a year and a half at Stony Brook when suddenly my mother became ill. I was needed in my mother's house. I nursed my mother. I could not accept that she was dying. I loved my mother. She was the entire world to me. And then she passed. It turned out to be cancer. In a month's time she was gone.

"This was the hardest thing that I had known. I was grown, a married woman with a child, but I felt that I was drawn back to my childhood again. Oh, my mother was my idol. I was scared to go on in the world alone. I believe I had a nervous breakdown but I was too sick to understand. I did not realize what was wrong.

"My brothers took me to the priest. The priest said that my mother had been taken from me as a punishment because I loved her more than God. I believe I went into a long withdrawal. I did not know what was happening to me. The priest said they should bring me to the burial plot. It was very difficult for me. I had to see the tablet on the stone. I had to know that she was gone. So then I knew that she had passed.

"My husband and I had purchased a three-family house in Queens. We had tenants. It was our home. When I was ill I couldn't work. We couldn't meet the payments. They foreclosed.

"Being here, you fight against depression. You know that you are in a struggle and you know you cannot yield. This is

what you have to tell youself: This is your home. *This is home.*
If it's the Martinique Hotel, it is your home.

"I do miss my home in Queens. If you are from Massachusetts I'll explain to you what Queens is like. It's like a neighborhood of Springfield, Massachusetts. You might say, serene. This
room is costing $1,600. For this money, we could buy a house
and live together. We could have another chance to have a
home. Houses in Queens cost $60,000 to $100,000. If I had a
home I would go back to work. I could work at night and save
the money to return to school. When I first came here I believed
that all these things were in my future still. I had a picture of
my life. So all of this seemed real. After you're living here a
while you begin to lose hold of your dream. You start to tell
yourself that it's forever: 'This is it. It isn't going to change. It
can't get worse. It isn't going to get better.' So you start to lose
the courage to fight back.

"You do spend a lot of time in line. You spend a whole day
at the washer. You spend another whole day at the welfare. You
go there at 9:00 A.M. You wait sometimes until 5:00 in the
afternoon. Then you get this check and then, of course, you
know you won't receive a dime. It's written out to you and the
hotel. When you have been living here two years, wouldn't you
think that they could have that check all ready when you come?

"Then you also have to look for housing. Being as I come
from Queens, I go there on the train. I walk for hours. I am
looking for a house I can afford. Welfare allows me $244. I look.
I make appointments. I go out there every morning once my
daughter goes to school. I take the baby with me. If it was $350
or $400 I'd be out of here by now. It's not easy for $244.

"Doing laundry does take you a lot of time. I spend $35
every two weeks washing clothes. Across town, it would cost
me $20, maybe $25. Pulling a shopping cart so far, my baby here
at home alone—I cannot do it. I can't go so far. They do charge
an awful lot for those machines. I don't like to say this—I am
not the kind of person to call somebody dishonest; but, to me,
they are not dealing with an honest deck."

Her husband, Bill, lives with her. Forbidden to live here
openly, he lives here by the subterfuge imposed on almost every
father by the welfare system. He's earning a small salary. It's

not enough to pay prevailing rents in New York City and it wouldn't be enough to handle the expense of food and clothes and health care for the children and for Gwen. If it's known that he is here, however, Gwen may lose her welfare check, food stamps, and Medicaid; she may also be ineligible to stay here at the Martinique. Forced to sneak and lie, therefore, she and Bill feel soiled by the organized deception they must carry out in order to remain together as a family.

Bill and Gwen are on a list for public housing. What they do not know is that 200,000 names are on that list ahead of theirs. They believe that, if they do things right, they will soon be living in a project. What they do not know is that the waiting period is eighteen years. Driven by economic forces she cannot control and is not sufficiently informed to understand, Gwen obeys the rules, fills out the forms, goes each day to search for an apartment she cannot afford, diligently combing a diminished housing market in which minimal rents exceed the limit she's permitted by at least $100. Like a well-conditioned animal within a research lab, she pursues each channel of improbability that is presented. Every channel she explores returns her to the place where she began.

While we're speaking, her husband knocks and comes into the room. Heavily dressed against the cold, he removes a woolen cap, stoops down beside the bed, picks up the baby, and, while he holds him in one arm, reaches his other arm to shake my hand. After that one interruption, he defers to her and lets her talk. He takes the baby over to the bed beside the window, cradles him, and looks outside.

"Schoolwise, this is hard for her." She gestures to the eight-year-old beside her. "She went to Head Start and parochial school in Queens. Here, she has thirty-three children in her class. I follow everything: her lessons, homework, and her grades. For these children I have the highest hopes. I tell the principal I want my son to go to college and become a doctor. I tell him that I want my daughter to become a nurse. He says to me: 'Well, Mrs. Abington, certain children can adjust to this and certain children can't.' I do not know if they should adjust to something if it's bad.

"That's my Bible on the bed behind you. My daughter has

her Bible too. I know the Bible very well. The Bible is what taught me how to read. When I read those 'thee's' and 'thou's,' I have this dream: God comes to me. He calls me 'thee.' I call Him 'Thou.' I tell myself that God is speaking to me. Yes. I do believe in God. I am a Catholic. There is a Franciscan church on Thirty-first Street. I go there when I'm feeling scared. On Sundays I prefer to go back to my church in Queens. It was my mother's church and I was baptized in that church. My mother is buried in the cemetery there."

2

Grieving for a Lost Home

Gwen's voice lingers in my mind. For the money spent to keep her here she said that she could buy a home and lead a normal life. The room is costing almost $20,000 every year. Is it necessary for the city to spend all this money to keep families here?

City officials say that they are powerless to strike a better bargain with the hotel owners. "It is," says the mayor, "a question of supply and demand."

What is the power that the hotel owners hold? Research by the *Village Voice* and other New York papers has elicited some information. Total costs for giving shelter to the homeless families of this city are about $150 million. Almost half, $72 million, is spent to house over 3,000 families in hotels. Of this total, $14 million goes to a business partnership, identified with a man names Morris Horn and several others, who own or operate seven hotels.*

Some, but not all, welfare hotel owners make large contributions to political campaigns in New York City. Mr. Horn and his partners, who receive the largest business, make the largest contributions.

One of their hotels, the Jamaica Arms, was selected by the city to house ninety families with sick children. This building

---

* Data here and elsewhere in this book are for the time span indicated in the text. Many of these items fluctuate from year to year.

belonged to the city in 1982; it had been seized from former owners in default of taxes. Instead of keeping the site to operate a humane shelter, the city sold it to a private corporation for $75,000. It was then resold to its present owners for $200,000. "The city," writes the *Voice*, "now pays about $1.2 million a year to house families in a building it owned four years ago."

Since 1980, the owners of this building have contributed over $100,000 to the electoral campaigns of city officials, several of whom determine housing policy.

The sums of money paid to these and other hotel owners have been reported widely. The second largest partnership— that of the Sillins family, owners of the Martinique—is reported to have grossed $11 million in the year in which this narrative takes place. The Martinique alone received at least $8 million. The owners of a smaller hotel, the Holland, grossed $6 million the same year. It is not known how much is paid to the Prince George Hotel. What *is* known is that this hotel, which houses more homeless families than any other in New York, is operated by South African investors.

Journalists in New York City have repeatedly unearthed reports of influence wielded by, or favors granted to, some of these owners. These matters, while disturbing, are tangential to the housing crisis. A matter that is not tangential is that so much money has been paid to so few people to provide such wretched housing for poor children.

In 1970, when Mr. Koch was still in Congress, he was stirred by the death of a child in a hotel in his district. He sent a telegram to John Lindsay, then the mayor of New York City, demanding that the city stop assigning families with children to hotels that he called "fleabags"—on another occasion, he called one such hotel a "hellhole"—at what he described as "Waldorf-Astoria prices." In that year the city spent $10 million to give shelter to 1,100 families in hotels. The city now spends seven times that much to house three times that many families in the same kinds of hotels.

A member of the New York City Council notes that universities which find themselves in need of dormitory space house their students in New York hotels for an average of $355 a month: about one-fifth the city's monthly payments to hotels that house the poor.

Why, in view of all this published information, does the city keep on wasting public funds to shelter homeless people in such dangerous hotels? Neither private greed nor the potential power of the hotel owners can explain this. Better explanations are much less sensational. Perhaps for this reason, they are given less attention.

New York, like almost every major city, has seldom made provision in advance for the most elemental needs of its poor people: even, indeed, those needs that city leaders have themselves projected.

"City policy toward the homeless," according to a task force of the American Psychiatric Association, "is best described as one that lurches from court order to court order. . . . Harvests of waste rather than economies of scale are reaped when crisis management becomes the modus operandi. . . ." This, in the opinion of most homeless advocates in New York City, is the first important explanation.

Reverend Tom Nees, director of the Community of Hope, a nonprofit shelter in Washington, D.C., speaks to the same point in describing the response of government officials in that city. "They're just putting out fires," he observes, "and picking up the bodies." This is an inevitable result when crisis management replaces wise, far-sighted planning.

A second explanation is provided by Kim Hopper and Jill Hamberg in a paper written for the Community Service Society of New York. Their words, although directed to the crisis in New York, apply to the entire nation.

"The pace, form, and vagaries of contemporary relief efforts," they write, "—their reputed 'failures' in short—may be read as signaling the re-emergence of an older disciplinary agenda. Specifically, they portend the return to a style of assistance that, while alleviating some distress, accepts humiliation as the price of relief and upholds the example of its labors as a deterrent to potential applicants for help."

Not by the malevolent intentions of one person, or of many people, but by regressive public policy enacted through the workings of municipal institutions, the disciplinary agenda is advanced. Low-income housing is not constructed or renovated fast enough to meet the needs our cities annually predict. Shelters, whether city-run or private—whether barracks, family shelters, or hotels—remain destructive institutions. Nonprofit model shelters are profusely praised but are not emulated. It is now and then suggested that the government, with private-sector help, might somehow replicate such shelters. This notion is discussed. It is proposed. In New York City, in one instance, it has even been initiated; but it has not been pursued with perseverance. Enlightened policy is not persistent. It is spasmodic. For this reason, it does not prevail.

What does prevail is an agenda of societal retaliation on the unsuccessful. When tragedies occur, good civic leaders honestly regret them; but tragedies that have been germinating for long years have never been addressed.

The consequence is seen in stifling of hope among poor children. People in the shelters feel that they are choking. The physical sense of being trapped, compacted, and concealed— but, even more, the vivid recognition that they are the objects of society's avoidance or contempt—creates a panic that can't get air enough into their lives, into their lungs. This panic is endemic. The choking sensation is described repeatedly by many adults and their children. Physicians often hear these words, "I can't breathe," in interviews with homeless patients. I hear this statement again and again. Sometimes it is literally the case.

December 23: Annie Harrington is lying on her bed. She has bad asthma. It scares her and her fear is realistic. Her father died of asthma several years ago. Her daughter suffers from it too.

Her asthma has become much worse since living in the Martinique. Tension, she believes, contributes to it, but it is immediately provoked by climbing stairs. Her room is on the fourteenth floor. Despite continual requests, the hotel refuses to allow her to move to a lower floor.

Every time she has to go downstairs to use the phone (she is obliged to contact realtors almost daily to live up to the requirement of "searching for a home") she has to carry her baby on her hip, and then she has to climb all fourteen floors unless she wants to wait for 20 minutes for an elevator. She's been taken to Bellevue three times after bringing groceries upstairs.

On the night I visit she is in a state of misery with which I can identify, as I have asthma too. Climbing to her room, as I've done many times, forces me to use an inhalator.

Her husband is a student in a computer course. He does his homework somehow in this room. He seems to be tender and patient and a bit in awe of her. They have been married seven years. Their children are Doby (seven), Eleanor (six), and Edward (a year and a half).

For some reason, this has been a harder week for her than usual. She has had several bad attacks of asthma. While I'm in the room she starts to cry. Her husband holds her while the children stand and stare. She asks him to leave her for a while. He tries to dissuade her, joking about something; but she's stubborn. "Let me be alone."

He pulls on a sweater and a coat and now he's standing by the door. Doby has some kind of muscle weakness that affects his vision. He wears unusually thick lenses in big horn-rim frames. He stands between them, holding his mother's and father's hands at the same time.

Annie's husband finally shrugs, scoops up a notebook, and goes out the door. After he's gone she looks at me and says: "I have a hard time breathing in this room."

Sociologist Kai Erikson, describing families who have lost their homes after a flood in Appalachia and are now entrapped in very crowded temporary dwellings, writes that "the pressures of life have drawn in so tightly" that they often feel they cannot breathe. They feel, he says, "as though they are always smothering," and he quotes a woman in these words: "Sometimes . . . I'm just choking half to death . . . It's just like something was wrapped around my neck. I'm short of breath . . . It's just a choking feeling. Just like everything is . . . tightening up."

When I go back a few days later Annie's husband has returned. He's reading on the bed beside the window. Annie is leaning on her elbow in the bottom of the bunk bed near the door.

"It's been four years we've been in and out of the hotels.

Here for ten months. It seems like ten years."

She completed tenth grade, worked as a food caterer, met her husband when he was in military service. He had completed high school but did not have skills enough to find a job. The military offered to provide him with an education and job preparation, and he had believed this. They lived for three years at a military base in Texas. When his service was completed he could not find permanent work. The training he'd been given in the army was too narrow to prepare him for civilian jobs. He'd found some part-time jobs and, while these were sufficient to support two children in the south, they were not enough to pay for housing in New York. He makes some money now by working in a hospital while taking classes in the afternoon and studying at night to finish his computer course. How does he study in this room?

"He gets back from class at suppertime," Annie explains. "After dinner he helps me with the children. He's *good* with the children. He tries to do the things a father should. He helps with homework, helps me to bathe them, tells them stories, gets them into bed. Once they're asleep he does his books. He'll be working up to three or four . . ."

Doby, with his brown eyes magnified by his thick lenses, is an earnest little boy. One of the workers in the crisis center calls him "an owl—bright and studious," he says. But he's a year behind his proper grade because he lost so many months during the time in which the family had been shunted from one shelter to another. He comes into the crisis center with his briefcase after school each afternoon and climbs onto the lap of one of the good-natured crisis workers. He looks like an oversized teddy bear and seems to be favored somewhat at the cost of his more quiet sister. His father cuddles him a lot, scolds him a little, and seems amused by almost everything he does. They bought him and his sister heavy clothes and winter boots for Christmas.

"We had no money for a Christmas tree or toys. We buy them what they need so they will not feel different from the other kids at school. All the money that we have, it goes to them. They're *nice* kids. They deserve it."

Annie is twenty-seven but she looks like a teenager. Her

husband is the same age but seems older. He doesn't say much, but he's friendly to me and seems grateful that I take an interest in them and, even more so, that I seem to take an interest in their kids. When Annie says, "they're *nice* kids," I cannot help thinking: "You are a nice person too." And, although there is much more than this to say of Annie Harrington, it is to me the most important and most simple truth of all about this man and woman. They are good people: clean and honest. Diligent too. They love their children and each other. Nothing I've read about the culture of the underclass comes near the mark in stating what is elemental in this family.

"My mother is alive but very poor. My father is deceased. He died of asthma and heart failure. This is why I scare so easily when I have my attacks. My daughter's attacks are not as bad as mine. They scare me too."

She's given $13 every two weeks to pay for travel costs of hunting for apartments; but her rental limit is $270 and she understands, after four years of searching, that she'll never find a home until the limit is increased. "Places I see, they want $350, $400, $500. Out in Jamaica, recently, I met an older lady. She had seen me crying, so she asked me: 'What's the matter?' I explained to her how long I had been looking for a home. She said: 'Well, I own a couple of apartments.' The rental was $365. She said that she would skip the extra month and the deposit. I had told her what my husband does, my children. I had Doby with me. I believe she took a liking to me. So I was excited. Happy! And she handed me the lease and proof of ownership and told me I should take them to my worker, and she gave me her phone number. A nice lady. And you see—you do forget what is your *situation*. You forget that you are poor. It's like a dream: This lady likes me and we're going to have a home! My worker denied me for $365. I was denied. $365. My social worker is a nice man but he said: 'I have to tell you, Mrs. Harrington. Your limit is $270.' Then I thought of this: The difference is only $95. I'll make it up out of my food allowance. We can lighten up on certain things. Not for the children, but ourselves. We'll eat less food at first. Then I can get a job. He'll finish his computer course. The house had a backyard . . . They told me no. I was denied.

"Do you know that they are paying $1,900 every month for me to stay here? Sixty-three dollars every night. So for two nights you'd have the $95 right there. I told my social worker that. I said it don't make sense and he agreed with me but he is not the one that made the rules; and he was right.

"Next Tuesday is my birthday. I'm just praying God that somebody will offer me a home. Just go to some kind of real estate or broker and explain myself. Even if I have to start a little crying. Somebody will think: 'This family isn't going to destroy my place. They are nice people.' And he'll offer me a lease."

At first I think she means this is her daydream. But it turns out that this really is her plan. "I'm planning to wear my pleated skirt, my white blouse, my navy jacket and—I won't wear heels. I'll wear these shoes." She shows me flat, plain shoes that have a Saks Fifth Avenue label. "I have had these shoes for thirteen years. I take good care of things. My mother got them on a sale for me when I was a teenager."

Under the pillow she is leaning on there is a pack of Newport cigarettes. She smokes continually while we talk; and even though she knows it makes her asthma worse, she tells me that she cannot get herself to stop. She says it cuts her hunger.

"Last night I had a dream of an apartment. It was so real I keep on thinking that I went there in my sleep. My daughter had her own room, pink and white with something up over the bed. A *canopy* is what it's called, I think . . . The boys, they had to share a room. I painted that room blue; there was a spread over the bed that Doby slept in. It had football pictures on it. My kitchen had a phone, a stove, refrigerator, toaster, all of those nice things. My dining-room table was glass and it was simple, plain and clean. In my living room I had a pretty couch and lots of books, a big bookshelf, and there were plants beside the window, and the floor was what I call a *parquet* floor and it was waxed. My bedroom had a nice brass bed, a lot of books there too, and pillows covered with fresh linens, and the drapes were nice bright colors. Yellow. Like the linens. And the neighborhood was clean. The neighborhood was nice. The neighbors liked me. And the landlord liked me too. He said that we could use the backyard, so we bought a grill to barbecue outside on summer nights. Then I woke up. And all my dreams, all my wishing, it went down the drain. It was a dream.

"Four years ago I used to be the happiest girl you'd ever see. You'd see me smiling. I'm not happy anymore. Four years of my life went down the drain. Four years are gone. I lost it. [Cries.] Things inside of me, not things that you could see. *Inside* things, I lost it. I don't have it in my *inside* anymore.

"Yesterday I had to be at welfare. A lady came in with a little baby. She was sitting there all day. All she asked was for a place to take her baby so that they could sleep. They're probably still sitting there right now—or at the EAU. A tiny baby. All day long I look at them. I sit there and I shake my head. I'm thinking: Years ago they built those projects and this lady and her baby, they would have been put into a nice apartment in those projects. Do they build those places now? I read in the paper they are building something called mixed-income housing, and I studied it real close and what it said is that it's for the moderate, the middle, and the poor. They gave an income, an amount of money, for 'the middle' and 'the moderate' and another for 'the poor.' The poor were people who had $15,000. I said to myself: That isn't poor. That isn't no way near where I am at. What good will that do for somebody like me? If they'd just fix up some of these places, boarded buildings, they're all over—they are *every* place you go in New York City—I would love it. It don't need to have a backyard. It don't need to have no pretty floor. It don't even need to have a porch. It could be by dumpside city and it wouldn't bother me. I don't pay no mind if it had rats and broken windows just so long as it had heat. Do you know—I have filled out so many applications. Section Eight. Public housing. Subsidized housing. There'a a million of these things. They have us filling out these applications all our lives. Why don't they fix those buildings?

"A home to me would be like this: You have your dinner at the same time all together. You go out together—yeah, you go out to play bingo. Go to the ice cream, to the movies. Then you all go home together. You sit down in peace together. You read together. You say your prayers together. You go to sleep together and you don't have to be scared there'll be a fire. Here in this building, I don't sleep. What's on my mind? I'm thinking:

There's so many people, trash piled around. What if there's a fire on my floor? There's no fire escape outside this window. I'm on the fourteenth floor. To me it feels like prison. Only thing is I can walk out when I'm ready. But my children can't. So I lie up awake at night. I read. I'll read a book. I read my Bible mostly —start from front to back. Sometimes I read the psalms. When morning comes the radio goes off, it's 6:00 A.M., I have to get them set for school. I get up. I get them up. I make them hot farina. A hot cup of tea. Doby puts his homework in his brief-case and I wrap his scarf around him, button up his coat. Once there's something hot inside of him I know he'll be okay until he gets to school."

I ask about her asthma.

"What I got right now is not so bad. It's just a little tight-ness in my chest. It weakens me but it's not something that I fear. What I fear is when I cannot breathe at all.

"A month ago I had it bad. Started with me walking up the stairs. I got in my room and there was something smelling strong. It's ammonia, I think, but very, very strong. They use it in the stairs. I'm lying here. That stuff is in the air. I use my pump"—she takes it out and shows me; it's an inhalator—"but it doesn't work. I use it three times and it makes me shaky, but it doesn't always work. My husband's here. He runs downstairs. The ambulance comes. They take my pulse. They go down to use the phone and call the doctor and he says to give me some-thing—'three cc.'s'—they give me an injection and they strap me in the chair. Then they have to wait to get an elevator. One of them is working. When it comes they wheel me in and put me in the ambulance downstairs. Soon as we get there, to the hospital, they put me in Emergency. The doctor came in. He gives me two injections. First he put a shot up in my back, then in my arm. He told me to sit up and gave me oxygen. He told me to inhale it. I inhaled it—from a mask he held. I've been through it before . . .

"When I left he gave me a prescription. My husband was back here with the children and I couldn't get a cab. No cab would stop. The doctor said I wasn't s'posed to walk. I had no choice. The walking starts me feeling tightened up and scared. When I get back, the same thing: There's no elevator working.

So I take it slow. I stop at every floor. By the time I'm in the room I feel almost the way I was before. I just made some hot tea and put on a heavy sweater and I took the medicine they gave me. And the next day I was feeling kind of weak when I got up. I rested and I used my pump. I took my medicine. That's happened three times since I'm here. I ask them will they move me some day to a lower floor. I have the doctor's letter. I'm still here."

She said the asthma makes her scared. I ask her what she fears.

"I fear death. I feel like I'm falling in a wishing well, like falling in a deep dark place. All I see is darkness."

Her daughter, she tells me, had a bad attack of asthma just three nights before. "Same thing. No cabs. Leave the hospital at four, walk back home, get here at five. Make her a cup of tea. Put her to bed. Outside the window, sky is turning: black to blue. It's daybreak. One day before Christmas."

On Christmas, she said, they made the children dinner but were interrupted when a little boy who lives next door had a bad accident. "The little boy was playing and he split his head. His mother was so scared I volunteered to go with her. They took us to the Roosevelt Hospital. That's where I spent my Christmas."

In the days since my last visit I have read a book that has been given much attention in the past few years. The book is titled *Wealth and Poverty*. Its author is a scholar named George Gilder. *Newsweek* says the book is something of a bible now in Washington. The book refers to the "more primitive rhythms" of unmarried men and speaks of a "young stud" in its reference to a black man who disdains the obligations of paternity. Unmarried parenthood and the decline of the work ethic are two of the themes of Gilder's book. "But even an analysis of work and family," he says, "would miss what is perhaps the most important of the principles of upward mobility under capitalism—namely faith." Exploring the sources of difference "between entrepreneurial Orientals" and what he refers to as "less venturesome blacks," Gilder sees faith—its presence or its absence—as the key determinant: "faith in man, faith in the future, faith in the rising returns of giving, faith in the mutual benefits of trade, faith in the providence of God. . . ."

When I read this first, I thought of Gwen. If Gilder is correct, Gwen ought to be a very wealthy woman. Listening to Annie's finals words I think of Gilder's faith again.

"Do you pray?"

"Every day."

"Where do you pray?" I ask.

"St. Francis church."

"Why there?"

"They let you pray. And they have social workers there."

"When do you have time to go there?"

"In the afternoons. I go at four o'clock."

"What do you pray?"

"Pray God to make me strong. If it's a bad day I think of heaven."

"How do you think of heaven?"

"Like Jerusalem in Bible times. Peaceful. Quiet. People there are civilized and kind."

Suddenly she laughs and points to Doby. "A TV reporter asked what he would do if he had an apartment. Doby said: 'If I had an apartment I would make cheeseburgers!' The reporter laughed." Annie laughs. Her husbands laughs. Doby stares at them, inscrutable behind those funny glasses. It is the first time I have seen this woman smile in four hours. But her cheerfulness departs her quickly. "When I came here summer was beginning. Summer passed and autumn passed and winter's almost past and—[cries] I don't want to be here for another summer. Please, if you could do something to help us to get out of here . . ." She cries. Her husband sits beside her but she cannot be consoled. Doby climbs up on the bed and pats his mother's shoulder with his hand.

One year later they are still here in the same room—and are still together.

How does a family stay together under these conditions?

There is a wealth of literature about the loss of certain values that provide cohesion for the family in American society. Less is written of the role played by society itself in the undoing of those decent family ties that do somehow prevail in even the most damaging conditions of existence. How do bureaucratic regulations in themselves conspire to annihilate a family?

Annie says her husband has to live with her illegally. Because of her asthma she cannot go down each night to sign him in. He has to sneak in past the guards, unless a guard who knows him will allow him to sign in. Employees of the HRA tell me that the rules about cohabitation are erratically applied. Their implementation depends to some degree on the caprice of social workers. If a man is already on a woman's welfare budget when she first applies for shelter, and if they have children, he may be allowed to live with her. If he isn't on her budget but can prove he is her husband or the father of her child, he may be included in her budget at the time of placement in a shelter. "However," according to one social worker, "it is always *very* hard to get a husband on a woman's budget. In any case, if he is working, she will forfeit benefits and, if his earnings are concealed and then discovered, she will find her case is closed." Because the jobs available to men like Annie's husband are unlikely to be permanent, rarely offer health insurance, and could not support a family in New York, the forfeiture of benefits (or, worse, removal from the welfare rolls entirely) poses unacceptable risks. Thus, loyal fatherhood becomes a fiscal liability. The father becomes extinct within his family. If he wants to see his children he must sign in as a stranger.

In some cases, husbands are obliged to pay to visit with their children. In the Hotel Carter, for example, a woman I have interviewed tells me that husbands have to pay $12.40 for the right to spend an evening with their families. Other relatives or friends, she says, have to pay even more. If grandparents, for example, want to spend an evening with their daughter and grandchildren they pay $16.70. This policy, no matter how distasteful, is consistent with an ethos honored citywide.

Other fiscal disincentives to family integrity are even more severe: New York will spend a great deal less to support an AFDC child in the home of her real mother than to subsidize that child in a foster home. A twelve-year-old child living at home in New York city is allocated a maximum of $262 a month for all food, clothes, and rent expenses (1986). If this child were taken from her mother for "abuse or neglect," the child would then be allocated $631 monthly. If the placement were routine—not for abuse, neglect, or any other failure of the parent—the child would be assigned about $410. Either way, she would be financially much better off without her mother.

In this book we will meet a very poor woman who has considered giving up her children to the state so that they may be better fed. Unnatural as such behavior may appear, mothers faced with bare refrigerators and with hungry children often are compelled to contemplate this option.

A welfare mother who has no home and has yet to locate shelter runs another risk of being separated from her child. A lawyer in Los Angeles describes a scenario repeated daily in America: A homeless family applies for AFDC. The social worker comes to the decision that the children are endangered by their lack of shelter. The children are taken away and placed in foster care. The parents are no longer eligible for AFDC now because they don't have children. So the family *as a family* receives nothing. The children have been institutionalized. The family, as such, exists no longer. Measures as severe as these are rarely taken in New York, but the values that permit this to be done in any state are present everywhere.

Crowded living spaces have their own disintegrating force. With two or three children sleeping in the same room as their mother, sexual activity is never more than six or seven feet from their own beds. So either sexual activity must cease (it does in many cases) or it must take place under conditions that appear degrading. An intolerable choice is forced on those for whom existence is almost intolerable already.

The latter point, however, is a small part of a larger issue. This is the question of what constitutes "a home" in terms that foster and preserve a family's ties. A place in which a parent cannot cook a meal is, to begin with, something different from a home as most of us would understand that word. Sharing food has been traditionally regarded as the essence of a home or hearth in most societies. Cooking a meal within the Martinique can be a complicated task, calling for strategic skills that few of us can easily imagine. With only a hot plate in a crowded room, every item (meat, potato, vegetable) must be prepared in se-quence. So the children have to eat each item separately and must pass back their plates to be refilled. From start to finish, a single meal like this may take two hours.

In most rooms, moreover, there is not enough space for a mother, father and their children to sit down and eat at the same time. I have yet to see a room in this hotel that has a dinner table. I have never visited a room that had as many chairs as occupants. At best, the occupants may sit together on a bed or, if the bed's too crowded, on the floor to share their food. It may be a tribute to the stubborn dignity of many people that they do exactly that. Some even say grace and thank God for their blessings before dining off the carpet or linoleum.

Drawing a distinction between home and shelter is, I hope, more than an academic exercise. Shelter, if it's warm and safe, may keep a family from dying. Only a home allows a family to flourish and to breathe. When breath comes hard, when privacy is scarce, when chaos and crisis are on every side, it is difficult to live at peace, even with someone whom we love.

In the months in which I've visited the Martinique, I've seen several previously close couples torn apart by quarrels that evolve out of sheer human density within a single room. Children, of course, cannot be sent outside to play when parents are distraught. Where would they go? "Outside" is a hallway or an elevator landing strewn with garbage or a stairway frequented by guards and by narcotics dealers. Holding a family together in the face of these conditions is an act of nerve.

It would not be accurate to say that Annie's family is a happy family. No one living in the Martinique Hotel has ever hinted to me that he or she was happy. It is a genuine family nonetheless. It is affectionate and strong and warm. But how much battering they have to undergo—how many alarms and illnesses and tensions. I've been back to visit many times. I have never been within this room when somebody did not have trouble breathing.

3

Three Generations

There are families in this building whose existence, difficult though it may be, still represents an island of serenity and peace. Annie Harrington's family has a kind of pained serenity. Gwen and her children live with the peace of resignation. I think of these families like refugees who, in the midst of war, cling to each other and establish a small zone of safety. Most people here do not have resources to create a zone of safety. Terrorized already on arrival, they are quickly caught up in a vortex of accelerating threats and are tossed about like bits of wood and broken furniture and shattered houses in an Arkansas tornado. Chaos and disorder alternate with lethargy and nearly absolute bewilderment in the face of regulations they cannot observe or do not understand.

Two women whom I meet in the same evening after Christmas, Wanda and Terry, frighten me by their entire inability to fathom or to govern what is going on inside and all around them.

Terry is pregnant, in her ninth month. She's afraid that, when she gives birth, she may not be able to bring home her baby from the hospital because she is not legally residing here.

Wanda, curled up like a newborn in a room no larger than a closet, is three months pregnant, planning an abortion.

Would doctors say these women are emotionally unwell? They might have no choice. Were these women sick before they came here? I don't see how we could possibly find out. What startles me is not that they have difficulty coping but that neither yet has given up entirely.

Terry: twenty-eight years old. She has three kids. She graduated from a school in Flushing and has worked for eight years as a lab assistant. Burnt out of her home, she stayed for two years with her sister's family: three adults, eight children, crowded into four unheated rooms. Evicted by her sister when the pressure on her sister's husband and their kids began to damage their own marriage, she had to take her children to the EAU at Church Street in Manhattan. Refusing to accept a placement at a barracks shelter, she's been sleeping here illegally for several nights in a small room rented to her cousin.

When we meet, she's in the corridor outside the crisis center, crying and perspiring heavily. She sits on a broken chair to talk to me. She's not on Medicaid and has been removed from AFDC. "My card's being reprocessed," she explains, although this explanation explains nothing. She's not on WIC. "I've got to file an application." Her back is aching. She is due to have her child any day.

This is the reason for her panic: "If I can't be placed before the baby's born, the hospital won't let me take the baby. They don't let you take a newborn if you haven't got a home." As we will see, this is not always so; but the possibility of this occurrence is quite real. Where are her kids? "They're here. I've got them hidden in the room."

She takes me to her cousin Wanda's room. I measure it: nine feet by twelve, a little smaller than the room in which I store my files on the homeless. Wanda's been here fifteen months, has four kids, no hot plate, and no food in the refrigerator. She's had no food stamps and no restaurant allowance for two months. I ask her why. (You ask these questions even though you know the answer will be vague, confused, because so many of these women have no possible idea of why they do or don't receive the benefits they do or don't deserve.) She's curled up in a tattered slip and a torn sweater on a mattress with no sheet. Her case was closed, she says. Faintly, I hear something about "an application." Her words are hard to understand. I ask her whether she was here for Christmas. The very few words she speaks come out in small reluctant phrases: "Where else would I go?" She says her children got some presents from the fire department. There's a painting of Jesus and Mary on the wall above the bed. "My mother gave it to me."

A week later I stop by to visit. She's in the same position: drowsy and withdrawn. I ask her if she celebrated New Year's Eve. "Stayed by my lonesome" is all that I understand. She rouses herself enough to ask me if I have a cigarette. In the vacuum of emotion I ask if she ever gets to do something for fun. "Go to a movie . . ." But when I ask the last time she's been to a movie she says: "1984." What was the movie? *"Dawn of the Living Dead."*

When she says she's pregnant and is planning an abortion I don't care to ask her why, but she sits up halfway, props herself against a pillow, looks at Terry, shrugs, and mumbles this: "What you want to bring another baby into this place for? There ain't nothin' waitin' for them here but dirty rooms and dyin'."

Her children, scattered like wilted weeds around her on the floor, don't talk or play or move around or interrupt. Outside in the corridor I ask her cousin if the kids are sick. Terry says: "They're okay. They just didn't have no food to eat today." So I ask: "Did you?" She shakes her head. I go down to Herald Square, buy french fries and chicken at a fast-food store, milk and cookies at a delicatessen, and return. The minute I walk in Wanda sits up, clearheaded and alert. Her kids wake from their stupor. Fifteen minutes later, every bit of chicken, all the french fries, cookies, milk have been consumed. There is a rush of energy and talking in the room. The kids are pestering the adults, as they ought to.

"I have a problem," Wanda says. "My blood sugar goes down. It is called [pronounced very precisely] hypoglycemia."

I meet Terry one year later by sheer chance outside Grand Central Station. She's in a food line for the sandwiches distributed by a charitable group at 10:00 P.M. Her kids are with her. She's holding a baby in her arms. She tells me she's in another hotel near the Martinique. "Don't have no refrigerators there . . ."

I lose her in the crowd of people waiting for a meal.

In the subway station under Herald Square a woman who has seen me coming from the Martinique follows me and stops me by the stairs. Her hair is disheveled. Words spill from her mouth. She says that she was thrown out of the Martinique. Her children were sick with diarrhea. Someone "reported" her; for what I do not ask. After the Martinique she says that she was in a place I've never heard of called the Brooklyn Arms. Her youngest child, one year old, became much sicker there. City workers finally persuaded her to give up all three kids to foster care. She's living now in a crowded women's shelter where, she says, there are twelve women in a room. She shrieks this information at me on the platform not far from the shrieking trains.

"There's no soap, no hygiene. You go to the desk and ask for toilet paper. You get a single sheet. If you need another sheet you go gack down and ask them for some more. I sleep on an army cot. The bathroom's flooded."

Is she telling me the truth? Is she on drugs? Is she unwell? Why did she elect to tell me this? Why do the words come out so fast? I feel unkind to cut her off, but I am frightened by her desperation. I leave her there, pouring out her words into the night.

The nurse in the Martinique says this: "A mother gave birth last week to a baby that weighed just over a pound. She was in her seventh month. Her children rubbed her belly while she cried. I called an ambulance."

The nurse is kind, compassionate, and overwhelmed. "People are fractured by this system. I'm responsible for 500 families, here and in another building. Custody cases. Pregnant women. Newborn children. I can get them into WIC. I'm snowed . . ." She's on the telephone, buried in papers, talking with women, hearing their questions, trying to come up with answers. There are others like her in the crisis center who create a tiny zone of safety in the larger zone of fear. But twenty-five hardworking nurses like this woman would be scarcely equal to the miseries that flood across her desk out of this factory of pain and tears.

Far from any zone of safety lives a man named Mr. Allesandro. He's six feet tall and weighs 110 pounds—down 20 pounds from late September. When he came to the hotel a year ago he weighed 165. I first met him in the ballroom before Christmas when I handed him an apple. One bright apple. One week later he does not forget and, when he sees me in the lobby, asks me if

I have some time to talk.

His two daughters are asleep. Christopher, his nine-year-old, is lying on the top bunk, fully dressed and wrapped beneath a pile of blankets, but he is awake and vigilant and almost belligerently alert. It's a cold night and the room appears to be unheated. Mr. Allesandro shows me a cracked pane of glass that he has covered over with a sheet of garbage plastic and Scotch tape. The two coils of the hot plate offer a symbolic reassurance ("heat exists") but they do not provide much warmth. He's wearing a coat and woolen hat. His mother, who is seventy-three, lives with them; for some reason, she's not here.

There aren't many men as heads of households in this building; this fact, I think, adds to his feeling of humiliation. His story, quickly told, remains less vivid for me later on than certain details like his trembling hands, the freezing room, the strange sight of his watchful boy, unsleeping on the bed. The boy reminds me of a rabbit staring from a thicket or caught in the headlights of a car.

These, as Mr. Allesandro tells me, are the facts: He was one of several maintenance workers in a high-rise building in Manhattan owned by one of the well-known developers. It was early autumn and his wife, for reasons I don't learn until much later, just picked up one day and disappeared. He tried to keep his job and home by rising early, feeding the children, bringing them to school, then rushing to his job. But his shift required him to be on duty very early. He was reprimanded and, when he explained his problem, was permitted to stay on but cut back to a half-time job. Half-time work was not enough to pay the rent. He was evicted. In the subsequent emergency he had to take leave from his job.

"My mother went with me to the EAU. We asked them if we could be placed together. That way, she could get the kids to school and I could keep my job." Instead, they put him in a barracks shelter with the children but would not allow his mother to go with them. As best he understands, this is because she drew a Social Security check and was on a different budget from his own. Eligibility rules are difficult to fathom; but, even where the consequences are calamitous and costly, they are faithfully observed.

"So I'm alone there in this place with about 200 cots packed side by side. Men and women, children," he says, "all together. No dividers. There's no curtains and no screens. I have to dress my kids with people watching. When my girls go to the toilet I can't take them and they're scared to go alone. A lot of women there are frantic. So I stand and wait outside the door."

He went back to the EAU and begged once more. "In my line of work," he says, "you don't earn much of your money from the salary. The people in the building get to know you and you do them favors and they give you money in return. Christmas is the time you get your tips. They'll hand you an envelope. Twenty dollars. Fifty dollars. Some give you a hundred. These are very wealthy people . . ." So his disappointment was intensified by recognition of the fact that he could not get back his job in time to benefit from the expected generosity of people whom he'd known: "Some of those people knew me well. They liked me." He seems desperate to be assured that he was liked, remembered, missed, by people who had frequently befriended him.

The use of barracks shelters as deterrence to the homeless is not absolute. Assignments are made "on an ad hoc basis," as one social worker states it. But nothing that Mr. Allesandro said could bring the EAU to place his mother with him. His former boss, he says, had told him he would take him back if he could start the day at 5:00 A.M. "There's no way that I could do it. Would you leave your kids alone within a place like that at 5:00 A.M.? I couldn't do it."

The upshot is this: He loses the chance to go back to his job a few weeks before Chirstmas. Although he's worked for many years, he hasn't been on *this* job long enough to have accumulated pension benefits. Dispossession from his home has left him unemployed; unemployment now will render permanent his homelessness.

Having finally lost everything he had, he returns a few weeks later to the EAU. This time, having undergone "deterrence" and still being homeless, he is granted "temporary" placement at the Martinique. His mother can join him now. But he is no longer a wage earner; he's an AFDC father, broken in spirit, mourning for those lost tips which he will obsessively recall each time we talk. His job has been assigned to someone else. He loses self-control. He thanks God for his mother. This strikes me as a gruesome and enormously expensive instance of municipal assault upon a man's work ethic and familial integrity at the same time.

How does he feel not working?

"It's a nightmare. I'm Italian. You know—I don't mean this to sound prejudiced"—all of the white people here, I notice, are extremely careful and apologetic on this score—"my people work. My father and grandfather worked. My mother worked. I can do construction, carpentry. I can repair things. I'm somebody who's mechanically inclined. I would make beds, I would clean toilets. I'd do anything if I could have a decent job."

He searches the ads, walks the pavement, rides the subway; but he cannot find a job that pays enough to rent a home and feed three children. His rent allowance is $281. He's seen apartments for $350 and $400. If he takes an apartment over his rent limit he will have to make the difference up by cutting back on food and clothes. His mother's pension is too small to offer them a safety margin. "I wouldn't risk it. I'm afraid to take a chance. Even if I got a job, what if I lost it? I'd be back there with the children in the barracks."

So, like everybody else, he's drowning in the squalor of the Martinique Hotel but dreads the thought of being forced to leave.

"My mother helps to make it like a home. She tries. We got the kids a kitten, which is something that is not allowed. I don't like to break the rules, but you have got to give them something to remember that they're children."

Thinking of his hunger, I ask how he feeds the cat.

"We don't need to. We have never bought one can. She eats better than we do—on the mice and rats."

Around midnight I notice that Christopher is wide awake and watching from the bed: blue eyes, pale skin, blondish hair. Mrs. Allesandro cuts the children's hair.

Where is Mrs. Allesandro?

Mr. Allesandro calls her "grandma" and he speaks of her as if she were *his* grandmother as well. Grandma fell in the stairwell Friday afternoon. There had been a fire and the stairs were still slick from the water left there by the fire hoses. She's in the hospital for an examination of her hip. He tells me that she has a heart condition. "If anything happens to her [pauses] . . . I'd be dead. She's the one that's holding us together."

Other people in this building speak of Mrs. Allesandro in almost identical words. They count on her perhaps even a little more than on the nurse or on the other people in the crisis center. Unlike the crisis workers she is here around the clock. As short of food and money as the Allesandros are, I am told that she is often in the hallways bringing food to neighbors, to a pregnant woman, a sick child living somewhere on the floor. A man who knows her but does not live on this floor speaks of Mrs. Allesandro in these words: "Here she is, an old Italian lady. Here are all these women. Most of them are Puerto Rican, black . . . You will see them holding onto her, crying to her as if she was their mother."

Mrs. Allesandro, however, is not here tonight. Her son is on his own—a skeleton of hunger, disappointment, fear. I look at him, at the two girls, asleep, and at the boy—awake, alert. The boy's persistent gaze unsettles me. I ask him: "Are you sleepy?" He just shakes his head. His father is too proud to tell me that the boy is hungry. I feel embarrassed that it's taken me so long to ask. At my request he opens the refrigerator door. There is one packaged dinner, smuggled out of the lunch program. "There was something wrong with it," he says. It has a rancid smell. "It's spoiled." There's a gallon tin of peanut butter, two part-empty jars of apple sauce, some hardened bread. That's it.

Mr. Allesandro takes the $20 that I hand him to the corner store. Christopher sits up halfway and talks with me. He lists for me the ten largest cities of America. I ask him whether he likes school. He does not give the usual perfunctory affirmative response. "I hate it," Christopher says. I ask him what he does for fun. He plays ball on the sidewalk at the corner of the street across from the hotel.

"Is there room to play ball on the sidewalk?"

He explains: "We play against the building of the bank—against the wall."

He falls asleep after I think of giving him a candy bar. His father returns in twenty minutes with a box of Kellogg's Special K, a gallon of juice, half-gallon of milk, a loaf of bread, a dozen eggs, a package of sausages, a roll of toilet paper. He wakes his son. The boy has a bowl of cereal with milk. His father stands before the counter where he placed the food. He looks like a man who has been admitted to an elegant buffet.

Is Mr. Allesandro laden with anxiety? Is Christopher depleted, sick, exhausted? Yes, I suppose both statements are correct. Are they candidates for psychiatric care? Perhaps they are; but I should think a more important observation is that they are starving.

A few months after my evening with the Allesandro's, President Reagan meets a group of high-school students from New York. Between government help and private charity, he says, "I don't believe there is anyone that is going hungry in America simply by reason of denial. . . ." The president says there is a problem of "people not knowing where or how to get this help." This is what he also says of those who can't find space in public housing that he has stopped building.

His former counselor and now attorney general, Edwin Meese, concedes that people have been turning to soup kitchens but refuses to accept that they are in real need. They go to soup kitchens "because the food is free," he says, and adds, "that's easier than paying for it."

Marian Wright Edelman of the Children's Defense Fund makes this interesting calculation: If Defense Secretary Caspar Weinberger were to give up just a single Pentagon budget item, that which pays for him to have a private dining room, one million low-income school children could get back their morning snack—a snack denied them by administration cuts.

Hundreds of miles from Christopher's bedroom in the Martinique, a reporter describes an underground limestone cave near Kansas City: the largest surplus-food repository in the nation. In this cave and in some other large facilities, in the winter of 1986, the government was storing some 2 billion pounds of surplus food. To a child like Christopher, the vision of millions of pounds of milk and cheese and butter secreted in limestone caves might seem beyond belief. Storage of this surplus food costs taxpayers $1 million a day.

Getting surplus food from limestone caves to children's tables calls for modest but essential transporation costs. In an extraordinary action, termed illegal by the General Accounting Office, the president deferred funds allocated by the Congress for transporting food to homeless people. The sum involved, $28 million, is a small amount beside the $365 million spent to store this food in limestone caves and other warehouse areas. The withholding of such funds may possibly make sense to an economist. I do not know whether it would make much sense to Christopher.

November 1986: I'm in New York and visit with the Allesandros. Grandma's back. She says her health is good. But Christopher looks frighteningly thin. Food was scarce before. The situation's worsened since I was here last. Families in the homeless shelters of New York have been cut back on their food-stamp allocations. The White House has decided to consider money paid for rental to the hotel owners as a part of family income. By this standard, families in the Martinique are very rich. "Tightening of eligibility requirements" has an abstract sound in Washington. On the twelfth floor of the Martinique what does it mean?

I study the computerized receipts that Mr. Allesandro has received. In June, his food-stamp allocation was $145. In August, the first stage in government reductions lowered this to $65. In October: $50. As of December it will be $33.

Mrs. Allesandro does not speak in ambiguities about the lives of her grandchildren. I ask her what the cuts will mean. "They mean," she says, "that we aren't going to eat." New York announces it will help make up the difference but, at the time I visit, no supplemental restaurant allowances have been received.

4

Rachel and Her Children

Mr. Allesandro is too shaken to attempt to hide his frailties from me. He tells me: "When you're running scared you do some things you'd rather not . . ." He does not regard himself as saint or martyr. There are virtues, feelings and commitments he has forfeited during this long ordeal. Love is not one of them. His desperation for his son and daughters and his adoration of his mother are as solid and authentic as the marble pillars of the Martinique Hotel. The authenticity of love deserves some mention in discussion of the homeless.

Houses can be built without a number of ingredients that other ages viewed as indispensable. Acrylics, plastics and aluminum may substitute for every substance known to nature. Parental love cannot be synthesized. Even the most earnest and methodical foster care demonstrates the limits of synthetic tenderness and surrogate emotion. So it seems of keen importance to consider any ways, and *every* way, by which a family, splintered, jolted and imperiled though it be by loss of home and subsequent detention in a building like the Martinique, may nonetheless be given every possible incentive to remain together.

The inclination to judge harshly the behavior of a parent under formidable stress seems to be much stronger than the willingness to castigate the policies that undermine the competence and ingenuity of many of these people in the first place.

"Men can be unequal in their needs, in their honor, in their

61

possessions," writes historian Michael Ignatieff, "but also in their rights to judge others." The king's ultimate inequality, he says, "is that he is never judged." An entire industry of scholarship and public policy exists to judge the failing or defective parent; if we listen to some of these parents carefully we may be no less concerned by their impaired abilities, but we may be less judgmental or, if we remain compelled to judge, we may redirect our energies in more appropriate directions.

New Year's Eve.

She stalks into the room. Her eyes are reddened and her clothes in disarray. She wears a wrinkled and translucent nightgown. On her feet: red woolen stockings. At her throat: a crucifix. Over her shoulders is a dark and heavy robe. Nothing I have learned in the past week prepares me for this apparition.

She cries. She weeps. She paces left and right and back and forth. Pivoting and turning suddenly to face me. Glaring straight into my eyes. A sudden halt. She looks up toward the cracked and yellowish ceiling of the room. Her children stand around her in a circle. Two little girls. A frightened boy. They stare at her, as I do, as her arms reach out—for what? They snap like snakes and coil back. Her hair is gray—a stiff and brushlike Afro.

Angelina is twelve years old, Stephen is eleven, Erica is nine. The youngest child, eleven months, is sitting on the floor. A neighbor's child, six years old, sits in my lap and leans her head against my chest; she holds her arms around my neck. Her name or nickname (I do not know which) is Raisin. When she likes she puts her fingers on my mouth and interrupts the conversation with a tremolo of rapid words. There are two rooms. Rachel disappears into the second room, then returns and stands, uneasy, by the door.

Angie: "Ever since August we been livin' here. The room is either very hot or freezin' cold. When it be hot outside it's hot in here. When it be cold outside we have no heat. We used to live with my aunt but then it got too crowded there so we moved out. We went to welfare and they sent us to the shelter. Then they shipped us to Manhattan. I'm scared of the elevators. 'Fraid they be stuck. I take the stairs."

Raisin: "Elevator might fall down and you would die."

Rachel: "It's unfair for them to be here in this room. They be yellin'. Lots of times I'm goin' to walk out. Walk out on the street and give it up. No, I don't do it. BCW [Bureau of Child Welfare] come to take the children. So I make them stay inside. Once they walk outside that door they are in danger."

Angie: "I had a friend Yoki. They was tryin' to beat her. I said: 'Leave her.' They began to chase me. We was runnin' to the door. So we was runnin'. I get to the door. The door was stuck. I hit my eye and it began to bleed. So I came home and washed the blood. Me and my friends sat up all night and prayed. Prayin' for me. 'Dear Lord, can you please help me with my eye? If you do I promise to behave.' I was askin' God why did this happen. I wish someone in New York could help us. Put all of the money that we have together and we buy a building. Two or three rooms for every family. Everybody have a kitchen. Way it is, you frightened all the time. I think this world is coming to the end."

Stephen: "This city is rich."

Angie: "Surely is!"

Erica: "City and welfare, they got something goin'. Pay $3,000 every month to stay in these here rooms . . ."

Rachel: "I believe the City Hall got something goin' here. Gettin' a cut. They got to be. My children, they be treated like chess pieces. Send all of that money off to Africa? You hear that song? They're not thinking about people starvin' here in the United States. I was thinkin': Get my kids and all the other children here to to sing, 'We are the world. We live here too.' How come do you care so much for people you can't see? Ain't we the world? Ain't we a piece of it? We are so close they be afraid to see. Give us a shot at something. We are something! Ain't we *something?* I'm depressed. But we are *something!* People in America don't want to see."

Angie: "Christmas is sad for everyone. We have our toys. That's not the reason why. They givin' you toys and that do help. I would rather that we have a place to be."

Erica: "I wrote a letter to Santa Claus. Santa say that he don't have the change."

Raisin: "I saw Santa on the street. Then I saw Santa on

another street. I pulled his beard and he said something nasty."

Angie: There's one thing I ask: a home to be in with my mother. That was my only wish for Christmas. But it could not be."

Raisin: "I saw Mr. Water Bug under my mother's bed. Mr. Rat be livin' with us too."

Angie: "It's so cold right now you got to use the hot plate. Plug it in so you be warm. You need to have a hot plate. Are you goin' to live on cold bologna all your life?"

Raisin: "Mr. Rat came in my baby sister's crib and bit her. Nobody felt sorry for my sister. Then I couldn't go to sleep. I started crying. All of a sudden I pray and went to sleep and then I woke up in the mornin', make my bed, and took a bath, and ate, and went to school. So I came back and did my homework. And all of a sudden there was something *irritatin'* at my hand. I looked out the window and the moon was goin' up. And then—I had a dream. I went to sleep and I was dreamin' and I dreamed about a witch that bit me. I felt *dead.* When I woke back up I had a headache."

Angie: "School is bad for me. I feel ashamed. They know we're not the same. My teacher do not treat us all the same. They know which children live in the hotel."

Erica: "My teacher isn't like that. She treats all of us the same. We all get smacked. We all get punished the same way."

Stephen: "I'm in sixth grade. When I am a grown-up I be a computer."

Erica: "You're in the fifth. You lie."

Raisin: "When I grow up I want to be multiplication and subtraction and division."

Angie: "Last week a drug addict tried to stab me. With an ice pick. Tried to stab my mother too. Older girls was botherin' us. They try to make us fight. We don't fight. We don't start fires. They just pickin' on us. We ran home and got our mother. They ran home and got their mother."

Raisin: "Those girls upstairs on the ninth floor, they be bad. They sellin' crack."

Erica: "Upstairs, ninth floor, nine-o-five, they sellin' crack."

Raisin: "A man was selling something on the street. He

had some reefers on him and the po-lice caught him and they took him to the jail. You know where the junkies put the crack? Put the crack inside the pipe. Smoke it like that. They take a torch and burn the pipe and put it in their mouth. They go like this." [Puffs.]

I ask: "Why do they do it?"

Erica: "Feel good! Hey! Make you feel fine!"

Angie: "This girl I know lives in a room where they sell drugs. One day she asks us do we want a puff. So we said: 'No. My mother doesn't let us do it.' One day I was walkin' in the hall. This man asked me do I want some stuff. He said: 'Do you want some?' I said no and I ran home."

Raisin: "One day my brother found these two big plastic bags inside his teddy bear. Po-lice came up to my room and took that teddy bear." She's interrupted. "I ain't finished! And they took it. One day we was by my uncle's car and this man came and he said: 'Do you want some?' We said no. We told my uncle and he went and found the man and he ran to the bar and went into the women's bathroom in the bar. And so we left."

Angie: "I think this world is ending. Yes. Ending. Everybody in this city killin' on each other. Countries killin' on each other. Why can't people learn to stick together? It's no use to fightin'. Fightin' over nothin'. What they fightin' for? A flag! I don't know what we are fightin' for. President Reagan wants to put the rockets on the moon. What's he doin' messin' with the moon? If God wanted man and woman on the moon He would of put us there. They should send a camera to the moon and feed the people here on earth. Don't go messin' there with human beings. Use that money to build houses. Grow food! Buy seeds! Weave cloth! Give it to the people in America!"

Erica: "When we hungry and don't have no food we borrow from each other. Her mother [Raisin's] give us food. Or else we go to Crisis. In the mornin' when we wake up we have a banana or a cookie. If the bus ain't late we have our breakfast in the school. What I say to President Reagan: Give someone a chance! I believe he be a selfish man. Can't imagine how long he been president."

Raisin: "Be too long."

Angie: "Teacher tell us this be a democracy. I don't

know. I doubt it. Rich people, couldn't they at least give us a refund?"

Raisin: "This man say his son be gettin' on his nerves. He beat his little son 'bout two years old. A wooden bat. He beat him half to death. They took him to the hospital and at five-thirty he was dead. A little boy. [Interrupted.] Let me talk!"

Erica: "The little boy. He locked himself into the bathroom. He was scared. After he died police came and his father went to jail. His mother, she went to the store."

Raisin, in a tiny voice: "People fight in here and I don't like it. Why do they do it? 'Cause they're sad. They fight over the world. I ain't finished!"

Erica: "One time they was two cops in the hall. One cop pulled his gun and he was goin' shoot me. He said did I live there? I said no. So I came home."

Raisin: "I was in this lady room. She be cryin' because her baby died. He had [mispronounced] pneumonia. He was unconscious and he died." Soft voice: "Tomorrow is my birthday."

The children are tended by a friend. In the other bedroom, Rachel, who is quieter now, paces about and finally sits down.

"Do you know why there's no carpet in the hall? If there was a carpet it would be on fire. Desperate people don't have no control. You have to sleep with one eye open. Tell the truth, I do not sleep at night.

"Before we lived here we were at the Forbell shelter [barracks shelter on Forbell Street in Brooklyn]. People sleep together in one room. You sleep across. You have to dress in front of everybody. Men and women. When you wake, some man lookin' at you puttin' on your clothes. Lookin' at your children too. Angelina, she be only twelve years old . . .

"There's one thing. My children still are pure. They have a concept of life. Respect for life. But if you don't get 'em out of here they won't have anything for long. If you get 'em out right now. But if you don't . . . My girls are innocent still. They are unspoiled. Will they be that way for long? Try to keep 'em in the room. But you can't lock 'em up for long.

"When we moved here I was forced to sign a paper. Everybody has to do it. It's a promise that you will not cook inside your room. So we lived on cold bologna. Can you feed a child on that? God forgive me but nobody shouldn't have to live like this. I can't even go downstairs and get gack on the elevator. Half the time it doesn't work. Since I came into this place my kids begun to get away from me."

There's a crucifix on the wall. I ask her: "Do you pray?"

"I don't pray! Pray for what? I been prayin' all my life and I'm still here. When I came to this hotel I still believed in God. I said: 'Maybe God can help us to survive.' I lost my faith. My hopes. And everything. Ain't nobody—no God, no Jesus—gonna help us in no way.

"God forgive me. I'm emotional. I'm black. I'm in a blackness. Blackness is around me. In the night I'm scared to sleep. In the mornin' I'm worn out. I don't eat no breakfast. I don't drink no coffee. If I eat, I eat one meal a day. My stomach won't allow me. I have ulcers. I stay in this room. I hide. This room is safe to me. I am afraid to go outside.

"If I go out, what do I do? People drink. Why do they drink? A person gets worn out. They usin' drugs. Why they use drugs? They say: 'Well, I won't think about it now.' Why not? You ain't got nothin' else to do, no place to go. 'Where I'm gonna be tomorrow or the next day?' They don't know. All they know is that they don't have nothin'. So they drink. And some of them would rather not wake up. Rather be dead. That's right.

"Most of us are black. Some Puerto Rican. Some be white. They suffer too. Can you get the government to know that we exist? I know that my children have potential. They're intelligent. They're smart. They need a chance. There's nothin' wrong with them for now. But not for long. My daughter watches junkies usin' needles. People smokin' crack in front a them. Screwin' in front a them. They see it all. They see it everywhere. What is a man and woman gonna do when they are all in the same room?

"I met a girl the other day. She's twelve years old. Lives on the fourteenth floor. She got a baby the same age as mine. Her mother got five children of her own. I don't want my daughter havin' any baby. She's a child. Innocent. Innocent. No violence. She isn't bitter. But she's scared. You understand? This is America. These children growin' up too fast. We have no hope. And you know why? Because we all feel just the same way deep down in our hearts. Nowhere to go . . . I'm not a killer. My kids ain't no killers. But if they don't learn to kill they know they're goin' to die.

"They didn't go to school last week. They didn't have clean clothes. Why? Because the welfare messed my check. It's supposed to come a week ago. It didn't come. I get my check today. I want my kids to go to school. They shouldn't miss a day. How they gonna go to school if they don't got some clothes? I couldn't wash. I didn't have the money to buy food.

"Twice the welfare closed my case. When they do it you are s'posed to go for a fair hearing. Take some papers, birth certificates. So I went out there in the snow. Welfare worker wasn't there. They told me to come back. Mister, it ain't easy to be beggin'. I went to the Crisis. And I asked her, I said, 'Give me somethin' for the kids to eat. Give me *somethin'!* Don't turn me away when I am sittin' here in front of you and askin' for your help!' She said she had nothin'. So my kids went out into the street. That's right! Whole night long they was in Herald Square panhandlin'. Made five dollars. So we bought bologna. My kids is good to me. We had bread and bologna.

"Welfare, they are not polite. They're personal. 'Did you do this? Did you do that? Where your husband at?' Understand me? 'Cause they sittin' on the other side of this here desk, they think we're stupid and we do not understand when we're insulted. 'Oh, you had another baby?' Yeah! I had another baby! What about it? Are you goin' to kill that baby? I don't say it, but that's what I feel like sayin'. You learn to be humble.

"I'm here five miserable months. So I wonder: Where I'm goin'? Can't the mayor give us a house? A part-time job? I am capable of doin' *somethin'.*

"You go in the store with food stamps. You need Pampers. You're not s'posed to use the stamps for Pampers. Stores will accept them. They don't care about the law. What they do is make you pay a little extra. They know you don't have no choice. So they let you buy the Papmers for two dollars extra.

"Plenty of children livin' here on nothin' but bread and bologna. Peanut butter. Jelly. Drinkin' water. You buy milk. I bought one gallon yesterday. Got *this* much left. They drink it fast. Orange juice, they drink it fast. End up drinkin' Kool Aid.

"Children that are poor are used like cattle. Cattle or horses. They are owned by welfare. They know they are bein' used—for what? Don't *use* them! Give 'em somethin'!

"In this bedroom I'm not sleepin' on a bed. They won't give me one. You can see I'm sleepin' on a box spring. I said to the manager: 'I need a bed instead of sleepin' on a spring.' Maid give me some blankets. Try to make it softer."

The Bible by her bed is opened to the Twenty-third Psalm.

"I do believe. God forgive me. I believe He's there. But when He sees us like this, I am wonderin' where is He? I am askin': Where the hell He gone?

"Before they shipped us here we lived for five years in a basement. Five years in a basement with no bathroom. One small room. You had to go upstairs two floors to use the toilet. No kitchen. It was fifteen people in five rooms. Sewer kept backing up into the place we slept. Every time it flooded I would have to pay one hundred dollars just to get the thing unstuck. There were all my children sleepin' in the sewage. So you try to get them out and try to get them somethin' better. But it didn't get no better. I came from one bad place into another. But the difference is this is a place where I cannot get out.

"If I can't get out of here I'll give them up. I have asked them: 'Do you want to go away?' I love my kids and, if I did that, they would feel betrayed. They love me. They don't want to go. If I did it, I would only do it to protect them. They'll live anywhere with me. They're innocent. Their minds are clean. They ain't corrupt. They have a heart. All my kids love people. They love life. If they got a dime, a piece of bread, they'll share it. Letting them panhandle made me cry. I had been to welfare, told the lady that my baby ain't got Pampers, ain't got nothin' left to eat. I got rude and noisy and it's not my style to do that but you learn that patience and politeness get you nowhere.

"When they went out on the street I cried. I said: 'I'm scared. What's gonna happen to them?' But if they're hungry they are goin' to do *something*. They are gonna find their food from somewhere. Where I came from I was fightin' for my children. In this place here I am fightin' for my children. I am tired of fightin'. I don't want to fight. I want my kids to live in peace.

"I was thinkin' about this. If there was a place where you

could sell part of your body, where they buy an arm or somethin'
for a thousand dollars, I would do it. I would do it for my children. I would give my life if I could get a thousand dollars. What
would I lose? I lived my life. I want to see my children grow up
to live theirs.

"A lot of women do not want to sell their bodies. This is
something that good women do not want to do. I will sell mine.
I *will*. I will solicit. I will prostitute if it will feed them."

I ask: "Would you do it?"

"Ain't no 'would I?' I would do it." Long pause . . . "Yes. I
did.

"I had to do it when the check ain't come. Wasn't no one
gonna buy my arm for any thousand dollars. But they's plenty
gonna pay me twenty dollars for my body. What was my choice?
Leave them out there on the street, a child like Angelina, to
panhandle? I would take my life if someone found her dead
somewhere. I would go crazy. After she did it that one time I
was ashamed. I cried that night. All night I cried and cried. So I
decided I had one thing left. In the mornin' I got up out of this
bed. I told them I was goin' out. Out in the street. Stand by the
curb. It was a cold day. Freezin'! And my chest is bad. I'm thirty-
eight years old. Cop come by. He see me there. I'm standin' out
there cryin'. Tells me I should go inside. Gives me three dollars.
'It's too cold to be outside.' Ain't many cops like that. Not many
people either . . .

"After he's gone a man come by. Get in his car. Go with
him where he want. Takin' a chance he crazy and he kill me.
Wishin' somehow that he would.

"So he stop his car. And I get in. I say a price. That's it. Go
to a room. It's some hotel. He had a lot of money so he rented a
deluxe. Asked me would I stay with him all night. I tell him no
I can't 'cause I have kids. So, after he done . . . whatever he did
. . . I told him that I had to leave. Took out a knife at me and
held it at my face. He made me stay. When I woke up next day I
was depressed. Feel so guilty what I did. I feel real scared. I can
understand why prostitutes shoot drugs. They take the drugs so
they don't be afraid.

"When he put that knife up to my throat, I'm thinkin' this:
What is there left to lose? I'm not goin' to do any better in this

life. If I be dead at least my kids won't ever have to say that I betrayed them. I don't like to think like that. But when things pile up on you, you do. 'I'm better if I'm dead.'

"So I got me twenty dollars and I go and buy the Pampers for the baby and three dollars of bologna and a loaf of bread and everyone is fed.

"That cross of Jesus on the wall I had for seven years. I don't know if I believe or not. Bible say that Jesus was God's son. He died for us to live here on this earth. See, I believe— Jesus was innocent. But, when He died, what was it for? He died for nothin'. Died in vain. He should a let us die like we be doin' —we be dyin' all the time. We dyin' every day.

"God forgive me. I don't mean the things I say. God had one son and He gave His son. He gave him up. I couldn't do it. I got four. I could not give any one of them. I couldn't do it. God could do it. Is it wrong to say it? I don't know if Jesus died in vain."

She holds the Bible in her hands. Crying softly. Sitting on the box spring in her tangled robe.

"They laid him in a manger. Right? Listen to me. I didn't say that God forsaken us. I am confused about religion. I'm just sayin' evil overrules the good. So many bad things goin' on. Lot of bad things right here in this buildin'. It's not easy to believe. I don't read the Bible no more 'cause I don't find no more hope in it. I don't believe. But yet and still . . . I know these words." She reads aloud: " 'Lie down in green pastures . . . leadeth me beside still waters . . . restores my soul . . . I shall not want.'

"All that I want is somethin' that's my own. I got four kids. I need four plates, four glasses, and four spoons. Is that a lot? I know I'm poor. Don't have no bank account, no money, or no job. Don't have no nothin'. No foundation. Then and yet my children have a shot in life. They're innocent. They're pure. They have a chance." She reads: " 'I shall not fear . . .' I fear! A long, long time ago I didn't fear. Didn't fear for nothin'. I said God's protectin' me and would protect my children. Did He do it?

"Yeah. I'm walkin'. I am walkin' in the wilderness. That's what is is. I'm walkin'. Did I tell you that I am an ex–drug addict? Yeah. My children know it. They know and they understand. I'm walkin'. Yeah!"

The room is like a chilled cathedral in which people who do not believe in God ask God's forgiveness. "How I picture God is like an old man who speaks different languages. His beard is white and He has angels and the instruments they play are white and everything around is white and there is no more sickness, no more hunger for nobody. No panhandlin'. No prostitutes. No drugs. I had a dream like that.

"There's no beauty in my life except two things. My children and"—she hesitates—"I write these poems. How come, when I write it down, it don't come out my pencil like I feel? I don't know. I got no dictionary. Every time I read it over I am finding these mistakes.

Deep down in my heart
I do not mean these things I said.
Forgive me. Try to understand me.
I love all of you the same.
Help me to be a better mother.

"When I cry I let 'em know. I tell 'em I was a drug addict. They know and they try to help me to hold on. They helpin' me. My children is what's holdin' me together. I'm not makin' it. I'm reachin'. And they see me reachin' out. Angelina take my hand. They come around. They ask me what is wrong. I do let them know when I am scared. But certain things I keep inside. I try to solve it. If it's my department, I don't want them to be sad. If it be too bad, if I be scared of gettin' back on drugs, I'll go to the clinic. They have sessions every other night.

"Hardest time for me is night. Nightmares. Somethin's grabbin' at me. Like a hand. Some spirit's after me. It's somethin' that I don't forget. I wake up in a sweat. I'm wonderin' why I dream these dreams. So I get up, turn on the light. I don't go back to sleep until the day is breakin'. I look up an' I be sayin': 'Sun is up. Now I can go to sleep.'

"After the kids are up and they are dressed and go to school, then I lay down. I go to sleep. But I can't sleep at night. After the sun go down makes me depressed. I want to turn the light on, move around.

"Know that song—'Those Monday Blues'? I had that album once."

I say the title: " 'Monday Blues'?"

"I got 'em every day. Lots of times, when I'm in pain, I think I'm goin' to die. That's why I take a drink sometimes. I'm 'fraid to die. I'm wonderin': Am I dying?"

5

The Big Street

"The Death of the Hired Man" by Robert Frost is quoted in many essays on the homeless. Some of us may feel that we have heard too many times the words of the farmer talking to his wife. "Home," he says, " is the place where, when you have to go there, they have to take you in." His wife's words are more interesting but less often quoted: "I should have called it something you somehow haven't to deserve."

Public policy in the United States today does not accord with this idea. We do appear to feel a home must somehow be deserved or earned. We do seem to regard it as a "gift" of sorts, which now and then may be awarded for correct behavior. The consequent feeling voiced by many women I have met is that a home is something they must *prove* that they deserve, but they do not know how they can.

How does a woman prove she is deserving? How can she expect that anybody will believe her? Can Rachel prove her children are deserving? She may try—much of what she said to me is like a lawyer's brief on their behalf: "They're innocent. They're pure . . ." She has no reason to expect that her opinion of her children will be given a responsive hearing.

This question of "deserving" safe accommodations, food, forgiveness, love, freedom from fear, comes up in every conversation. Those who live in greatest darkness often are the least prepared to call themselves "deserving" and the least equipped to offer arguments that may persuade us that they are.

After I leave New York each time, I find my thoughts returning to the people I have met. I think most frequently of Rachel and I wonder what will happen to her children. What if the city takes her kids?

Several times in the subsequent weeks I have the wish to call her. This is, of course, impossible. She has no phone. There are phone booths in the lobby, but you cannot call a phone booth and expect to get a message to a woman in a room on the sixth floor. Messages I've phoned to the hotel desk have not been delivered. Letters sent to the hotel are sometimes long delayed before they reach a resident. It's easier to reach a friend of mine in northern Haiti than to get a note to Angelina's mother.

A month later I return. I go through the same ritual once more. Wait for the guards. Wait for the elevator. Give up waiting for the elevator. Climb six flights of stairs. Knock at the door. The rooms appear exactly as they did before. Nothing is different; but there is more tension in the air.

"They chargin' me with bein' a bad mother. You can see the letter that I got. It's in the bureau in the other room."

Angie has been arrested. Her brother Stephen was arrested too, but for a different reason.

"Angie was caught stealin'."

I ask: "What did she steal?"

"They got arrested stealin' food. They did it at a grocery. Why they do it?" Rachel says it was her fault: "I didn't get my check. Made some mistake. I was cut off. They was hungry. Told me they was goin' visit somebody downstairs. Came back with a chicken. I say: 'Where you get the chicken?' They say: 'We was packin' bags at A & P.' I know they was lyin' so I say: 'Tell me the truth.' She says: 'We stole it.' Next time that they did it, they got caught.

"Stephen, he got caught for something small. He tried to jump the turnstile in the subway 'cause he didn't have the token that he needs to get to school."

Jumping the subway stile is so common that it isn't treated as a serious offense; transit police are tolerant with children. Stealing from a supermarket is a different matter. What I have a very hard time keeping in my mind is that all these kids are really hungry and that some of them are hungry almost all the time.

An eight-year-old who lives in the hotel is sitting on the bed with Angelina. He tells me he panhandles when he's hungry. I ask him where. "The street," he says. Which street? "The big street," he replies. Rachel says that he means Broadway where it enters Herald Square.

Even though I've seen this often, I want him to tell me just exactly how he goes about it. I ask him what he does. Does he walk up to someone and put out his hand?

He tells me he cleans windows on the cars that stop for the red light on Thirty-second Street. If the driver's not annoyed or not afraid of him he rolls down the window and hands him a coin. He says he does it at rush hour in the afternoon. How much can he earn?

"Couple of dollars . . ."

"What do you do with it?" I ask.

"Go to the store. Buy some juice. Loaf of bread, quart of milk . . . Get me a box of cereal."

"What kind of cereal?"

"Cheerios!" He says it with a smile.

He's tiny, thin, has freckles and a cough. He's a student in the third grade. Raisin is his sister. Where is Raisin?

"Raisin's got the measles."

Children I meet like this are sometimes very shy at first and answer only in these short, staccato bursts. Then some kind of key is turned and an unexpected little narrative pours forth.

"This man that I met on the street, he says he'll give me twenty dollars."

He stops right there and waits for me to ask him something more. So I ask him: "What's he give you twenty dollars for?"

"If I take down my pants."

"Right on the street?"

"Yes," he says.

"Which street?"

"The big street," he says again.

I ask him: "When?"

"At two o'clock."

"Two in the afternoon?"

"No. When it's dark."

"What did you do?"

"I ran away. Came home and told my mother."

Rachel: "He ain't got no right to be out in the street at two o'clock. But they do it. And it happens. It don't need to be at night. Angie and her friend be out there in the afternoon. Man come up. She doesn't understand that he's a pimp. He treats them to a meal. Why do they want to feed a little girl? Fatten them up! Later he'll say: 'Remember what I done? You owe me somethin' in return.' "

Angie: "They was grown-up men. They told my friend, they said: 'Your friend is pretty.' So they say, do we want anything to eat. I was hungry. I said yes. They bought us hot dogs and a soda. So they said: 'Meet us on Friday night. We'll take you to the movie. You don't need to bring your brother.' I'm not stupid. I stayed home. I may be little but I have a brain."

Years ago I was a grade-school teacher and taught children just about her age. It's easy to imagine her surrounded by the other children in the classroom of a cheerful, clean, suburban school. It would be fun to be her teacher. She's alert and funny and the phrasing that she chooses is amusing. Even when the theme is human ruin I enjoy her skipping moods, her merriment and whim. Does she know that she is telling me the story of her own demise? Sordid though the story and disheartening and foul the four walls of the surrounding room, she lives in a child's garden still. Innocent, tonight, she may be transformed into a tough and lean and predatory woman in two years. Sitting here, it's easy to forget I'm not her teacher and she'll never be a student in a good suburban school.

"One day we were out in Herald Square. This old man, a white man, he say he was goin' to give me money. Gave me a five dollar bill. Then he ask me was I hungry and I was, so he says he is goin' to take me to the Burger King. So I went with him and we went to this parking lot and he pulled down his drawers. So I came home."

In the other bedroom later, with the door closed, Rachel tells me Angelina won't go outside any longer. "She won't step outside that door. She's scared. She's even scared to go to school.

"The letter I got from BCW—I got it hidden here." The

Bureau of Child Welfare has been renamed Special Services for Children; most of the mothers still refer to it by its original initials. The letter from an HRA caseworker is a warning that she's now under investigation. The letter includes a memo that refers to her abuse of alcohol.

Would these kids be better off if they were taken from her? Knowing what I do of foster care in New York City, I am certain that their lives would not be better. Even a home, sufficient food, a stove, a place to play, a neighborhood, real education in small classes in a first-rate school—would any of this make a difference now? Is it too late? It is impossible to know and our society, in any case, is not disposed to offer them this option.

One thing I know. Foster care cannot provide these children with the soaring loyalty that Rachel feels. The love that makes her language incandescent when she speaks of Angelina is her solace, but, because she cannot do what love instructs, it is her agony. Desire can be renounced, Ignatieff writes, and wishes bleached away. But the tragedy of need—the desperation of a mother's love—is that it can neither be renounced nor patiently endured.

"I didn't tell you this before. Angie—when they caught her stealin' at the store, they brought her here in handcuffs. I don't think you need to do that to a child. Once you see that, it do make things different. You do see your own self somewhat different from before. 'Well, if I done that, if I be bad, then why not go and do some more?' "

I never get to talk with her again. Someone has told her I have talked with the BCW. The next time she sees me in the lobby she turns instantly and hurries toward the stairs.

PART TWO

Failure to Thrive

But it is a dreadful place for child to pass the long days and nights in. This is rather hard treatment for a young witness, is it not?

—*Charles Dickens,* American Notes

1

Concealment

It is a commonplace that a society reveals its reverence or contempt for history by the respect or disregard that it displays for older people. The way we treat our children tells us something of our moral disposition too.

The rate of child poverty in 1986 was one-third higher than ten years before. The Children's Defense Fund states that poverty, which has increased 50 percent since 1969, now affects "nearly one out of every three children under the age of six."

In constant dollars, welfare benefits to families with children have declined 35 percent since 1970, according to the *New York Times.*

The Reagan administration canceled the White House Conference on Children for the first time in this century.

Children are paying a stunning price for these revised priorities. Housing discrimination against children is well documented nationwide. A federal study finds that children are "routinely excluded from a fourth of rental housing" and "from 60 percent" of housing built since 1970. New York City "may be worse," the *New York Times* reports. "Call us soft on children," writes the *Times.* "We think a society that harmfully discriminates against its young betrays its heritage and subverts it future."

The bias against children finds its most extreme expression in denial of essential health care and nutrition. In 1985, according to the *New England Journal of Medicine*, 35 million Americans had no health insurance. One million people had been cut from food stamps in the first year of the Reagan presidency. Six hundred thousand had been cut from Medicaid from 1981 to 1983. Children had been "hardest hit by cuts in Medicaid." Two hundred fifty community health-care centers had been closed in 1982. One million low-income children had been excluded from nutrition programs between 1982 and 1984. There had been "a nationwide increase in the number and percentage of women who do not receive prenatal care at all or before the third trimester" and a "large increase" in the incidence of anemia in pregnant women.

"Maternal anemia," according to the same report, "has been associated with low birth weight and with stunted cognitive and physical development in children." Women who do not receive prenatal care, the *Journal* said, are "three times as likely" to give birth to a low-birth-weight child. According to one study, "Low-birth-weight babies are 40 to 200 times more likely to die and three times more likely to have neurodevelopmental handicaps. . . ."

A "particularly ominous finding," said the *Journal*, was the recent increase in the incidence of low-birth-weight babies. In Boston, "14 percent of inner-city children"—or three times the normal rate—fell into this category. "Blood lead levels are also rising. Between 1982 and 1983 there was a 59 percent increase in the number of children with elevated lead levels and a 52 percent increase in the incidence of clinical lead poisoning." The incidence of measles had increased in 1984 "for the first time since introduction of the vaccine. . . ." A separate article in the same issue of the *Journal* spoke of the Reagan administration's "relentless efforts" to reduce health services to "low-income persons who are aged, blind, disabled, or members of families with dependent children."

Abnormally high numbers of the children of the homeless are low-birth-weight babies. We have been acquainted with the term "failure to thrive." The phrase, while it applies to children of the rich and poor alike, increasingly defines the status of the poorest chldren in our land. It also suggests some of the clinical detachment that permits us to attribute failure to the child rather than to the society that has endangered him. But the medical term may be applied more broadly. All but a few of the children in the Martinique and similar hotels will fail to thrive in any meaningful respect.

Early death or stunted cognitive development are not the only risks these children face. Emotional damage may be expected too. Ellen Bassuk, a psychiatrist at Harvard who has studied many homeless families, speaks of interviewing children who are more depressed than those she would expect to find in psychiatric clinics. She describes a nineteenth-month-old baby who has started having nightmares and stopped eating. A ten-year-old boy, ridden with anxiety, begins to mutilate himself. He has pulled out his permanent teeth.

Anger that does not turn in upon the child frequently turns out to vent itself upon society. Children liked Doby, Christopher and Angelina live with a number of good reasons for intense hostility and with very few for acquiescence in those norms by which societies must live. Such children, if they do not cause disruption in the streets and hotels, may do so in the public schools. Even the most enlightened teachers in an urban school are likely to take recourse to severe and punitive measures to contain a child's wrath and to preserve some semblance of serenity in which to educate the other children in the class.

In classes that contain large numbers of such pupils, education often must be forfeited almost entirely. Discipline problems dominte the teacher's time. An atmosphere of martial law prevails. Teachers faced with pedagogic situations of this sort often flee the education world for more rewarding work. This, in itself—the loss of excellent teachers and the loss of decent education for all children—is one of the incalculable costs that we incur.

What happens to children whose behavior in the school is so disruptive that they simply can't be handled anymore? What of the child who begins to drift into the streets and never gets to school at all? That child runs the risk of being placed in jurisdiction of the courts. A child in this situation enters a legal netherworld, or category, commonly referred to as that of the "status offender." The status offense is not a form of criminal behavior (it is not the child but the child's status that offends us), but it does compel the state to introduce a child to the legal system.

A month before my visit to the Martinique I was asked to speak before an audience of justices of New York's Family Court at a weekend convocation held in Tarrytown. Conversations with a number of the judges, children's advocates, and welfare workers present at this meeting left a stunning portrait of the long delays and vast expense in time and labor needed to bring children through the labyrinth of the courts.

The dollar costs of juvenile placement are the least important; even these are quite astonishing. The cost of placement for a child who is too severely damaged to be suited for an ordinary foster home—one who requires placement, for example, in a low-security institution—ranges from $25,000 up to $50,000 yearly. In cases where children are believed to need more careful supervision, costs may be as high as $80,000.

Shortages of space in juvenile homes, moreover, frequently compel the court to place the child in an institution which is also home to serious offenders. The status offender and the genuine offender (one who, were he older, would have been condemned to prison) live together in such institutions. The status offender learns survival strategies from those with whom he dwells and must contend. Soon enough, the categories that divide them become academic. The child whose sole offense had been a status that compelled compassionate attention from the state now becomes apprenticed to those who are competent in real offenses. He learns to struggle, to connive, to lie, and to fight back.

With few exceptions, children placed in institutions of this sort mature in time into adult offenders. The cost of their adult incarceration may be less than that of juvenile detention ($40,000 yearly is an average cost for prison maintenance of adults at the present time in New York City), but there are additional expenses that cannot be measured: damage to victims and to property; costs required to provide police protection for the law-abiding citizens; costs of litigation, prosecution, and defense; and all the other billions squandered as the seemingly inevitable price of our initial willingness to countenance the institutional assault upon these children in their early years.

The power of peer pressure to instruct a child in the use of

violence is most readily perceived in juvenile detention but prevails, often with equal force, in places like the Martinique. "My
kids ain't no killers," Rachel said. "But if they don't learn to kill
they know they're goin' to die." The lessons of violence are all
around them. Exiled from the family of society, they may see
few reasons to respect the family's rules.

A letter from a woman in the Martinique brings me this
information: "A security guard got killed right on my floor last
week. It's been on the news since Sunday morning. It seems a
man was beating up his wife. Security was called. The man was
told to leave the room. He came back with a shotgun and he
shot the guard right in the face. He ran to get some help and he
collapsed and died beside the elevator. Half his head and brains
were on the floor around the corner where he had been shot."

Can we expect that children do not see these things? "They
see it all," Rachel observed. "They see it everywhere." We have
now seen Angelina coming home in handcuffs. More important,
she has seen *herself* in handcuffs. The end of innocence for
Rachel's children seems to be at hand.

New York City spends a huge amount of money to build
prisons and a great deal more to house the prisoners within
those buildings. A year after my visit to the Martinique, I am
told the New York prison population is approaching 15,000. In
desperation to find further space, the city has converted a ferry-
boat to hold another 160 men. It now announces plans to build
a vast new prison that will hold 4,000 inmates. The prison will
be built on Staten Island. The Staten Island borough president,
who has opposed a plan to build four homeless shelters in his
borough, indicates his preference for the prison. "A jail is pref-
erable to a shelter," he explains, "because it's self-contained."
He notes that "it doesn't spill over" into the surrounding neighborhood.

An equation, then, already exists between the homeless
population and the inmates of a jail. The theme of containment
is applied to both; the jail contains its inmates more efficiently.
His phrase—"it doesn't spill over"—is suggestive. "Spillage" is
applied more frequently to sewage than to human beings. But it
is unrealistic to believe that any containment of this "spillage"
is within the power of the city. New York will never be able to

build new prisons fast enough to hold all of the turbulence and
anger that are being manufactured daily in the Martinique Hotel
and in the more than sixty other buildings that contain its
homeless children.

In reviewing a book on the alleged genetic origins of crime,
Mayor Koch writes that "people who try to blame society for
criminal behavior look pretty foolish." He cites the authors'
"fundamental insight" that "an indivdual commits crime because of enduring personal characteristics." These innate factors
include, among others, "level of intelligence, genetic inheri-
tance, "anatomical configuration. . . ." He says the authors "effectively destroy the shibboleth that poverty causes crime" and
quotes without demurral their assertion that "chronically criminal biological parents are likely to produce criminal sons. . . ."
He describes such persons as "this legion of habitual predators."
He notes that "the number of convicted felons in New York
prisons has more than doubled" since he came to office.

The number of homeless families has increased more than
500 percent in the same years.

What of the children who do not become entangled in the
legal system but remain to do their best in the hotels and public
schools? Many do not get to school at all. Transient existence
cuts them from the rolls. If readmitted to their former schools,
they may face a long ride on a bus or subway twice a day. If the
bus or train is late, they arrive at school too late for breakfast
and must struggle through their lessons on an empty stomach.
If transferred to another school close to their temporary residence, they still face the other obstacles that we have seen. Just
getting up and getting out may be a daunting task.

At P.S. 64, on New York's Lower East Side, 125 children
from the Martinique were registered in February 1987. Only
about 85 arrived on any given day. This estimate indicates that
almost one third aren't in regular attendance but does not include those who, because of bureaucratic complications or parental disarray, have never been enrolled. I would guess, based
on a head count of the school-age children in the ballroom of
the Martinique at lunch, that *more* than a third of the children
in this building do not usually get to school.

What of those who do make it to school? Teachers speak of

kids who fall into a deep sleep at their desks because conditions in their hotel rooms denied them a night's rest. How much can such children learn? Stanley Goldstein, principal of P.S. 64, estimates that a quarter of the hotel children are between two and three grades behind their peers in academic skills. This, he observes, makes them still more reluctant to appear at all. "They feel like idiots . . . ," he says. "Can you blame them?"

A reporter describes a nine-year-old in the third grade, already a year behind his proper grade, who cannot read, cannot tell time, and has a hard time adding and subtracting numbers of two digits. He has been classified "learning disabled" and "emotionally disturbed." Many of the hotel children, school officials say, are becoming "deeply troubled" and exhibiting the symptoms of withdrawal. Others are becoming hyperactive.

Mr. Goldstein notes that it is difficult to reach the parents of a child. (Families in the Martinique seldom have phones.) He adds that, even when attendance officers attempt to visit parents at the Martinique, they are often unsuccessful. He says that sometimes no one answers—"Or sometimes there's no one there." What does the attendance officer do? He can leave a message at the desk, but parents tell me there is a good chance that it will never be received.

"You're not dealing with the Pierre, you know . . . ," says Mr. Goldstein. "We have children who just disappear from the face of the earth."

The New York Board of Education does not know how often children of the homeless lose out on an education; nor does it keep records of how well those who are registered in school perform. Nor has it any central policy to dictate to the schools how homeless children should be treated.

For children in the barracks shelters, pedagogic damage may be worse. In these situations, rudimentary classsrooms are provided as a substitute for school. In some of these shelters, according to the *New York Times*, "the one-room schoolhouse —a fond bit of Americana—has been revised and updated to serve the city's dispossessed." There is nothing fond, and little of Americana, in the setup that the city has contrived to fill the days, if not the minds, of these unlucky children. One courageous teacher, given few supplies, does the best she can with a forty-year-old encyclopedia, donated desks, and storybooks on loan. "I've had three children and I've had forty-five . . . I never know, from one morning to the next, who will be here or how many." Sometimes her biggest job, she says, is calming the kids down.

The problem is not limited to the five boroughs of New York. Homeless children in Westchester County undertake extraordinary journeys to get to their schools: Of 860 dislocated children living in motels, half or more must travel up to forty miles twice a day. Many travel longer distances. Because of shortages of space in Westchester motels and (according to one press report) beause motels in other counties offer cheaper rooms, 454 children have been sheltered in motels in four different counties.

Each morning, they are put on buses—or, where there are not enough of them to justify a bus, in taxis—and they ride from town to town, county to county, in their search for education. Often these taxis take a number of different children to a number of different schools. "This results in children arriving at school either very early or late," reports a school psychologist in Peekskill. Many of these children rise so early that they don't eat breakfast and arrive at school carsick and hungry. "In our school" he says, "we have children as young as four years old traveling over thirty miles. . . ."

There is unintended irony in this. A society that vocally rejects the "busing" of poor children over distances of two to seven miles to achieve desegregation finds it acceptable to ship a child forty miles to be sure she goes to school where she originally lived. One homeless twelve-year-old at school in Peekskill says that she has been commuting from Poughkeepsie since the age of ten. A ten-year-old at school in Yonkers rides sixty miles *twice a day* from a motel in Newburgh. Because the system lacks coordination, schools in Mt. Vernon have children who commute from Yonkers while Yonkers schools have children who commute from Brewster. Westchester County, according to the *New York Times,* is trying to devise "a computer program" that would "keep track" of the children and their parents, "cross-referencing the homeless. . . ."

In provision of transportation, as of basic shelter, money

may be made out of despair. A long taxi ride costs $10 a day per child: $1,800 for the academic year. A bus ride, priced at $1 per child per mile, costs up to $80 a day. In one extreme case, a homeless child relocated in Poughkeepsie has to commute to school in Yonkers at a state expense of $180 a day—$32,000 if projected for the academic year. For one-third this sum, the child could be sent to private school. For a great deal less, she could be sent to school with children from Poughkeepsie. Is there a reason she must ride to Yonkers every day?

The owner of a motel housing thirty homeless children sees an opportunity for profit. He recently bought four buses and obtained a contract with Westchester County to transport the kids to school. He gets a dollar a mile for each child. "I would anticipate we will be picking up from more motels . . . ," he says. "I don't think homelessness is going to disappear."

Finding shelter for homeless families with children in New York becomes more difficult on weekends because, on Fridays and Saturdays, prostitutes have more business and the homeless must compete with them for space. In Washington, D.C., in 1986, the problem is more easiliy resolved. Children and prostitutes are housed in the same building.

"The number of homeless families seeking emergency shelter" in the District, writes the *Washington Post,* "increased more than 500 percent during the last year," pushing the city to house thirty-nine homeless children with their parents in a rooming house for prostitutes known as the Annex.

In the Annex, mothers put milk on windowsills to keep it cold. Families are confronted with drug paraphernalia in shared rest rooms. Children mingle with the prostitutes and clients. The owner of the rooming house describes it as unfit for children. "This is a pigpen," he tells a reporter. But the city keeps the children in the "pigpen" for almost a year.

A member of the city's Commission on Homelessness visits the "pigpen" and sees homeless children playing in corridors while, twenty feet away, prostitutes and clients take turns waiting to make use of the same room. Exit signs for the fire excape are in front of a locked door. Smoke detectors don't work. The ropes from the window sashes have been confiscated by drug users to tie up their arms. "This is one of the worst things anybody could do to any family," says a woman who has lost her home after losing her job. But she says she doesn't dare complain. "If I lose this I have nothing."

The city's excuse, the *Washington Post* writes in January 1987, "is, as usual, that it had no choice." But says the *Post*, there have been sufficient warning signs. When the city attempts to justify this as a temporary answer to an unexpected need, the *Post* observes that city officials have been putting families in the Annex "since last March." The *Post* editorializes that responsible officials ought to be removed. Embarrassed by the sudden press attention, a city official moves the families to another building. "This," she says, "is just to get the situation out of controversy."

The situation in Washington seems neither worse nor better than that in New York. Homeless families, according to the rules in Washington, must go every day to a decrepit place known as "the Pitts Hotel," where they receive their meals and room assignments for the night. If the Pitts is full, they're given bus fare and sent to one of two other dismal shelters. The next day they return to the Pitts and must begin the process once again.

"We have a more efficient system in the U.S. to deal with stray pets," says New York Congressman Ted Weiss, "than we have for homeless human beings."

Do we know what we are doing to these children?

Knowingly or not, we are creating a diseased, distorted, undereducated and malnourished generation of small children who, without dramatic intervention on a scale for which the nation seems entirely unprepared, will grow into the certainty of unemployable adulthood. The drop-out rate for the poorest children of New York is 70 percent. For homeless kids the rate will be much higher. None of these kids will qualify for jobs available in 1989 or 1995. But every one who is a female over twelve is qualified already to become a mother. Many only thirteen years of age in hotels like the Martinique are pregnant now. Hundreds more will have delivered children, brain-damaged or not, before their sixteenth year of life. They will not be reading books about prenatal care. They will not be reading or observing warnings about damage done to infants by the alcohol or drugs they may consume. When their hour of labor comes, many will not even understand the medical permission forms they sign before they are sent into anesthesia. What, then, will happen to *their* children?

Those who are tough-minded may berate the mothers of these children. They may lacerate their fathers for not finding the employment that does not exist, or for which those educated in the schools provided to poor people cannot qualify. No matter how harsh, however, how will they condemn the children? Will they accuse these children, too, of lacking the resilience to stand tall? Some of these children are so poorly nourished, their confidence so damaged, or their muscle tissue so deteriorated, that they have a hard time standing up at all.

Visitors remark that places like the Martinique Hotel remind them of a penal institution. Prisons are for those who have committed crimes. What crime did the children in the "pigpen" or the Martinique commit? These children haven't yet lived long enough to hurt us. They have not grown big enough to scare us. They have not yet learned enough to hate us. They are as yet unsoiled by their future indignation or our future fear. The truth is, they offend us only in one manner: by existing. Only by being born do they do injury to some of us. They take some of our taxes for their food and concentrated formula, their clothing, and their hurried clinic visits and their miserable shelter. When they sicken as a consequence of the unwholesome housing we provide they cost a little more; and, if they fail utterly to thrive, they take some money from the public treasury for burial.

So they offend us not by doing but by being. We pity them enough to put them in a warehouse, but we do not mark these buildings in a way that will attract attention. You could walk from Broadway to Fifth Avenue on Thirty-second Street a dozen times and never notice that there is a building on the left side of the street in which 400 families are concealed.

The Martinique Hotel is an enormous building and should not be easy to disguise; but the sign has no illumination and it's hard to see the name of the hotel unless one studies it from across the street. For this reason, and because of the bleak lighting in the lobby and the filthiness of the glass doors, it is difficult to recognize this as a residence. It resembles less a dwelling place than a dilapidated movie house or a bus station. One would not imagine from the sidewalk that this building might be home to 1,800 human beings.

Concealment is apparently important.

Stereotypes

The use of the unrestrictive term, "the homeless," is in certain ways misleading. It suggests a uniform set of problems and a single category of poor people. The miseries that many of these people undergo are somewhat uniform. The squalor is uniform. The density of living space is uniform. The fear of guards, of drugs, and of irrational bureaucracy is uniform. The uniformity is in their mode of suffering, not in themselves.

No two people in the Martinique are quite alike; but no two people could be less alike than Rachel and a woman I call Kim. Kim stands out from almost every other person I have met here. Her energy may be a helpful and instructive counterpoint to much of the hopelessness and panic we have seen.

She's in her twenties, has some education, and lives with her children in a room on the eleventh floor. She tells me that, before becoming homeless, she was living in a building she was trying to restore. She was a preschool teacher and was working to support her children when her enterprising spirit met its match in the cold weather of New York.

The plumbing and heating in the house weren't operating well. She had managed some repairs and was planning to replace the heater and install new pipes once she had saved the necessary funds. The heater ceased to function in December. She had no affluent relatives or friends to help her out.

Living in substandard housing on a tight and careful budget in the 1980s leaves no room for breakdown of the heating system in midwinter. In a matter of weeks she was reduced from working woman and householder to a client of the welfare system. Like many others, she was forced to sit and wait for hours with her children at the EAU. Like others, she was finally assigned to the Clemente shelter in the Bronx, one of the largest barracks used for housing homeless families at the time. Better informed than many mothers, she rejected placement at Clemente.

"There were people with tuberculosis in those barracks. I refused."

In 1984, Kim and her children were assigned a placement at the Martinique, where they now dwell.

Kim, because she's educated and articulate, is often interviewed by visiting researchers. When she is asked why she is here she says that it's because her heating system doesn't work. This answer is frustrating to researchers. Looking for more complicated data, they regard her answer as facetious—or a screen for something she is trying to conceal.

" 'What would it take to get you out of here?' they ask. Like, what would it take to get my family values reconstructed? I tell them: Maybe ten or fifteen thousand dollars. 'What would it take to get you back to work?' I tell them: 'Help me get a loan to fix up one of those abandoned buildings.' "

The city, state and federal government pay to the Martinique year after year the money that she might have used to have restored her home. Kim was doing, and would like to do again, exactly what the government ought to have been doing for the past ten years. She wasn't waiting for the government. She wasn't looking for a federal grant. She wasn't asking anything for free. She gave her sweat. She could have used a loan.

The New York City Council calculates (1986) that it would cost between $4,500 and $30,000 for the rehabilitation of each of 100,000 vacant units that the city owns in buildings seized for nonpayment of taxes. Others estimate that total ("gut") rehabilitation of some of these units may run higher—up to $65,000 each. An average rehabilitation cost may be $30,000. Even this—a one-time cost—is scarcely more than what the city spends each year to house a mother with four children in the Martinique.

"I know Mr. Tucelli." She speaks of him more comfortably than many tenants do. " 'I'll put you out of my hotel,' he says. 'You talk too much and give me too much trouble.' I tell him: 'Look, do you think that I like it here in your hotel? I am here because I have a broken furnace.' "

Mr. Tucelli carries a pistol. Many women speak of this with fear but Kim does not. "It doesn't bother me," she says. "Listen! Mr. Tucelli's pistol didn't put these people here. Mr. Tucelli's not my enemy. The guards and social workers aren't my enemies. The system that puts all of these poor people in this building is what makes me scared. In a way, I kind of *like* Mr. Tucelli. I see him sometimes looking worried—or unsure . . . I believe this whole thing makes him *very sad.* Does anybody like to run a prison?"

Like others, she reminds me that the Martinique is not the worst of the hotels. She speaks of another hotel, the Brooklyn Arms: "There are families there who say they have *no* heat and *no* hot water. There are people who have been there for two years. After they've been there that long they begin to tell themselves that it's forever. They stop getting dressed. They feel afraid to go outside. Once you're out, no matter where, you don't want to go back."

She says this about the Brooklyn Arms: "The building is so dangerous that welfare workers won't come to your room. You have to go down to the desk and beg for little things like toilet paper. The guards sell drugs. The place is run by somebody important. He's married to an opera star. He gives a lot of money to the politicians. When things go wrong, when something terrible occurs, who do they blame? They blame the residents. They're not going to blame someone with connections!"

Kim's words are later confirmed and amplified by stories in the press and by the New York City Council. The hotel draws attention when a fire breaks out and incinerates four children. At that point, the press cites residents' complaints that there was no fire-alarm system in the seventeen-story building and reports that rotting garbage is strewn about in roach-infested halls, that the owner is indeed the husband of an opera star, that his attorney is a former New York mayor named Robert Wagner. The press also confirms her point about political contributions by the operators of the Brooklyn Arms. A police investigation in July finds fifteen walkie-talkies allegedly used by hotel guards and others working for narcotics dealers. A report by members of the city council in November notes that, in order to call an elevator, "one must kick the door to the elevator shaft and yell . . ." Residents, the city council adds, "must negotiate . . . for toilet paper at the desk."

In a final confirmation of Kim's words, the death of the four children, one of whom was less than two years old, is blamed upon their parents. The mother and father, it appears, had left the children in order to go out into the streets and search for cans and bottles that they could turn in for cash, perhaps in order to buy food. They are charged with "endangerment" and put in jail before their children can be buried. The city's response is not to criticize the hotel management but to increase funds available for burying poor children.

Kim: "There are worse hotels than that. The Allerton is worse. Same thing there: You have to beg for toilet paper in the lobby. The Bayview—that's in Brooklyn. . . . Owned by a criminal. It costs a lot. I think it's something like $100—more than here. One hotel, the Holland, makes $3 million every year. Most of these people owe the city money in back taxes. Does the city seize their buildings? No. But they'll put a woman on the street because she owes $200 to her landlord."

As she observes, however, hotel owners are not the real issue; giving more than brief attention to such individuals diverts from more important problems. Cities, moreover, can deal with such exposures easily. It is a common practice of officials everywhere, once an atrocious situation has been publicized, to make amends in a determined but selective manner. For this reason it is possible that the Brooklyn Arms or Martinique may have been shut down before too many years. It is also possible that the Martinique which has received unusual scrutiny, may in time be turned into a showpiece of benevolence and order to discredit those who have condemned its recent practices.

There is another reason for believing this is possible: Mr. Tucelli, I am told, would like to see himself as a humanitarian and to be so regarded by others. Kim's relatively generous perception of her landlord is, admittedly, voiced by few others in the building. Most residents are in too much turmoil to attempt to see the human side of someone who holds so much power over them. But at least one other woman has described some kindly things that he has done: small favors or a thoughtful word to somebody in trouble. Even if the Martinique, however, should someday be utterly transformed, there will still be more than sixty other buildings in New York that offer an equivalent regime of degradation. The real question is why the city, any city, will allow itself to do this.

"Government policy," according to the New York City Council, holds that if homelessness is made "too comfortable," the homeless "will want to remain homeless." The mayor believes that the hotels have acted as a magnet. His concern is that a family doubled up or living in substandard housing sees hotels as the first step to better housing. "New buildings," he says, "are like highways—they attract occupants." For this reason, he explains, "we are going to, whenever possible, put people into congregate housing [which] is not something people might rush into. . . ."

"The mayor's words are very hard on people living here," says Kim. "I don't know what's in his heart. But his sarcasm hurts a lot of people."

She tells me of a child in the Martinique who has had an opportunity to testify in Washington. In his testimony before Congress, he reported he was often hungry when he went to school. He said that he had trouble concentrating and sometimes he had to rest his head against his desk because, he said, "it hurts to be hungry." The mayor replied that the child's family (six persons) received a budget of over $20,000, not including the hotel bill. Thousands of city employees, he observed, earn less than that. "And," he said, "they all work for a living. I wonder why they bother."

Kim: "What he seems to mean is that the people here are lazy. I don't believe the mayor is being fair. When he added up that budget, he included the allowance for apartment rent. People in a hotel don't receive it. He added Medicaid. Right there, those two items add about $8,000. Subtract $8,000 and the budget comes to something like $6 for each child for one day. Is that enough to feed your child in New York?"

A reporter later asked a similar question to the mayor. "You bet it is," he said.

The mayor's views have changed somewhat in recent months. His present position, summarized in the final pages of this book, has been described by homeless advocates as less severe. Whatever one may think of this, it may be worthwhile to recall Kim's words about Mr. Tucelli. Individuals did not create these prisons. Systemic inequities are the real issue. City officials throughout the nation, faced with the results of such inequities, resort to words and measures that seem punitive.

Why do they do it? "They have to do it," George Orwell wrote in 1931. "If they made these places too pleasant you'd have all the scum of the country flocking into them." That is apparently what cities fear.

"As to conditions at the hotels," the HRA reports, "the city . . . has a stringent Family Hotel Inspection Program. Violations of building and health codes are identified through regular inspections. . . . Corrective action plans are both required and enforced. . . ."

It is true that there is an inspection program. Inspections in the Martinique, however, are announced ahead of time. Families are told to hide their hot plates or their toasters in a drawer. Residents tell me garbage bags are handed out by the hotel to hide a hot plate too large for a bureau drawer. The ritual has the effect of leaving residents responsible for fires or for any injuries to children that result from cooking in a crowded room. The hotel is protected by the notice that prohibits cooking, given to people on arrival. The city is protected by the pretense of inspection. The residents are unprotected.

"When I came here first," says Kim, "I found I'd lost the right to vote. A group of people had to sue the city to regain the franchise. Even with the vote we're disenfranchised. We're like cripples in this city. But I thought that the denial of our right to vote was pretty raw.

"Other rights go by the board. You're not supposed to talk to a reporter. There's no written rule, but it's well understood you run the risk of being thrown out of your room if you say something that gets into print. You can publish a newsletter but it's censored. There was one newsletter issued by the nurse. They did an item about legal rights, the way to fight eviction. Very brief—they simply gave a number to reach Legal Aid. The hotel confiscated the entire issue. How do TV stations get into the building? They hide their cameras, one reporter hid the camera in a baby carriage."

She shows me a copy of the banned newsletter that she salvaged from the trash. The item about Legal Aid is followed by this admonition: "Please do not leave your children unattended. If you absolutely cannot take them with you, get a responsible baby-sitter. Otherwise, fires could result. . . . Your children [could be] taken away by the police. Things could get worse. . . ."

She laughs. "That's true. They could. You could be in a hotel that doesn't have refrigerators. We had to fight for those. Food for children couldn't be refrigerated. You couldn't open a can of infant formula and save it overnight. If you didn't use it all you'd have to throw it out.

"I'd been through one summer here with no refrigerator. Living in this building in the summer—it was steaming in these rooms. A woman upstairs agreed to talk to a reporter. A man who saw the story offered to provide her a refrigerator. He asked: 'Does anybody else there need refrigerators?' She said: 'Every mother in the building does.' So he told her: 'Get a list together.' I worked on it with her. We found diabetics in the building keeping insulin under the water tap. There were children who were ill and needed daily medication. Some needed injections. We made the list. On the day they came, Mr. Tucelli wouldn't let us bring them in. The truck was there. TV reporters came. Once he saw them he agreed. If you confront him, he'll back down."

The hotel added a dollar to the rent each night for the refrigerators. "Later he supplied them to all residents. They're half-size refrigerators. I believe they cost less than $200." She does not regard this policy as sinister but simply part of a predictable routine. "Why not? Hey! For him, it isn't a bad deal."

She tells me what happens when the rent is overdue: "First you lose your right to visitors, clean linens . . . Mr. Tucelli comes to your door at 6:00 A.M. He bangs on the door. You open up. There he is in the hallway with his gun. 'Where's your rent?' "

I ask her why a parent doesn't go and get the rent a day or two before it's due.

"That would make sense," she says. "But that's the problem. It is not permitted. You cannot get your rent check even *one* day early. You have to go and pick it up the day it's due. Even then, they don't begin to type the checks until four in the afternoon. If someone's sick, a crisis, anything like that, you're overdue. If the rent is three days overdue, they'll send up a guard at 1:00 or 2:00 A.M. He bangs at the door 'Your rent is due.' It wakes the children. Then you can't get back to sleep. Six A.M. He bangs again. Mr. Tucelli. 'Where's your rent?' " She shakes her head. "There's got to be a better way to do this . . ."

Kim is a lively woman with an angry and investigative zeal. But none of her anger is turned in upon herself. It is turned out; and in that turning out, that venting of a well-defined and well-supported rage, she finds a fair degree of energy and health.

Political anger isn't high on any list I've seen as a solution to the ravages of homelessness; but it is notable that those who seem to hold up best under the pressures and who seem the best defended against alcohol or drugs are almost always those who have some kind of overview—a "lever" or an "edge." The rise in drug use in poor neighborhoods of inner cities, those at least with which I am familiar, parallels the sharp decline in organized political activity that makes it possible to galvanize a neighborhood to fight for its collective good. Those who celebrate the passing of the urban protest of the 1960s, but deplore the heightened fratricidal violence and use of drugs among the very poor, may not be persuaded that the loss of one fosters proliferation of the other. I believe they are connected and that Kim's defiant sanity is an example of the energy that finds its nutriment in focused indignation. The consequence is not a better room or an exemption from continual assault by sometimes hostile overseers; but it does protect her from self-laceration and it also seems to have protected her from the despair that leads so many people in this building to collude in their own ruin.

It's also interesting to me that Kim is one of the few people here who doesn't demonize her landlord. Her evenhanded comments on Mr. Tucelli, salted with a bit of irony and humor, demonstrate some capability for balance. Political awareness seems to rescue her from hate and self-hate both. She voices anger at injustice, not contempt for individuals.

Self-hate is common among many women here. If a woman feels she is despised, and has no recognition of the forces that demean her, perhaps it is inevitable that she will feel despicable. If nothing can affirm her dignity (if she is, like Terry, forced to beg and sweat and tremble in the hallway of the Martinique, hiding her children in a tiny room for fear of being cast out on the street) it seems understandable that she may see herself as worthy of contempt. Drug use in the Martinique strikes me repeatedly as a routinely exercised attempt at self-annihilation. If we are persuaded that society would dearly wish that we did not exist, might we not assist society in our undoing? These tendencies are not particular, unique, but shared by many. Epidemiology may be of more help to us than classical psychiatry in understanding why so many people whom we dare not touch regard themselves as toxic and unclean.

Kim: "Why don't people in this place complain? Because they're so damn scared. If the city will do this, they think, it might do something even worse. . . . There's a woman on the seventh floor. She's like a broken stick. You ought to meet her. She's so timid and afraid. She thinks that all of this is something she deserves. Some kind of punishment from God. She asks for something and it's never done. She loses her benefits. She gets cut off—this happens all the time—because she cannot read. She's quiet. They ignore her. Why do you think nobody intervenes? They'll intervene after she kills herself. She takes her children to the hospital. They don't explain things. They throw papers at her. She can't understand. Nobody says: 'Wait a minute. Something here is wrong.' They leave her there to rot. Why don't they teach her how to read? I *know* her. This is something that she *wants.* If they had a decent day care setup in this building, I'd go down and teach her. There's no day care, nothing you can count on. No literacy—there are volunteers but nothing energized enough to do the job. No library. No quiet place to meet and talk. Not even a pleasant place to sit and read a book.

"Why don't people in the city ever look around this building? Why don't they figure out who's here, who's got some skills, who could help someone else? They look at us to see what isn't there, and not what *is*. They see us like a lot of empty bottles that they don't intend to fill. Listen! There are gifted people in this building. Why don't they wake up? Do they think that they won't have to pay for this?"

It seems astonishing, with all the arbitrary cruelties or illegalities we have observed, that Kim must be interrogated by psychologists in order to decode her poverty and ascertain the secret failing in her soul—behind the broken furnace.

"Imagine," says Kim, "with all these children, all these people concentrated here within one building, all the useful things that you could do. I mean, you *have* these people here. You don't have to beat the streets to find them! The city is supposed to have a literacy program. Lots of press. You must know about it. 'Where can we locate those in need? Why don't they come forward?' Here they are!

"You could do some good things here in those empty rooms. Lectures. Movies. Every night you could have education going on. Doctors could come and talk, explain things women need to learn. Imagine all the decent things that you could do with just a little common sense if you were not thinking of this situation as a penalty for failure."

3

The Penalties of Failure

Kai Erikson describes a feeling, voiced by dislocated families he has met, that they have lost "a certain natural immunity" to misfortune. He speaks of a growing conviction that the world is no longer "a safe place to be." One of the "bargains men make with one another," he observes, "in order to maintain their sanity is to share an illusion that they are safe even when the physical evidence in the world around them does not seem to warrant that conclusion." Without this bargain he wonders whether life would be endurable.

There are only a few people in the Martinique Hotel of whom it would be accurate to say that life has ceased to be endurable. Kim spoke of one such person. She described her as "a broken stick." When I return a few nights later she has arranged for us to meet.

The woman—I will call her Laura—is so fragile that I find it hard to start a conversation. Before I do, she asks if I will read to her a letter from the hospital. Her oldest son has been ill for several weeks. He was tested in November for lead poisoning. The letter tells her that the child has a dangerous lead level. She's told to bring him back for treatment. She received the letter some weeks ago. It's been buried in a pile of other documents she cannot understand.

Although she cannot read, she knows enough to understand the darker implications of this information. The crumbling plaster in the Martinique Hotel is covered with sweet-tasting chips

103

of paint that children eat or chew as it flakes off the walls. Infants may be paralyzed or undergo convulsions. Some grow blind. The consequences may be temporary or long lasting. They may appear at once or not for several years. This final point is what instills so much uneasiness; even months of observation cannot still a parent's fear.

This, then, is her first concern; but there are others. The bathroom plumbing has overflowed and left a pool of sewage on the floor. A radiator valve is broken. It releases a spray of scalding steam at the eye level of a child. The crib provided by the hotel appears to be unstable. It may be that it was damaged by another resident or perhaps by one of Laura's children. One of the screws is missing. When I test it with my hand, it starts to sway. The beds in the room are dangerous too. They are made of metal frames with unprotected corners; the mattresses do not fit the frames. At one corner or another, metal is exposed. If a child has the energy or playfulness to jump or do a somersault or wrestle with a friend, and if he falls and strikes his head against the metal ridge, the consequences can be serious. A child on the fourteenth floor for instance, fell in just this way, cut his forehead, and required stitches just a week before. Most of these matters have been brought to the attention of the hotel management; in Laura's case, complaints have brought no visible results.

All of this would seem enough to make life difficult for an illiterate young woman in New York, but Laura has one other urgent matter on her hands. It appears that she has failed to answer a request for information from her welfare office. She's been cut from benefits for reasons that she doesn't understand. The timing is bad: It's a weekend. The crisis center isn't open, so there's nobody around to tide her over with emergency supplies. Her children have been eating cheese and bread and peanut butter for two days.

"Those on welfare," writes the Community Service Society of New York, may be suddenly removed from welfare rolls "for reasons unrelated to their actual need" or even to eligibility standards. This practice is called "churning" by the New York City welfare system. Laura and her children now are being churned.

The room is lighted by fluorescent tubes fixed high above us on the ceiling. They cast a stark light on four walls of greenish paint smeared over with some sort of sludge that drains from someone's toilet on the floor above. There is an infant girl, two boys with dark and hollowed eyes. A third boy is outside and joins us later. The children have that washed-out look of children in the half-light photographs of Walker Evans that accompanied James Agee's book *Let Us Now Praise Famous Men*.

There are four beds—those with the metal frames—a grimy sofa, the crib, two chairs and a refrigerator. There is a television set that doesn't work. A metal hanger is attached instead of an antenna, but there is no picture on the screen. Instead, there is a storm of falling flakes and unclear lines. I wonder why she keeps it on.

There are no table lamps to soften the fluorescent glare, no books, no Christmas tree, no decorations. She tells me that her father is of Panamanian birth but that she went to school in New York City. Spanish is her first language. I don't speak Spanish well. We do the interview in English.

"I cannot read," she says. "I buy the *New York Post* to read the pictures. In the grocery I know what to buy because I see the pictures."

What of no-name products—the generic brands that have no pictrures but could save her a great deal of money?

"If there are no pictures I don't buy it. I want to buy pancakes, I ask the lady: 'Where's the pancakes?' So they tell me."

She points to the boys: "He's two. He's five. Matthew's seven. My daughter is four months. She has this rash." She shows me: ugly skin eruptions on the baby's neck and jaw. "The carpets, they was filthy from the stuff, the leaks that come down on the wall. All my kids have rashes but the worst she has it. There was pus all over. Somewhere here I have a letter from the nurse . . ." She shuffles around but cannot find the letter. "She got something underneath the skin. Something that bites. The only way you can get rid of it is with a cream."

She finds the letter. The little girl has scabies.

"I been living here two years. Before I came here I was in a house we had to leave. There was rats. Big ones they crawl on us. The rats, they come at night. They come into our house, run over my son's legs. The windows were broken. It was winter. Snow, it used to come inside.

"My mother lived with us before. Now she's staying at my grandma's house. My grandma's dying in the bed. She's sixty-five. My mother comes here once a week to do the groceries. Tomorrow she comes. Then she goes back to help my grandma.

"I know my name and I can write my name, my children's names. To read I cannot do it. Medicines: I don't know the instructions.

"I was living here when I was pregnant with Corinne. No. I didn't see no doctor. I was hungry. What I ate was rice and beans, potato chips and soda. Up to now this week we don't have food. People ask me: 'Can you help? Do you got this? Do you got that?' I don't like to tell them no. If I have something I give it. This week I don't got.

"I can read baby books—like that, a little bit. If I could read I would read newspapers. I would like to know what's going on. My son, he tells me I am stupid. 'You can't read.' You know, because he wants to read. He don't understand what something is. I tell him: I don't know it. I don't understand. People laugh. You feel embarrassed. On the street. Or in the store." She cries. "There's nothing here . . ."

She gestures in a wide arc, but I can't tell if she means that gesture to take in the room or something more: all of her life, all of the city, all the cities of the earth. Then she makes her meaning clear: "Everything I had, they put it on the sidewalk. When I was evicted. I don't know if that's the law. Things like that—what is the law, what isn't? I can't read it so I didn't understand. So I lost everything I had."

Erikson writes of the belongings lost by people when they are uprooted: "These goods are more than a form of decoration or a cushion against want; they are . . . the furniture of self." To lose the sum of one's belongings, he observes, is to lose evidence of who one is: "In that sense, too, the terrain has become undependable."

For few people anywhere on earth could the terrain seem less dependable than for this woman: "I sign papers. Somebody could come and take my children. They could come. 'Sign this. Sign that.' I don't know what it says. Adoption papers I don't know. This here paper that I got I couldn't understand.

She hands me another letter. This one is a notice from the management of the hotel: "This notice is to inform you that your rent is due today. I would appreciate your cooperation in seeing to it that you go to your center today." Another form she hands me asks her to fill out the names and ages of her kids. "Papers, documents—people give it to me. I don't know it: I don't understand.

"I'm a Catholic. Yes: I go two weeks ago to church. This lady say they have these little books that learn me how to spell. You see the letters. Put them together. I would like to read. I go to St. Francis church. Go inside and kneel: I pray. I don't talk to the priest. I done so many things—you know, bad things. I buy a bottle of wine. A bottle of beer. That costs a dollar. I don't want to say to God.

"I get $173, restaurant allowance. With that money I buy clothes. Food stamps: I get $200. That's for groceries. Subway tokens I take out $10. Washing machine, I go downstairs. Twenty-five dollars to dry and wash. Five dollars to buy soap. Thirty dollars twice a month."

These costs are about the same as those that Gwen reported. Another woman at the Martinique calculates her laundry costs at my request. She comes out to nearly the same figure. These may be the standard rates for a midtown location. The difficulty of getting out and traveling across town to find lower prices, whether for laundromats or groceries, cannot be overstated. Families at the Martinique are trapped in a commercial district.

I ask Laura who stays with the children when she does her chores.

"My mother keeps the children when I do the wash. If she can't, I ask somebody on the floor. 'Give me three dollars. I watch your kids.' For free? Nothing. Everything for money. Everybody's poor.

"This is the radiator. Something's wrong." She shows me where the steam sprays out. I test it with my hand. "Sometimes it stops. The children get too close. Then it starts—like that! Leak is coming from upstairs down." I see the dark muck on the wall. "The window is broke. Lights broke." She points to the fluorescent tubes. They flicker on and off. "I ask them: Please, why don't you give me ordinary lights? They don't do nothing. So it been two weeks. I go downstairs. They say they coming up. They never come. So I complain again. Mr. Tucelli said to come there to his office. Desks and decorations and a lot of pictures. It's above the lobby. So the manager was there. Mr. Tucelli sat back in his chair. He had a gun. He had it here under his waist. You know, under his belt. I said: 'Don't show it to me if you isn't going to use it.' I can't tell what kind of gun it was. He had it in his waist. 'You are showing me the gun so I will be afraid.' If he was only going to show it I would not be scared. If he's going to use it I get scared.

"So he says: 'You people bring us trouble.' I said: 'Why you give my son lead poison and you didn't care? My child is lead poisoned,' He said: 'I don't want to hear of this again.' What I answer him is this: 'Listen. You live in a nice apartment. You got a home. You got TV. You got a family. You got children in a school that learn them. They don't got lead poison.'

"I don't know the reason for the guards. They let the junkies into the hotel. When my mother comes I have to sign. If it's a family living good they make it hard. If it's the drug dealers, they come in. Why they let the junkies in but keep away your mother?

"The guards, you see them taking women in the corner. You go down twelve-thirty in the night, they're in the corner with the girls. This is true. I seen it.

"How I know about the lead is this: Matthew sits there and he reach his fingers in the plaster and he put it in his mouth. So I ask him: 'Was you eating it?' He says: 'Don't hit me. Yes, I was.' So then I took him to the clinic and they took the blood. I don't know if something happen to him later on. I don't know if it affects him. When he's older . . ."

I ask her why she goes to church.

"I figure: Go to church. Pray God. Ask Him to help. I go on my knees. I ask Him from my heart: 'Jesus Christ, come help me, please. Why do you leave me here?'

"When I'm lying down at night I ask: Why people got to live like this? On the street, the people stare at you when you go out of the hotel. People look. They think: 'I wonder how they live in there?' Sometimes I walk out this door. Garbage all over in the stairs. When it's hot, a lot of bugs around the trash. Sometimes there are fires in the trash. I got no fire escape. You have to get out through the hall. I got no sprinkler. Smoke detector doesn't work. When I cook and food is burning, it don't ring. If I smoke it starts to ring. I look up. I say: 'Why you don't work? When I need you, you don't work. I'm gonna knock you down.' I did!" She laughs.

There is a sprinkler system in the corridor. Several women tell me it is unreliable. I ask her if the older children are enrolled in school.

"This one doesn't go to school. He's five. I need to call tomorrow. Get a quarter. Then you get some papers. Then you got to sign those papers. Then he can start school.

"For this room I pay $1,500 for two weeks. I don't pay. The welfare pays. I got to go and get it." The room, because it is divided, is rented as a two-room suite. "They send me this. I'm s'pose to sign. I don't know what it is. Lots of things you s'pose to sign. I sign it but I don't now what it is."

While we speak Matthew comes in. A dark-eyed boy, he sits beside his mother. He lowers his eyes when we shake hands.

"Looking for a house, I got to do it. I can't read so I can't use the paper. I get dressed. I put my make-up on. If I go like this they look afraid. They say: 'They going to destroy the house!' You got to dress the children and look nice. Owners don't want homeless. Don't want welfare. Don't want kids. What I think? If they pay one thousand and five hundred dollars every two weeks, why not pay five hundred dollar for a good apartment?"

She hands me another paper. "Can you tell me what is this?"

It's a second letter from the hospital, telling her to bring her son for treatment.

"Every day my son this week, last week, was vomiting. Every time he eat his food he throw it right back out. I got to take him to the clinic . . .

"Christmas: they don't got. For my daughter I ask a Cabbage Patch. For my boys I ask for toys. I got them stockings." What she shows me are four cotton stockings. They are tacked into the wall with nothing in them. "They say: 'Mommy, there's no toys.' I say not to worry. 'You are going to get something.' But they don't. They don't get nothing. I could not afford. No, this isn't my TV. Somebody lended it to me.

"No. Christmas tree I can't afford. Christmas I don't spend it happy. I am thinking of the kids. What we do on Christmas is we spend it laying on the bed. If I go outside I feel a little better. When I'm here I see those walls, the bed, and I feel sad. If I had my own apartment maybe there would be another room. Somewhere to walk. Walk back and forth."

I ask her: "How do you relax?"

"If I want to rest, relax, I turn out the light and lie down on the bed.

"When I met his father I was seventeen. One night he bought me liquor. I had never tasted. So he took me to this hallway. Then my mother say that what I did is wrong. So I say that I already did it. So you have to live with what you did. I had the baby. No. I did not want to have abortion.

"The baby's father I still see. When he has a job he brings me food. In the summer he worked in a flower store. He would bring me flowers. Now he don't have any job. So he don't bring me flowers."

Again that gesture: "Nothing here. I feel embarrassed for the room. Flowers, things like that, you don't got. Pretty things you don't got. Nothing like that. No."

In the window there's a spindly geranium plant. It has no flowers but some of the leaves are green. Before I leave we stand beside the window. Snow falling slantwise hits the panes and blurs the dirt.

"Some of the rooms high up—they got a view. You see the Empire State."

I've noticed this, seen it from a window. It towers high above the Martinique.

"I talk to this plant. I tell him: 'Grow! Give me one flower!' He don't do it." then, in an afterthought: "No pets. Goldfish. No. You don't got. Animals. They don't allow."

It occurs to me that this is one of the few places I have been, except a hospital or a reform school, where there are 1,400 children and no pets. A few people like the Allesandros keep illegal cats.

"I wish I had a dog," she says. "Brown dog . . . Something to hug."

"It is utterly part of our nature," writes Robert Coles, "to want roots, to need roots, to struggle for roots, for a sense of belonging, for some place that is recognized . . . as *ours*." It is bad enough, he says, "that thousands of us, thousands of American children, still go hungry and sick and are ignored and spurned—every day and constantly and just about from birth to death. It is quite another thing, another order, as it were, of human degradation, that we also have thousands of boys and girls who live utterly uprooted lives, who wander the American earth . . . but who never, never think of any place as home, of themselves as anything but homeless. There are moments, and I believe this is one of them, when even doctors or social scientists . . . have to throw up their hands in heaviness of heart . . . and say in desperation: God save them, those children; and for allowing such a state of affairs to continue, God save us too."

Coles wrote those words in 1969. He was speaking of the children of the migrant workers in the Appalachian states. What might he say today, were he to visit in the Martinique Hotel?

Mobility is common in America. Families change homes frequently, the move occasioned often by career demands. Their children may be briefly traumatized; most manage the transition in good stride. When a child is torn from his home, when he sees his family's belongings piled on the sidewalk by a landlord or the agent of a bank, when he is left to wait and wither for long months within a series of unhealthy places like the Martinique Hotel, he may not literally die, but his survival is endangered and his childhood has, to a large degree, been taken from him. He either regreseses or is forced to grow up very, very fast. Average length of stay in New York's family shelters, we have seen, is thirteen months; sixteen months within the Martinique. This is a long time to exist in arid soil.

There's little in Laura's life of joy, nothing of indulgence. Anything like luxury or fun is not simply absent from this bleak existence. It's as far away as daisies—or a brown dog—on a hillside in New Hampshire. Her longings are so dreadfully austere. She wishes she had a room where she could see the symbol of New York that mocks her pitiful existence. She'd like to see that plant do what a plant is supposed to do—give her one flower. She wants to read. She feels ashamed to go out to the store. "I would like to know what's going on," she said. She doesn't have the least idea.

A night in March. I wait in the lobby for Kim to sign me in. As soon as we're in the stairs, she tells me: "Something terrible has happened. Laura's gone."

Once in her room, she lights a cigarette and tells me this: "Everyone sees her as a simple person, plain and dull, nobody of interest, even to a man. Well, I could have told you what would happen. Somebody finally told her she was pretty. He bought her some clothes and took her out. She put on make-up. I had never thought of her as glamorous. Neither did she. She saw herself as someone colorless and drab. Now a man likes her, buys her a dress. He gives the kids a TV and some toys. Two days later Laura's gone. Things happen fast. He was a pimp. He gave her drugs. Nobody's seen her since. Her mother came to the hotel. She's staying with the kids."

I go down to visit with her mother. Her father's there too— a man in his fifties. Her mother tells me that she's forty-five.

"When I was called, they told me she was taking men to a hotel. I asked what was she wearing. They said she was wearing a red coat. I went out to look for her. I went to the bars. I went in the hotels. I spent the night on Forty-second Street. Times Square. All over. I can't find her. Then somebody says he saw her on Fifth Avenue—a place where women take the men to a hotel. I went to the hotel. A man in the hotel, he asked me who she was. I said that she's the one in the red jacket and he said: 'Oh yeah! She's here.' She was upstairs.

"She came downstairs to speak with me. I told her I had come to bring her home. She said: 'I have a better life here now. I have these things. This jacket. See?' I couldn't get her to come home."

So Laura's mother is stayinig here to take care of the kids until she figures out a way to find a home. Her own mother has a place in Flushing but is near the point of death and cannot take them in. Laura's father walks with a cane; he's permanently disabled. They've applied for custody of Laura's children.

"The baby's sick. She has a fever. Matthew has an ear infection. I'll take them to the hospital tomorrow. I'm responsible. It's in my hands."

March 21: I'm visiting with Kim. A woman I have never seen bangs at the door. She's come upstairs from Laura's room to ask for help. When Kim and I arrive the mother's kneeling on the floor. She's in a state of near-hysteria. As she explains it, this is what took place: She had noticed that the crib was swaying and was worried that it might collapse. She had therefore lifted the baby out and placed her on the bed. A moment later, as she turned to warm some milk, the baby somehow toppled over, striking her head against the metal frame.

"I put her here. I told her: 'Do you want some milk?' I went to warm the milk. I turned around and she was bleeding. Her head was swelling up, like this. Her eyes are getting big. She's changing colors. I said: 'She is dying.' "

The child was taken to the hospital. Her grandfather is with her, waiting there for the report. The other children sit nearby, not understanding. On a shelf above the crib there is a lion, a stuffed panda, and a bear. A small pink elephant lies with his four feet in the air beside the metal bed. There is a color photo of the baby on the door.

The child survives the night. Her future is unclear. A few days later, Laura's mother is served papers—charged with child neglect. No charges, to my knowledge, have been brought against the Martinique Hotel.

4

The Road to Potter's Field

Tragedies like that of Laura's baby rarely cause much public controversy. When they do, it is often the result of a particularly vivid news report. One such story drew attention at the time that I first visited the Martinique. Although the mother was no longer living in the building, her story was known to several residents because she had been living here when she was pregnant and she had gone into labor here. Her child's weight at birth was dangerously low and, because he had grown very ill soon after birth, he had been kept in the hopsital for several months. He had been discharged on Christmas Eve of 1984. Subsequent events within his life led to a threat of legal action.

With the help of members of the Coalition for the Homeless who had come to know the child and his mother, I was able to meet her and to learn firsthand what she had undergone. Finding her was, in itself, a challenge. It required many phone calls and a long and complicated search that does not call for recapitulation here. It is enough to say that, when we finally spoke, she wanted very much to meet and talk. She told me she was living in a shelter, in a section of Manhattan that I did not know. On a day in the later winter, following directions she had given me, I found her temporary home.

If the reader has not visited New York City, or if you have visited but never been as far downtown as Houston Street, you need to imagine a wide-open, unprotected stretch of road with

114

very few stores or houses and with little else on either side other than a number of high-rise housing projects spotted here and there, not far from the East River.

On a very cold afternoon the wind that sweeps in from the river numbs your face and brings tears to your eyes. Silent men hunch over in the doorways of deserted stores. A group of homeless men and women stand around a barrel with their hands extended to the flames that rise out of a mass of burning trash.

Wiping my glasses with my sleeve, I enter the side door of the building. There's no elevator. I walk up to the fifth floor.

Holly Peters lives in the Henry Street Settlement House for now—a homeless shelter, but a better one than she has ever known since she was pregnant in the Martinique Hotel. She introduces me to her two children and her husband, David, and invites me to sit down. She's thin and small and rather nervous at the start. While we talk she braids her hair.

I've already been informed that she is twenty-four and that she was taken from her mother as a child and put into foster care. She tells me that she spent most of her childhood in state-run institutions and in several foster homes throughout New York. Despite the many interruptions in her education caused by frequent transfers from one home or institution to another, she stayed in school until twelfth grade. She became pregnant that year and quit school.

By this time, she had been reunited with her mother and was living with her. After her child was born she entered a program of job training. It appears she had a good employment record for the next few years. "I worked for Stouffer's. Now that was an interesting job. You got these carts: sandwiches and coffee, even a cash register, it's right here on this wagon. You're in an office building. So you go to every floor. You got a little bell. You ring your bell. If anybody on the floor wants something, they come to the wagon. Order a chef's salad, that's $2.60. Add the coffee, fifty cents. So that's $3.10. Give you five, you give them back their change. That's how it was."

Early on, however, she encountered a problem faced my many young and pretty women with their male employers. "One job I had—you got to wonder if it's you or if it's just the way some people are. I had been there as a waitress for some time. The owner told me that he had an opening for a cashier. He had restaurants all over. Every borough of New York. He said he was goin' to take me to the one in Queens so the girl could show me how to do it. Maybe I'd start workin' there. I said okay.

"It was in the summertime. I wanted to go dressed appropriate. He told me: 'You can wear your regular clothes.' So he come there in a van and we go drivin' out to Queens. All of a sudden he pull up in front of this hotel. He offered me a hundred dollars if I go inside. I told him no. I wasn't goin' for it.

"Ever since that day he had me workin' like a slave. Never once in this here job did I receive more than a hundred dollars. He was gonna pay me that much just to go inside of the hotel."

Her daughter was nearly two by now. Another child was born one year later. She says she had returned to school to get her G.E.D. (high school equivalency), but that she was forced to interrupt her studies when her mother was evicted. Holly was obliged to turn to welfare for emergency assistance. She lived for eight months in two homeless shelters in Manhattan, only to be transferred to the Holland—viewed by many people as the worst of all hotels for homeless families in New York. While living there, she learned that she was pregnant for a third time.

It was winter. The hotel was poorly heated and, as she reports, the place was rat infested. "Just about this hour—you see how it is outside?—they startin' to come out. Evening sun be goin' down, they playin' on the floor. We sit on the bed. We didn't move. They right there on the floor. Go [stamp!] like this! They race around. They *right* there on the floor."

After the Holland, Holly's wanderings become unclear. At various points in the subsequent year she lived in at least seven hotels and, for certain nights at least, she slept in EAUs. "They tried to send me once to the Clemente shelter, but they wouldn't take me in. I got as far as the front door. They told me: 'Go back to the EAU and tell them not to send you here.' "

Holly moved into the Martinique in early 1984 and was living there until the day that her third child, Benjamin, was born in late September. Mothers at the Martinique had no refrigerators at that time. Information given me by other women living there that year indicates that conditions in the Martinique were even worse than at the time of my first visit.

"Yes, I believe that it affected him," she says without assertiveness but with a quiet note of acquiescence in accomplished fact. "How do I know? You do *not* know. I only know that life in that hotel was hell. I can't say that living in the Martinique Hotel is why this happened. But I do believe a woman ought to have a better place to stay when she is carrying a child. If I would have had a little more, the proper medical care, the proper housing—if had a place like this, I believe he would have had a better chance than what he did."

She finds a cigarette, talks to her children in the bedroom, says something to her husband in the kitchen, and returns to find a match to light the cigarette.

"He was born on Saturday. He weighed four pounds, eight ounces. When I came downstairs to see him Sunday, he was in the incubator. When I came on Monday, they was giving him IV. When I came the next day, he had oxygen. Then they had to start giving him blood. I had to go around to people gettin' blood . . .

'Then from there he stayed, you know, inside the incubator. I used to cry. Sometimes I'd pray. Something I've always done is pray. If I meet somebody—they start talkin' that there ain't no God, you know, I don't be bothered. Anyway, I used to go to see him and he laid there for three months. He didn't move."

Why was she forced to leave the Martinique? Holly says at first that she was robbed repeatdly while she was there. From her later conversation it appears that the real reason had to do with David. She was afraid to be alone, especially while Benjamin's condition remained so uncertain. David was also scared to be without her. I believe it was his presence in her room that finally led to her eviction or departure.

"So I was in the Hotel Mayfair, near Times Square." She tells me of walking from Forty-ninth Street to Beth Israel, standing by the baby's bed for hours. "I would stand there by his bed and pray. I have a Bible but I didn't need it. I prayed from my own.

"I had him baptized in the hospital. They asked me would I like a priest to bless him. I said yes 'cause he was critical. The doctor said: 'Point-blank, I'm gonna tell you. I'll be honest with you—'. She said Benjamin was not s'posed to live.

"I was not on WIC. Each time for my appointment, each time I got ready, he was in the hospital. Medicaid, he wasn't on my card. I don't know why. Maybe, if a baby's in the hospital, they belive that he's provided for. He wasn't on my budget."

Some of her suppositions seem at first to be implausible. It does not make sense to me that Benjamin was not on Medicaid and not on Holly's budget. When she tells me this, I mark her statement in my notes with a large question mark. An HRA report later confirms her words: "Infant not on IM [welfare] budget or Medicaid. . . . Social worker working on this."

The facts, as best I understand, are these: Some days after Benjamin was born he contracted a viral infection. The virus left him partially blind, brain-damaged, deaf, hydrocephalic. He is also said to have developed a "seizure disorder." Three months after birth he was released by hospital officials and was taken to the Mayfair. Holly says that he was having seizures at the time. She had been told to give him phenobarbital, but she says she had to pay for it out of her other children's food allowance since he wasn't yet included on her budget. His weight was seven pounds.

I ask her if they had refrigerators at the Mayfair.

"Not in the Martinique. Not in the Mayfair. Nope."

She was evicted from the Mayfair five weeks later. The reason again, she says, was her request that David stay with her and the refusal of the hotel to permit this. So it was winter, four months since the child's birth, a year since his conception. They were homeless.

"After that, they couldn't find no place for me to live. I was a little everywhere." She lists a number of hotels: the Madison, the Prospect, and (again) the Holland. "So we have been all over. I would carry all his things—disposable bottles, Pampers and his clothes, his phenobarbital, his toys, pregested milk. I carried it in bags each place we went. By that time he was completely blind."

The city reports that Benjamin did not have phenobarbital from January 4 to January 8 and that he had twenty seizures in those days. On January 15, Benjamin had not been given Meicaid. A temporary card was issued on that date.

"All this time I had been looking for apartments. I saw lots of places that I didn't have the money for. Two hundred seventy dollars was my budget limit. I used to tell them: 'All the money you will pay for me to stay in a hotel? You can't give me half that money *once* to pay the rent and rent deposit? I could get me an apartment. You won't ever see me anymore!'

"Even at the project the committee turned me down. They ask me if I ever been evicted. If you ever been evicted they hold that against you. I said no. I have never been evicted 'cause I never had my own. I had only had my mother's home. Then because I had the kids, they say: 'We don't want them writin' on the walls.' I said: 'Look. My daughter's five. My son is three. Benjamin is four months old. Do you think this baby will be writin' on your walls?' They turned me down."

Benjamin was readmitted to Beth Israel twice during this time. Four nights before his second admission, the HRA reports: "Baby stays overnight at EAU." On his release from the hospital on March 13, Holly was at the Holland Hotel for a second time. On March 20 she was told she had to leave the Holland, according to the HRA, "because of a City policy that only allows families to stay 28 days." Two days later, after she had left the Holland, the HRA temporarily lost track of her: "case to be closed due to circumstances." Five days later, Benjamin was readmitted to Beth Israel.

Holly: "It was near the end of March. The baby had to go back to the hospital again. His skull was widening. The fluid, I believe, was putting pressure on his brain. I stayed there with him in the hospital. EAU can't find me nothin' so I slept there with him in his room. David came to visit but he stayed out with his mother and the other children on Long Island. David's mother has a heart condition. She can't do but so much—I mean, takin' care of children, puttin' up with noise and the confusion. But this was a crisis so we had no choice. She done the best she can . . .

"So I was alone now with my baby. Apart from having no place else to stay, I wanted to be with him at this time. I would get up each mornin' and I'd bathe him. I would wash his clothes. I preferred to care for him myself than anybody else. The people in the hopsital can care for him but just so much. I wanted to be *with* him. Period!

"Even though I was afraid, it is the truth to say that I was happy. I was happy to be with him in a place where he was safe and where we could not be evicted. Only place he had a home in all those months was in the hospital. That be one place where they don't evict you.

"David came to be with me while Benjamin was in the surgery. We waited for him to come out—in recovery. They brought him up. They said: 'Well, we will see how he will be.' They wouldn't know if it was a success until a couple days."

Medical records indicate the hospital had put a "shunt" into the baby's skull on April 22 to drain off fluid. Holly describes it to me vividly: "The shunt is a tube that goes into the brain. It goes under the skin, under one layer of the skin, and it goes down to the stomach. It was like a plastic tube, a fat tube, you could see under the skin. Goes to the stomach. You could see it, you could see the print of it under the skin."

On May 1, the hospital told her they were going to release him. This information startled her and it would later startle many people in the press. A spokesperson for Beth Israel Hospital later said the hospital would never have released the baby had it known he had no proper shelter. The hospital, however, had provided Holly with a note to be submitted to her welfare worker. The letter asked that she be given shelter.

Holly tells me: "I was worried if it was too soon. 'Well, Mrs. Peters, he will be all right.' But I was feelin' scared. First, because the shunt was in his head. Second, even with him bein' like he was they couldn't find no place for me to be."

Because of the controversial nature of this story, I will add one observation here. I do not believe the probity of health officials should be called in question. Holly speaks with obvious affection of her doctor. It is unimaginable that any of those who came in contact with the child wished him ill or that officials consciously released him to the street. Hospitals all over the United States, faced with hundreds of thousands of unsheltered people and with millions of the very, very poor, do the best they can, and sometimes do so quite heroically. The issue is not medical or bureaucratic mishap in Manhattan. It is destitution.

"I told my social worker: 'I don't have no place to take

him.' So she said that, if I had no home, then I could leave him and they'd put him in an institution. I said: 'You are tellin' me that you can't help me in no kind of way? You know that I have no place to stay. Are you tellin' me ain't nobody can help me? I been tellin' you for weeks that I don't have no place to take him. Now you say that you are takin' him away? I am leavin' with my baby and you *know* that I ain't got no place to live.''

"So there was the two of us, Benjamin and me, we was discharged, and it was evenin', like about four-thirty, five o'clock, and we was walkin' in the street.

"It was rainin', as a matter of fact. Not a warm night, kind of cool. I had to go straight to the EAU. When I got there I went in and I explained: 'My son has had an operation.' I had brought the letter from the doctor. I had had that letter from day one. It didn't help me. I was on the street. For seven days, a whole week, I was on the street. That was in May. He come out from havin' surgery, shunt was in him, I was pretty weak. The EAU, to me, is in the street.

"I would sit from nine to five, the welfare center. They'd come out and give me a referral: 'Here, go to the EAU. We couldn't find no place for you tonight.' Benjamin was in his carriage and I had the letter with me and we sat from nine to five there in the center and from five to eight o'clock at EAU. I lay him down. I was sleepin' in the chair. He was in his carriage. They say in the paper that he died there on the floor. That isn't true. I lay him in his carriage.

"All the time that we was on the street we carried all his things. Carryin' everything, his milk, his phenobarbital. In the mornin' I would wake up in the chair. By that time I had the other children. David's mother couldn't keep them anymore. She was a sick woman. So David was with me—and the children. We were at the EAU. Get up in the mornin', wash 'em in the bathroom, comb their hair . . . I be scared he have another seizure.

"Only time they placed us was for two nights at a nice hotel in Queens. This hotel is not for welfare and they let you know that right away. Tell you that you're there one night and you cannot come back. We stayed for two . . .

"You can say we got two nights, but it is not like *nights*

because we didn't get there until 3:00 A.M. How much sleep, then, is a child gettin'? Two children and a baby that has had an operation? Is that gettin' any sleep? So we get up and get the train. The rest of the time we stayed there in the center."

The city reports that, on the day of Benjamin's release after his surgery, Holly brought him to the EAU in early evening. She was sent to the Turf, a Queens hotel, at one-thirty in the morning. Two nights later she was sent back to the Martinique but was turned away, she said, because there was no vacancy. She returned to the EAU at four-thirty in the afternoooon on May 4 and waited there with Benjamin for *about ten hours.* At two-forty-five in the morning, they were assigned to a hotel. Benjamin and Holly spent the entire next night at the EAU.

"So he was goin' in the cold and rain. I was givin' him all that I could. They wasn't givin' me a stable place for him to be. The place the shunt went in, his wound had gotten bad. It was sunk in and you could see his skull. His eyes was sinkin' too. And I said: 'David, look at him.' He looked at him. His father looked. And there was dark around his eyes. His eyes was dark and sinkin' in.

"Nothin' that I tell you, when it comes down to that baby, is untrue. You could look at him and tell. One lady at the welfare that I didn't know her name, when I said that he was sick would she come over she would not come there to look. She would *not* come over there to see my son was sick. So I begged her: 'Please, my baby's dyin'.' I had brought the letter I was s'posed to. I said: 'David, look at Benjamin's eyes is sinkin' in.' 'Cause you could look at him and tell.

"That was the seventh of May. Then the lady in the welfare said: 'The baby looks like it is dyin'.' So we raised him up. We lifted him again and looked and you could see it. You could *see.* He had these scars from the IV. He had a scar up here. There was a hole like where the needle was put in. We was sittin' in the EAU, in Brooklyn, on the right-hand side.

"I said: 'David, take him to the hospital. I'll sit here and wait and see in case they find a place for us to stay.' He asked someone if they have the money for a cab. Takin' the train meant switchin' trains. I didn't think we had the time. But they said no. They did not pay money for no cab. They did offer us to call an ambulance. That was no good. The ambulance would take you to the nearest hospital. Brooklyn Hospital's the nearest hospital to EAU. We had to get him to Beth Israel. That's where all his records was. If we took him to another hospital, by the time they find out what is wrong he would be dead. I said we was gonna take him to the hospital that know him from the day he was born. The hospital that *knows* his situation."

David, who has interrupted only once or twice up to this point, fills in the rest: "I got ten dollars from a friend who knows me and I took a taxi to Beth Israel. I brought him in. As soon as I come in they ask me what had happened, where he was? I said: 'We've been out there at the welfare.' The doctor said: 'Are there sick children there?' And I said yes. At welfare there is nothin' but sick children. Little kids with coughs and runnin' noses runnin' up and down. They're runnin' everywhere. You know? So he said: 'The baby caught a stomach virus.' That explains why he had diarrhea. He was sick to start with. When you add the stomach virus . . . He had been dehydrated so bad. The skin on him was dry, like this. That was seven days since he come home. So he was in the hospital again. He stayed there after that."

After a silence, he goes on: "I came back to Brooklyn, to the EAU. Holly says: 'They found a place for me to stay.' I was thinkin' they have pity for her now—and ever since. She don't need no sympathy no more. She needed it back then. Now he dyin', now you offer her a place to live."

After Benjamin's death, the city seemed to place much of the blame upon his parents. Holly, said the city, had been beaten by the father of her other children. As a consequence, the *New York Times* reported, "the baby was not fed for several hours." Holly denies both accusations. But, assuming that these things are true, it remains incomprehensible that a disaster fostered, countenanced, ignored for over half a year should retroactively be blamed upon parental failure—an alleged delay of "several hours" in the feeding of a child—at a point at which his health had been already damaged past repair.

The city also maintained it gave the family shelter, transportation, food. In fact, according to the Legal Aid Society, the city galvanized itself to action only on the night before her baby was brought back into the hospital to die and only after Legal Aid, having been alerted to the child's plight, had telephoned the HRA, demanding that the child be afforded suitable shelter.

HRA officials placed a special emphasis upon the fact that Holly was repeatedly evicted from hotels because of David's presence or that she rejected placements in hotels where he would not have been allowed to stay. Holly places far more emphasis upon the dangerous conditions in the various hotels and on the fact that she was forced to sit and wait so many hours on so many evenings at the EAU while Benjamin was gravely ill. But, granting that the statements of the HRA are true, we may wonder at an agency of government that, even unwittingly, punishes a mother in a time of crisis for her desperation to remain close to the one adult in the entire world who seems to love her. Why would a society alarmed by the decline in family values try to separate a mother from her child's father at the time she needs him most and when he displays that willingness to share responsibility whose absence we repeatedly deplore?

This, then, is a case not of the breakdown of a family but of a bureaucratic mechanism that *disintegrates* the family, tearing apart a mother and father in a time of shared ordeal. Sharing pain does not merely bring relief to people under siege; it often forms a bond that gives them stronger reason to remain together later. So the efforts of the city, as belated as they were, to offer Holly shelter if she would agree to shed her child's father, like its offer to remove her as a parent altogether and to place the child in an institution—not because the child *needed* institutional care but because the city could not give her a safe home —represent destructive social policy on several levels.

I have deleted some of the words that David spoke while Holly told me of the months after her baby's birth. He is recounting the events of early January of 1985 after Benjamin was discharged from Beth Israel. They were living in a hotel near Times Square. It appears, from what he says, that Benjamin may not yet have been entirely blind.

"Nighttime he'd be with us in our bed. I'd be here. Holly be there. He be in the middle. Plenty of nights I'd jump because I had forgot that he was there. He would work his way down in the bed. Sometimes he would get under my arm and go to sleep.

"He used to smile—sit and smile. He would gurgle and make sounds like he was tryin' to speak. He'd go [sings a long, contented baby's sigh] and then he'd go to sleep. Go *right* to sleep. He never cried but once.

"When she would go out I'd stay with him, give him his bath. Feedin' him, I'd sit him on my lap. I would talk to him. He would make sounds like he was talkin' back. Once I had him in the bath tub with me, washin' him, and he start slidin' down. I pick him up, he slide back down. I let the water hit 'bout to his neck. He sit there in the water and he move his head and look at me like 'What you doin' to me?' So I fed him and I got him dressed to take him for a walk. Go in the stroller. Go around the block. I have some friends. I liked to show him off.

"So I was goin' to take him out. He fell asleep on me! I put him in the bed. I watch him. This is how he moves: He use his head.

"That mornin', like I say: a split-second reaction. I turned around and he was slidin' off. I could see his little feet just danglin' in the air. I reached down. I picked him up. That was the first time that he ever cried! I just looked at him. I was amazed. I was shakin'. Four months old and he had never made a cry till then. I just sat there lookin' at him, hopin' that he'd cry again.

"So I set him back in bed and I laid down tryin' to sleep. I pat him softly on his back to make him go to sleep. Soon as I close my eyes I'd open them and he is starin' at my eyes. Then he'd close his eyes, I'd open mine, then he'll close his, and every time I open mine he close his eyes. I just had fun with him, that's all. I had a lot of hope during that time."

Eight P.M. The wind is howling outside on Houston Street. I picture those men around the flaming barrel that I passed five hours before. Holly finds another cigarette, curls up on the sofa, strikes a match, and poses the question I had hoped to ask when she was done.

"Later, a reporter asked me this: 'How do you feel? Do you feel it was the city's fault?' I say: 'Yes, that's true. I do. Hospital was the only home he ever knew. Minute he was admitted they had found me a hotel. I said: 'Oh, that's good! That is real good! Now he be dyin' . . .'

"Seems like they do everything a little bit too late. I couldn't get him on my Medicaid when he was livin'. Mind you, *now* he's on my card!" She takes out the card and reads his name. "Why do they bother with it now? When did he need it? Then? Or now? *Now* they give it to me! He be gone now almost for a year . . .

"So they sent me over and I went there and I had two weeks. The Hotel Carter. First they put me on the ninth floor. They had gotten me a room. It was a nice room. It had carpets on the floor. Understand that, even though the chance was slim, I was living like he'd make it still. So I thought at last I have a place for him to live.

"After a few days I came downstairs. The manager said I had to move down to a different room. He gave me this key and I went there to look. I went there to see it and it didn't have no knob. It didn't have no heat, no lights, and it was springtime but the nights sometimes in springtime do be chill and I was thinkin' like my baby would be with me soon. So I asked him: 'Are you tellin' me I got to take my baby there? I can't take my baby there in his condition. Nor the other children either.' In my thinking he was with me still.

"I told the man: 'If you had a son in his condition would you put your son into that room?' And he said: 'No. I wouldn't.' But he said I didn't have no choice. He tell me that I have to wait till Monday to do something about electricity. I said: 'Are you tellin' me you want me to stay in that room with both my children until Monday mornin' in the dark?' There was no electric switch to switch the light. You had to use your finger. There was wires but no switch. The wires that go in the box that holds the switch, the light switch that goes up and down, you could push those wires together but you get a shock. No doorknob on the door. You *push* the door . . .

"I saw a woman—I think it's his wife or daughter workin' down there at the desk. I thought, bein' she's a woman, she would understand. So I told her that my son was sick. She said: 'What's wrong with him?' I told her. She says: 'Why you want to bring him here?' I said: 'Can I stay please in a room that's got a light switch and some heat? My baby has an illness.' She just look at me and says: 'I'll tell you what you do. You pack up your stuff and leave right now. You can take this room or else you go.' I said: 'Well, I'll have to go.' So I bundled up my kids and I went back to EAU, and after that they sent me somewhere else.

"You know, there is something that I do not understand. With all this money that they have here in this state, in New York City, it should not be no one homeless with the money that they have. The money they take spending on these condominiums—they could be building places such as this." She gestures with her hand. "They are out there building condominiums—beautiful places, cost five hundred dollars, that poor people can't afford. Five hundred dollars. Way they goin'—you remember when there use to be a time when it was *high* class, *middle* class, then *poor?* Now it's only high and poor. And gettin' worse. If the government was doin' what it s'posed to do, you would not be puttin' people into places with no doorknob and no heat."

Evicted from the Carter, she returned to welfare and was told to go back to the EAU. "I said to them: 'By the time that I get out of here it's goin' to be too late. Let me call the hospital and see if he's okay.' If I couldn't be there I would call the hospital three times a day. On the phone the woman told me: 'Mrs. Peters, come right now.' So I said: 'What is it?' I was thinkin': They are goin' to remove the shunt. I will have to sign a paper. I said: 'Can't you tell me on the phone?' She said: 'No, I have to tell you this in person.' I went out and got a train and I went to Beth Israel. I had gotten a cold feelin'.

"On the train I said: 'No. I ain't goin' to think like that.' So when I got to the hospital I went to his room. The bed was made. I ain't seen none of his things, none of his toys or nothin'. I said: 'Where's my baby?' And she looked at me. So I said: 'Where's my son?' She like ignored me. So I said: 'Look, I am askin' you: Where is my baby? Did you move him to another floor?' She said then: 'The doctor will talk to you.' So then his doctor, she came over. 'Is there someplace we can go that's quiet?' So I say: 'Please tell me here.' So she said: 'Well, umh . . . during the night or else this morning somehow, he, the baby got congestion and he choked. We did everything we could, but it was just too late.' I just sat there and I started cryin'. They had took his stuff and boxed it up in boxes. I said: 'Look. I have to go.' So I got up and left.

"I had to make the funeral arrangements on my own. Welfare gave $250. The Coalition for the Homeless paid the rest. A man that worked at the Carter had a son who was a preacher. He preached at my baby's funeral. I cannot recall his name. Reverend somethin'. He was good. Umhum! I don't remember what he said. There was one part he got out of the Bible. One last paragraph he said, he read it from the Bible. But the rest was from his own."

Coalition representatives confirm her memory of the expense. The city allotted only $250 at the time to bury the dead children of poor people. An HRA employee called the Coalition and requested the remaining funds required for the funeral.

"I was cryin'. Went from there to welfare. Then to EAU. I still didn't have a place to stay. I could not go to the burial. It was some place on an island. I was thinkin' I would go this year. Go for his birthday. As a matter of fact . . . we had no money to get out.

"After that the doctor said I had a nervous breakdown. I was cryin'. I was *tired.* I gave up on everythin' from then. Everythin', on him, on me, the kids . . . I knew I cared about my other kids but now that Benjamin was gone and he was something precious that I lost . . . I was hurtin' bad so when I lost him I just said . . . Because I had the other kids. Don't get me wrong. But I had built my world around him for so long. I had built it in my mind: Nothin' would happen. He was here and he would live and that was *it.* You know, I blocked it out of mind. When it happened I would not believe that he was gone. Even when I saw him in the casket I did not believe that he was gone.

"That was like almost a month. Bein' that I had all of his clothes there and his carriage and his toys, I used to sit there every day and look at them and cry. It took me a long time. Even now I wake at six o'clock. That is the *exact* time that I used to wake and feed him, six o'clock. And do it now. When I wake I know that he's not there. I *know* he isn't. Only that I'm used to lookin' for him that I still get up at six.

"Let me tell you, when he died, that man upstairs: I cursed

Him out. I said: 'Why did you have to take my baby?' Then, you know, I said: 'It's over.' So I prayed and asked for His forgiveness. Then I say: 'He did it for a reason.' I ain't sayin' He intended it. I'm just sayin', if He took my baby, then He did it for a reason. Well, my son was sufferin' real bad . . .

"It's an island. I forget the name. I don't think that I am ready yet. I'm not gonna say I got it stable in my mind. I'm not goin' to tell you I accepted. In my dream, when I do dreamin', I think that he's there. I wake up and look for him. I do it plenty of times. Searchin' for him. Searchin'. He's not there.

"After I calm down, then I believe in Him again. Most definitely. I believed in Him back then, it's just that I was wantin'. I was wantin' him real bad. With my other two I loved them all the same, but at the time he was so sick I would of had to show a little more for him because of his condition. I wouldn't love him more than I love them, but I would give him more because of his condition. But, um, that was in my heart.

"My daughter, she was took real hard after he died. She cried. You had to talk to her. When he went into the hospital she took it bad. She would sit awake and cry. Umhum! Act more like she was the mother and I was the child. Like *she* was his mother. It was hard. Every night when they would go to sleep I used to tell them: 'Say a prayer now for your brother.' For a long time after that my son would say: 'When is the baby comin' home?' I had to tell him he's not comin' but he still don't understand. Even sometimes now he'll say: 'When is the baby comin' back?' He'll ask me that. My son. Umhum. My daughter tell him that the baby's dead and he's not comin' back. He in heaven. She know more than lot of people understand."

I ask her how she pictures heaven.

"Peaceful . . . glorious . . . paradise . . . That's the place where you can rest in peace eternally. And that's another thing. I know my baby's restin' now. Can't nobody or nothin' hurt him anymore. He don't have to suffer anymore. No welfare, EAU. No nothin'. No more can hurt him now he's in His hands now and can't nobody harm him. *Nobody.* And *nothin'* . . . He's in peace."

5

Distancing Ourselves from Pain and Tears

Men and women from the Coalition for the Homeless, who befriended Holly, note that, in the period she has described, her capability for making wise and long-term judgments seemed impaired.

This seems a realistic observation. I'm not sure it tells us much of Holly. It does tell us something of the impact of the shelter system on a homeless woman.

"You *think* only of the next day when you're *trained* to think only of the next day." These words were spoken by a homeless man with whom I spoke last year. "Be at the EAU by five. Be at your welfare office on the other side of town by nine . . ." When every moment in a woman's struggle for survival calls for an alacrity in seizing the next opportunity for placement, for a medical appointment, or (when all else fails) for an appointment to obtain the money for her child's burial, it may be a bit unfair to ask for long-range plans.

A friend who knows this story raised a somewhat different point: "I don't believe you can exonerate the city. Nonetheless, you have to ask yourself: Why did she have another child? After all, she wasn't married when the older two were born. She couldn't support them. She hadn't finished school. Why does she have a child if she knows she can't provide him with a home? It seems a little harsh of me, perhaps; but isn't this a fundamental question that has got to be addressed?"

It is a fundamental question and it needs to be addressed;

but it is not the issue in this book. This is a book about the fact of dispossession—*homelessness*—not teen pregnancy, illiteracy, poor education, or the evolution of an underclass. We do not know what we ought to do about an underclass. We do know that we should not manufacture one. We do not know how to bring an end to poverty and inequality in our society. We do know children shouldn't live in subways. We also have a good idea of how to build a house—or many houses, each of which has many heated, safe, well-lighted rooms, doors with doorknobs, electric switches that go on and off, a stove that can be used to cook nutritious meals, a refrigerator in which food for children can be stored. Overwhelmed by knowledge of the things we can't do, we are also horrified that we do not do what we can. I suspect that one of the ways we deal with this is to get angry—not at ourselves, but at the mother and, by implication, at the child.

It is easier to be impatient than to live with sadness. Finding fault with Holly may divert us from the thought of what we might have done—or what the people we elect to office should have done—to have prevented this disaster. It may also be a way of distancing ourselves: "She's not like us. This nightmare could not happen in our lives or to our children. There must be something wrong with her—some flaw we do not share." In this way perhaps, we find some consolation for the grief we feel and some assurance that our own lives are secure.

A middle-class woman who sees a homeless woman on the street in New York City shares her fears with a psychiatrist. "If I don't do something about my life," she says, "I could be like that. Who would take care of me?" Another response, says the doctor, is an inability to cry: "They say, 'What's wrong with me that I could walk past these people and feel nothing? How cold have I become?' "

Many of us wrestle with this question.

Is Holly's story unique in any sense? If it is, then it makes sense to ask hard questions about Holly. If it is not, then it would make more sense to ask hard questions of ourselves.

"Some 800 homeless infants" in New York City, according to documentation published by the Coalition for the Homeless in 1985, "routinely go without sufficient food, cribs, health care and diapers." The lives of these infants, writes the coalition, "are put at risk because of the reckless negligence" of welfare personnel. The coalition states that "high-risk pregnant women" are routinely sent to barracks shelters, others to EAUs: "Coalition monitors, making sporadic random checks, found eight women in their *ninth* month of pregnancy sleeping in EAUs. . . . Two women denied shelter began having labor contractions at the EAU."

The coalition is an advocacy group and, for this reason, may be viewed as partisan in its defense of homeless children. The New York City Council is not an advocacy group. A letter dated April 30, 1984, written by Carol Bellamy—president of the city council at the time—notes that social work departments at six of the city's public hospitals indicate that they would discharge women with newborns to barracks shelters or hotels "only as a last resort"—but that frequently they have no choice. "In those cases, they generally referred the families to Special Services for Children as potential abuse and neglect cases because of the substandard housing."

What this seems to mean is that an option open to the city is to charge a mother with abuse of her own child if it sends them to an unsafe shelter. Who, then, has abused the child?

The *New York Times* (1984) reports that "mothers and young children" have been sleeping "on chairs, counters and floors" of city welfare offices. A year later, the city concedes, about 2,000 children have been forced to sleep in EAUs during a single three-month span.

Some of these situations have improved. Others have not. In September 1986, the Legal Aid Society was forced to go to court to stop the city from assigning pregnant women and infants less than six months old to barracks shelters. One plaintiff in the case, according to court papers, had suffered a miscarriage in the communal bathroom of a shelter in the Bronx. The woman had asked that she be transferred from the shelter when she learned that she was pregnant—a request that was apparently ignored. On the night that she miscarried, she lay on the bathroom floor for half an hour.

According to the *New York Times*, a state regulation forbids the referral of pregnant women to such shelters.

There are thousands of poor women who could tell us similar stories. If we try, I suppose that we can find a flaw in every one of them. But all the flaws that we may find in Holly—or her counterparts in Washington, Chicago, or wherever homeless women wander in America—cannot justify the larger flaw in national priorities. Devastated mothers may well blur some details or confuse them. Infant mortality figures do not lie.

"The first thing that has to be said about the homelessness problem," writes Thomas J. Main in the *New York Times*, "is that solving it is going to take time. There are no quick fixes. . . ." The author criticizes those who wish "to improve allegedly 'damaging' conditions" in the shelters. His concern is less with the conditions in the shelters than with those who live there. "Homeless families," he writes, "seem to have greater behavioral and psychological problems than similar nonhomeless families." He speculates that "such families" are "less able to adapt" to a tight housing market than the rest of us.

This is correct. Families whose welfare rental limit is $270 in New York City do not adapt well to a market where the lowest rents begin around $400. Heads of families not on welfare, earning minimum wages of $560, don't adapt successfully to rentals that consume three quarters of their income.

"Can anything be done?" The writer answers that we need more research: "Such work could do for the study of homelessness what the development of the poverty line did for the study of poverty; it does not solve the problem but it imposes a sorely needed discipline . . . on the discussion."

What does it do for someone with no home?

We may wonder if the author would propose such patience if he were, just once, in Holly's situation. We know, of course, that he would not be patient in that case; he would act with the dispatch of any frightened parent. But the distance he has already created by his clinical finality makes it impossible for him to see himself in Holly's situation. This is one reason why I think we ought to view the use of psychiatric labels, especially by those who aren't physicians, with considerable caution. It can too easily create a distance that does more than to alleviate our fears; it may at length permit us to be rather cruel and, even worse, a little smug and comfortable in our detachment.

Labeling a homeless woman as defective ("less able to adapt," to use his words) also leads us to avoid some of the documented causes of her suffering.

"A Cold-Blooded Assault on Poor People." This headline in the *Washington Post* precedes an article by William Raspberry. "Programs for low-income Americans," he writes, represent "just over a tenth of the federal budget," but are "ticketed" for one third of the 1987 Reagan budget cuts. "Are appropriations for low-income housing so excessively generous," he asks, "that it makes sense to cut them by a third?" Do indigent people waste so many of our dollars on "imagined illness," he asks, "that a $20 billion cut in Medicaid over the next five years" is justified? "Do housing repair grants, rural housing programs, emergency food assistance, legal services and the Work Incentive Program" represent such foolishly misguided policies that "they should be terminated altogether, as the president proposes?"

The essay by Mr. Main speaks of the "behavioral and psychological problems" of the homeless. What of the behavioral peculiarities of those who place a child in a "pigpen" a few minutes from the White House? What of the behavior of a president who tells us that there is no hunger in the land, while children die of diarrhea caused by malnutrition, or because their mothers were malnourished—both the consequence, at least in part, of policies he has advanced?

" A continuously rising level of child abuse and homelessness," writes New York City Council President Andrew Stein, "is not a force of nature. . . ." This is a point he is compelled to make because we tend so easily to speak of homelessness as an unauthored act: something sad, perhaps the fault of those who have no homes, more likely that of chance. Homelessness "happens," like a flood or fire or a devastating storm—what legal documents, insurance forms, might call "an act of God." But homelessness is not an act of God. It is an act of man. It is done by people like ourselves. It is done to people such as Benjamin.

Phrases such as "no quick fix" do more than to dilute a sense of urgency; they also console us with the incorrect impression that we are, no matter with what hesitation, moving in the right direction. All available statistics make it clear that this is not the case.

"Federal housing assistance programs have been cut a full 64 percent since 1980," according to Manhattan Borough President David Dinkins in a study released in March of 1987, "from $32 billion to $9 billion in the current fiscal year."

In 1986, the Department of Housing and Urban Development subsidized construction of only 25,000 housing units nationwide. When Gerald Ford was president, 200,000 units were constructed. Under President Carter, 300,000 units were constructed.

"For each dollar authorized for national defense in 1980, nineteen cents were authorized for subsidized housing programs," according to another recent study. In 1984, only *three* cents were authorized for housing for each military dollar. This is neither a "quick fix" nor a "slow fix." It is an aggressive fix against the life and health of undefended children.

Mr. Stein poses a challenging scenario. "Imagine the mayor of New York calling an urgent news conference," he writes, "to announce that the crisis of the city's poor children had reached such proportions that he was mobilizing the city's talents for a massive rescue effort. . . ." Some such drastic action, he asserts, is warranted "because our city is threatened by the spreading blight of a poverty even crueler in some ways than that of the Great Depression half a century ago."

We hear this voice of urgency too rarely. Instead, we are told that all these children we have seen—those who cannot concentrate in school because they are too hungry and must rest their heads against their desks to stifle stomach pains, those who sleep in "pigpens," those who travel sixty miles twice a day to glean some bit of education from a school at which they will arrive too late for breakfast and may find themselves denied a lunch because of presidential cuts—must wait a little while and be patient and accept the fact that there is "no quick fix" for those who are too young to vote and whose defeated parents have no lobbyists in Washington or City Hall.

There is a degree of cruelty at stake when those who aren't in pain assume the privilege to counsel moderation in address-

ing the despair of those who are, or when those who have resources to assuage such pain urge us to be patient in denial of
such blessings to the poor. It is still more cruel when those who
make such judgments are, as they are bound to be, articulate
adults and those who are denied are very frail and very small
and very young.

No quick fix, the essayist decrees, for Laura's children. No
quick fix for Raisin or for Doby or for Angelina. There is no
quick fix for those we do not see as having human claims upon
us. We move fast for those we love, more patiently for those we
neither love nor know nor feel that *we* could ever be. This is the
great danger in the clinical detachment that allows us to assign
the destitute their labels.

The debate persists as to how many homeless people are
the former patients of large mental hospitals, deinstitutionalized in the 1970s. Many homeless *individuals* may have been
residents of such institutions. In cities like New York, however,
where nearly half the homeless people are small children, with
an average age of six, such suppositions obviously make little
sense. Six-year-olds were not deinstitutionalized before their
birth. Their parents, with an average age of twenty-seven, are
not likely to have been the residents of mental hospitals when
they were still teenagers. But there is a reason for the repetition
of such arguments in face of countervailing facts. In a sense,
when we refer to "institutions"—those from which we think
some of the homeless come, those to which we think they ought
to be consigned —we are creating a new institution of our own:
the abstract institution of an airtight capsule ("underclass," "behavioral problem," "nonadaptive" or "psychotic") that will not
allow their lives to touch our own. Few decent people or responsible physicians wish to do this; but the risk is there. The homeless are a nightmare. Holly's story is a nightmare. It is natural
to fear and try to banish nightmares. It is not natural to try to
banish human beings.

The distancing we have observed receives its most extreme
expression in the use of language such as "undeserving." This
is, in some sense, the ultimate act of disaffiliation and the most
decisive means of placing all these families and their children
in a category where they can't intrude upon our dreams.

A classic nineteenth-century distinction draws the line between two categories of the poor: those who are "fit" to survive, and those who aren't. Of the latter, Herbert Spencer wrote: "The whole effort of nature is to get rid of such, to clear the world of them and make room for better." Few people would use such words today; but several prominent authors do accept the basic notion of a line between two categories of the indigent: those who merit something in the way of mercy or forgiveness, those who don't. If such a distinction may be made at all without some injury to our humanity, we need at least to ask if those who fall into the former category (the "deserving") have deserved—and, if so, how they have deserved—precisely the abysmal treatment they receive.

Holly and Benjamin presumably are two of the deserving. Annie Harrington and Gwen and Mr. Allesandro and their children may also be regarded as deserving. If they are, I should think that they deserve a little better than they get. It is true that they receive "a free lunch," holidays and weekends not included. They also get "a free ride" if they can survive for thirty months within the Martinique Hotel in order to be eligible to use a public van to search the city for apartments. This much is permitted the deserving. What, then, of the ones who are the less deserving? The deserving group receives so little that it isn't easy to imagine what remains to be denied. Life itself, perhaps, may be denied. That would then become the final penalty for failure.

Even if some of us feel comfortable with such extreme distinctions and are not embarrassed to wield quite so sharp a blade, will we not feel hesitant to let that blade fall also on the child of the adult who has been found lacking? For an answer to this question, we may listen to the words of a conservative author named Charles Murray. "The notion," he writes, is to reduce the reproduction of poor children by intensifying the unpleasantness of circumstances that precede their birth, rendering "unwed parenthood," in Murray's words, "contemptible." But how does one apply this stigma to the parent without savaging the child too? Undesirable existence is the child of contemptible conception. One word of contagion necessarily entails the next. The social worker does not enter into dialogue with Benjamin but with his mother. If the mother is contaminated in his eyes, the child's likelihood of finding a benign reception in the world is undermined as well.

Murray also makes an argument for restoration of the poorhouse as a substitute for income maintenance provided to poor mothers with small children. "Granted Dickensian horror stories about almshouses . . . ," he writes, then asks us to believe that "there were good almshouses." The prospect of living in such an institution ("a good correctional 'halfway house' " is his term) might serve as an incentive for an unwed mother, if she has no money, to accept abortion or to give her child to the state.

Finally, he argues that a thorough extirpation of the social benefactions that evolved from Franklin Roosevelt's time into our own would remove unnatural incentives to unadmirable behavior: "Take away all governmentally-sponsored subsidies for irresponsible behavior. . . . The natural system will produce the historically natural results."

Murray's ideas have been received well in the White House. The harshness of the wording he employs reflects a mood that may be dangerous for our society. "Some people are better than others," he writes. "They deserve more of society's rewards. . . ." The obverse of this statement, when applied to children such as Benjamin, is chilling.

Why is it that views like these, so alien to our American tradition and Judeo-Christian roots, should have received acceptance in this decade? Weariness and frustration, I have said, may lead some people to impatience and, at length, to anger at some of the mothers whom we have described. The fear of seeing our own nightmares acted out upon the sidewalk right before our eyes may be another reason for our willingness to place the indigent at a safe distance from our lives. For some of our fellow citizens, however, I believe there is a darker side to this.

There is, in certain intellectual circles, an increasingly explicit sense that some of us have a more authentic claim, not just to a comfortable life but to life itself, than do some others. The definition of the meritorious has gradually been codified in recent years. A close identification between worth and toughness, between "hardness" ("leanness") and desirability, increasingly defines the sort of person we regard as a true asset to our social order and precludes such virtues as the capability for gentleness, unselfishness, or love. Those, like Annie Harrington, who demonstrate the latter characteristics but are lacking in the former are not only less respected but provided disincentives to give birth to other persons like themselves.

Current discourse offers multiple examples of this narrowed definition of a person's worth. Two words—"lean" and "mean"—are often used in tandem, and the rhyme appears to resonate with socially attractive implications. It is noted that the decade which has seen fit to apply more stringent standards to the poor, and to reduce their life supports to the bare bone, is also that in which the cult of "fitness"—an obsession with thin bodies and hard minds—has overtaken the American imagination. Winning is all; the solitary runner, tuned to a headset that excludes the cries of his less fortunate competitors, becomes a national ideal.

The adjective "lean," suggestive as it is, is also used by government officials in defense of what is designated a "spare" budget for the poor. "Cutting away the fat" is the familiar term for fiscal measures which make life a little less endurable for those who are already the least favored, and render their children, who have already far too little fat upon their bodies, still more likely to remain in skeletal condition. A conservative educator speaks with pride of the less democratic, more exclusionary university or college as "a more lean and mean machine." He is not reprimanded, even by his adversaries, for this choice of words.

The jargon brings to mind an astronaut or military hero. Such a man is made, we have been told, of "the right stuff." But, if there is a "right stuff" then there has to be a "wrong stuff" also, and we know too well how such determinations will be made. The right stuff tends to be Caucasian, slender, self-reliant. The wrong stuff is an indigent and pregnant woman, possibly of dark skin, who depends on welfare and most certainly does not run laps or do aerobics. Even our conscience has been honed by current moods to a lean style. Conscience may be viewed as admirable still, but it must be disciplined, unsentimental, taut. We seldom berate our politicans for an agile cynicism but deplore the excess baggage of compassion. Jimmy Carter's conscience was not welcome in America. We voted for a rigorous simplicity, not self-examination. We travel light, in airplanes and in social policy. Leanness of body comes to symbolize austerity of heart, severity of mind.

So we grow a little bit impatient about Holly. We notice her errors, her confusion, sometimes her ineptitude. We want to shout at her, perhaps, and tell her there's a better way to handle things. Above all, we do not want to be labeled sentimental. She isn't the right stuff. Nor, assuredly, was Benjamin. I believe that our unwillingness to forgo toughness and submit to our own instinct for compassion speaks ill of democracy. It betrays the best things that America should stand for.

6

About Prayer

On the day after my meeting with Holly, I return to Houston Street to talk with her again. By the time I leave it's dark and very cold. It's only seven minutes to the subway station at Delancey Street. In the wind that cuts across the open spaces in this section of New York, it seems much longer. At 8:00 P.M. I pick up my bags and take a taxi to La Guardia.

Boston is even colder than New York. In the nearly empty terminal of Eastern Airlines I go to the phones. I want very much to see Elizabeth. I call her to be sure that she is home.

"Where are you?"

"I'm in the airport," I reply.

"Come on over here," she says. "I have a box of tea."

Elizabeth is not the poorest woman that I know; her home, however, is hardly elegant. Every other house along her street has been demolished. Half of her three-decker house was gutted a few years ago by fire. On this night it seems the safest place on earth. It's like a halfway house between the worlds of everything and nothing.

When I arrive the children are asleep. Winnie, her twelve-year-old, awakes and comes out to the kitchen in her night-gown. Smelling of sleep, she kisses me and is sent promptly back to bed. Elizabeth gives me a plate of food. She pours us each a cup of tea.

"How can they pray?"

"You have to pray. You have no choice," she says.

141

"You don't pray."

"I do. I never told you that. I do. Every morning, ever night, all of my life, I go down on my knees. I hold my hand like this. I close my eyes. When I wake up I wash my face, I sa my prayer, and then I find my clothes. When I go to bed, *befor* I go to bed, I say my prayer. You have known me twenty-thre years. I never told you that I do that, but I do. It's true."

"Do your children pray?"

"They do."

"Does your mother pray?"

"She do."

I ask Elizabeth this question: "How can you pray to some thing you don't know? How can poor people do it? How doe *anybody* pray?"

"The ones you know don't answer prayers," she says. "Yo pray to God because He don't say no. You are hungry. You can pay the rent. You cannot buy the shoes your child needs. Yo cannot understand the rules. You cannot keep the cat or the TV You need to pray! Help me, God! Help me to see the day! Hel me to see the light! Help me to go over. Don't forget me. Pleas do *not* do that!

"God tells you in the Bible: I do not hate ugly. I do not hat beauty. I accept you. I don't read the Bible but I *knows* the Bibl I have knowed it since I was a child. How do I know it? I hav knowed it from a child in a tent. I am that child. Preacher tel you: 'Everybody say amen!' You have to say it! You don't got n choice. You have to say amen!"

I ask Elizabeth why Winnie and the other children go t Catholic school.

"I do that because the school is good. It isn't for religion."

"Do you believe the Bible?"

"No. I don't. I tell you why: It don't make sense. God sa that a rich man cannot enter through a needle. That's not righ Ain't nobody can enter through a needle! I can't do it! You can do it! Nobody can do it! God can do it. No one else.

"The Bible isn't like a book of fact. It give you stories an examples to take heed by. If a man be good, he can go throug the needle."

She looks at the table, sips her tea. "Many of these wome

you have met—they don't have fathers. Or they didn't know their fathers. God is like a father for poor people. He may be neglectful. He may be demanding. He may not do what he is s'posed to do, but He do not disown you. He accepts you. Do these people know they are rejected? 'Course they do. If they isn't crazy then they know they be despised. God is the only one who don't despise. He *got* to be there. Jonathan, you cannot *live* with nothing to believe."

I tell her about Benjamin and Holly. I tell her about Rachel and her kids. Elizabeth says: "They be treated wrong. They be despised. They be contempted. What do the city say? It say: 'We do not want to see you, so we cut you out.' The city do not want these children to exist. It do not want them to be in existence. City tell you: 'You are not allowed to reproduce your kind. If you do this, we will cast you out.' The city say: 'We cast your child out.'

"When I pray I do not pray for things of gold. I see advertisements for furniture and cars on the TV. They don't excite me. Not me, not my kids. Expensive things, some people want them, I suppose. I can't identify. I do not want them! I don't need them! I can be my own self in my own house. I do like some pretty things. This saucer have blue daisies on it. This is the teapot that go with it—it have daisies too. After the children go to school I have a cup of tea. After the children go to sleep I have have a cup of tea.

"Television ads, I do not need it. I tell Winnie: 'Do not watch it! You can be brain damage. Turn it!' You be tired from New York. It make you sad. You didn't drink your tea . . .

"I watch TV. I won't deny. When they show me Dr. King, it make me cry. I was not a part of the participation. I am black. It make me cry. I tell Winnie: 'Turn it!' So she cut off the TV.

"Winnie, she's got a beautiful way. You don't see it often anymore. It's in her air. She's sweet! She be twelve but she's like nine years old. I be thinking during the night: If I had the money I would send her to a better school. Not a lot. Enough to help a little girl get over."

"Over what?"

"Over—to a better place," Elizabeth replies.

"This here is a mason jar my mother gave me. Down South

in the neighborhood where I was born, you go into any house any poor person's house you find two things: a Bible and a mason jar. You go into their house, you see maybe two-dozen jars. The mason jar is a natural form. I keep a little money in it Not a lot. I just like enough to help her to get over."

I tell her about Laura. I tell her that, because she couldn' read, she was afraid of signing an adoption paper by mistake.

"The world is words," Elizabeth replies. "If you canno read, you do not know. I have a friend. He cannot read but I be nice to him. He say: 'I want you to come visit in my house. takes bus number 23.' So I say: 'Where do it go?' He say: 'It go up the avenue.' I say to him: 'Where you get off?' He tells me 'On the street.' He do not *know!* 'You get off and you come down and you walk for a block and that's my house.' I say 'What is the *name* of this here street you live?' He say that he don't know. Jonathan, you write this down: That's what's taking place here in America! He know where he's going but he don't know where he *be!* I say: 'My God in heaven!'

"Well, he's older than myself. So I feel sympathy. He told me that he go down to Connecticut. I think: How in hell he ever get there?"

"When he's wrong, do you correct him?"

"Yes I do. You cannot play a game. If I said something to you that was not right and you didn't tell me it was wrong and then I learned it later on, I would be angry. I would think: He' laughing. He thinks: 'She is using the wrong word.' It isn't doin anybody any good to lie. You need to *know.*

"I be thinking of the lady in New York. That do make you sad to cry. She be scared they take away her baby. What do she have more precious in the world?"

Elizabeth tells me her mother has been sick. She is seventy four years old. She lives in Newport News, Virginia. "M mother asked me how is it that you and I be friends? I tell her I'm not going to explain it. I have known you twenty-three years. Why are we friends? My mother want to know. Why? It' a puzzle. Why are we friends? Who knows the reason? You don' know it! I don't know it! Only God can know. I don't question Twenty-three years and we are friends. That's it! So I don' worry about nothin' . . .

"The little boy that ate lead paint. Now, I can tell you that ain't something new. Twenty years ago they did newspaper stories. It was going to be fixed. Ten years ago they did the same newspaper stories. It was going to be fixed. They lie to you when they pretend it's something new. Don't they ever read the things they wrote? I guess that it do make them feel better . . ."

I have know Emmie, Elizabeth's oldest daughter, since she was a child. She works today at a shelter for the homeless. "One of the babies is lead poisoned," Elizabeth says. "Emmie say she see her in her walker. She be blind but she can tell when Emmie's in the room. She turns her head. Emmie say she stand before the window. She just stand there and she stare into the sky. Maybe she see something we don't know.

"One of the nuns say this. She say: 'I wish those people who parade around with pictures of abortions—of the fetuses— I wish they cared as much about the living as the dead.' Emmie agree. Some of those people are the ones who want to cut the foods stamps for the welfare children. They will bless you if you die but they will kill you if you live. Emmie agree."

I look at my watch. It's after 2:00 A.M. I find it difficult to leave. I am thinking about Holly going back and forth between the welfare office and the hospital and EAU. I tell her about the funeral.

Elizabeth closes her eyes and she says this: "I be hungry and you gave me not to eat. I be thirsty and you gave me not to drink. I was naked and you did not clothe me. I was a stranger. You did not take me in.

"Jonathan, you write this down. When a child is allowed to die because he has no place to live, what is it? It is murder. Write it down."

I get my pen out of my pocket and do as she says.

"Why do people pray? I'm going to tell you for a natural fact. We talkin' about me. If you're not born rich and you are my complexion, you know that it's going to be hard and it ain't going to get better. If you have a dream, then you have something you can hold. You may be low. You may be beaten down. But you say, 'Maybe, someday—' So this dream don't let you die.

"The lady ask you is she dying? She be right: We dying all the time. She dying. So are you. Everybody, rich and poor, we all be scared to die."

I put on my coat. She wraps the teapot with blue daisies in newspapers and she puts it in a cardboard box. "When you are in New York you bring her this. I can get another one in time." Then I go down the stairs. Elizabeth goes with me. At the door she kisses me. It's hard to say good-bye.

PART THREE

The Natural Results

Who are these people if not tokens of mass dispossession of a sort not seen since the lean years of the thirties? And what is their likely fate if this is their plight in the midst of an economic recovery?

—Kim Hopper and Jill Hamberg,
Community Service Society of New York

1

Seasonal Concerns

Homeless people and their advocates notice with frustration that the press appears to focus on the issue of the homeless only, or particularly, in the weeks preceding and just after Christmas. There is some truth in this, although it may be less true now than during 1985 when I first visited the Martinique Hotel.

The ebb and flow of seasonal concern applies not only to the press but to much of the population. I am sure that it was not by accident that I was initially attracted to the Martinique not on a fine spring day but in the week preceding Christmas. After that first visit, and a longer visit the next week, I remained in Boston, thought about the families I had met, and then returned to spend a number of nights in further conversations in late January and, again, on four occasions between February and the start of May. After that, I visited only once, in mid-July, before cold weather drew me back the following November. It may be that there is something seasonal in the attraction that these stories hold.

Autumn 1986: The building that houses the city's central EAU is on Church Street in lower Manhattan. At about eleven-thirty on a night in late November, I watch a woman walk into this building.

Dark-eyed, pregnant, carrying some paper bags of clothing, Susan comes into the room with a good deal of hesitation. Her husband, a tall man with reddish hair, walks beside her. Seated in one of the molded plastic chairs, she holds a crumpled tissue in her hands. When she isn't weeping, she leans back and shuts her eyes and twists the Kleenex in her hands. She and her husband, both of whom appear to be in their late twenties, do not speak to each other but stare at a TV set fixed to the wall before them.

I later learn that she is eight months pregnant. They have been staying in the home of friends. Their friends, already overcrowded, have been threatened with eviction if they stay. They were finally asked to leave. They have been here before. They have been in other shelters. They haven't had a real home for six months.

She sits patiently, crying some and coughing a great deal. On the wall above her head there are these printed words: "If you are eligible for emergency housing you will receive a referral to shelter and transportation to get there. If you do not accept the shelter and transportation you are offered, you have to leave. . . ."

Near this sign there is another, somewhat more alarming. It advises families who have formerly been placed in one of the city's largest family shelters that their children ("six years or younger") should be tested for lead poisoning. The shelter, nearby on Catherine Street, has been in the news a great deal recently. Opened in December 1985, it was found in February 1986 by the Legal Aid Society to be hazardous to children and to pregnant women. The New York City Health Department noted that the water heater leaked carbon monoxide. The kitchen was strewn with garbage. Heating facilities for food were found to be inadequate. An outbreak of infant diarrhea, twenty-five cases in one week, had been noted by residents and provoked the city's health inspection. The city at first declined to close the shelter because, officials said, the problems weren't "life threatening."

In March, a pediatrician from Montefiore Hospital had studied the shelter. Terming conditions there "abominable," he reported that the walls were covered with lead paint. Paint was also flaking off around the windowsills and radiators within reach of children. Worse, large chips of paint removed by painters doing renovation had been left in open piles and plastic bags where children and adults could breathe the lead. The paint on the walls, examined by an independent testing agency hired by Legal Aid, contained "ten times the amount of lead permitted by law," according to a Legal Aid attorney. Contamination from exposed asbestos had also been present. Children and adults, the doctor said, had been endangered since the shelter opened.

The city refused to close the shelter until April, when it was so ordered by the courts. It reopened the shelter in September, but instead of getting rid of the lead poison, it had simply covered it with lead-free paint. This cannot prevent the further flaking off of chips, which may expose a child to the poison that remains beneath.

The chairman of pediatrics at the State University Health Science Center in Brooklyn supplied some added information. Medical treatment of lead-poisoned children, he observed, is "generally disappointing because it occurs after the fact of brain damage. . . ." Damage "to intellectual function," he added, is often irreversible. "Using children to discover bad housing is analogous," he said, to the use of a canary by coal miners to discover noxious fumes. "We can afford to lose some canaries in a good cause." Subjecting children to such risks, he said, was "not appropriate."

The city, however, continued to send families to the shelter. Almost 500 people, over half of whom were chldren, were still housed at Catherine Street in late November. The HRA agreed that pregnant women and children under seven would not be placed there.

Susan tells me she is a high school graduate and had a clerical job before becoming pregnant. Her husband, who held a low-paid job, lived with her and their daughter in an apartment that her father helped to pay for. Evicted after her father's death, she has been homeless since. Ten days with friends. Two weeks in one homeless shelter. Two weeks in another. She's been on her feet for half a year, riding at night on subways to the EAU, going at two or three o'clock to a hotel. Her rent allowance when her child is born will be $244. Because of dislocation she has lost her Medicaid. She hasn't been housed in any one location long enough to get herself enrolled in WIC. She expects her child in three weeks. She has not received prenatal care. Last week, she says, she came here twice. Her child, who is six, was with her.

"I slept here two nights on that bench. They let my daughter use the crib. They gave her tuna fish and juice."

The first night, after having waited until 5:00 A.M., she and her daughter had been sent to Catherine Street.

"At Catherine Street, they wouldn't let me stay. They don't take pregnant women. They let me sleep there in some kind of office, on a cot. We had to leave after about an hour." The next night, when they told her they were sending her to Catherine Street again, she grew alarmed. "I wouldn't go. They put me in handcuffs—over there. They said I was upset."

Handcuffs for a pregnant woman who refuses to be sent into a shelter where the city has already promised not to send a pregnant woman seems a bit extreme. When she tells me, almost with embarrassment, "They said I was upset," I think of certain women who are close to me—my mother, sister, friends. I try to picture what they'd do or say in such a situation.

She points to a corner of the room: "I threw up—right over there."

At 1:00 A.M., a man dressed in a suit and tie, a handsome overcoat and hat, opens an office door and comes to speak with her. He asks her why her daughter isn't here. She answers that she left her child with her mother. For some reason this disturbs him. He tells her this was irresponsible. She explains that she was here last week for two nights with her daughter.

"They sent me to Catherine Street. They wouldn't let me stay. My daughter couldn't sleep." She says she thought that it was more responsible to leave her daughter with her mother, who agreed to keep the child for the night. Once they find a place for her to live she'll bring her daughter.

The man's response is puzzling. Is there something here that I don't understand? "This is irresponsible," he says again. "I'll bet that you won't show up at your welfare office in the morning. You'll get there late. Tomorrow night I'll see you sitting here again." He shakes his finger inches from her eyes. "There's something lacking in you. You have to be up at 7:00 A.M. You have to get into your welfare office."

Over his head there is the printed warning about Catherine Street. "Here you are—it's after midnight. How much sleep do you expect to get?"

Intimidated by his words, weary with six months of sleeplessness, recurrent nausea, aching limbs, she looks down at the floor. He lectures her again about her irresponsible behavior. She looks up at the sign above his head.

The man's demeanor, self-assured, impeccable, bewilders me. He seems convinced that he is doing something good for Susan by reducing her to tears. "Destructive forms of conscientiousness," wrote Erik Erikson: "the most deadly of all possible sins."

At one-twenty another man emerges from an office. "We're sending you to Catherine Street," he says. "Do you accept?" She shakes her head. "Then you refuse?" Again, she shakes her head. He disappears into the office.

At 2:00 A.M. the second man returns. It seems they have relented. They are sending her instead to a hotel in Queens. He drops into her hand four subway tokens. She is admonished to be at her welfare office, with her child, in seven hours.

With the help of her husband she gets up from the plastic chair. Her husband hands her one of their paper bags. An elderly policeman who has been observing this steps forward to assist her as she straightens up her back. She thanks him, and in doing so, her face relaxes for the first time in two hours into a real smile.

When I recount this story later to an academic friend in Boston, he looks at first bewildered. Then, in a bemused way, speaking very slowly, he asks me what appears to be an unrelated question: "Have you ever heard of a venturi?"

I tell him I don't know the word. He says it is a term in physics. A venturi, he explains, is a constricted passage in a tube or tunnel through which air or fluid moves. The flow of air or fluid may be smooth and unimpeded both before and after the venturi; but, in the region of constriction, turbulence develops. Anything—a fleck of dust, a bit of paper—will be swirled about and torn apart. He says the word comes from the name of the Italian physicist who first devised it.

"This place—this EAU," he says, "it seems to have the same effect on human beings."

The metaphor is somewhat esoteric (it is for me, as least, since I have never heard the word before) but it may be useful nonetheless. It may help explain the turbulent behavior, often with a lapse in customary shrewdness and strategic skills, that many of the people I've described seem to display. Even the most rational of men or women may well lose their bearings, or good judgment, once they have been introduced into a virtually closed system from which almost any exit seems implausible or when they are asked to answer questions to which any possible reply will be irrational. This applies not only to the EAU but to the shelter system as a whole.

Homeless families in the Martinique Hotel, as we have seen, are told they must not cook within their rooms. They are then assigned a "restaurant allowance" which, however, they are told, it would be unwise to use in restaurants. In time, they realize that the restaurant allowance is intended to buy groceries they cannot cook in kitchens they don't have and must therefore try somehow to cook on hot plates they are not officially permitted to possess. If they use the restaurant allowance in a restaurant, their children will soon starve. If they cook within their rooms, they break a rule to which they have agreed. If they are discovered in infraction of a rule, they are at the mercy of the guard who has discovered their offense.

Another example of immersion in irrationality: A mother of three children, living on the twelfth floor of the Martinique Hotel, is told that she must demonstrate her capability for self-reliance by doing all she can to find a permanent apartment. If she fails to do so, she may learn her "case" is closed, her room given to someone else, her children cut from sustenance or taken from her custody. She must therefore clip advertisements from the newspapers, use one of the telephones twelve floors below her in the lobby, travel to a realtor's office, fill out forms, look at apartments, and return to the hotel with evidence that she has carried out what is, effectively, the "job" of homeless people.

The social worker who assigns this task also tells her that her rent allowance is $270. Realtors tell her that apartments at

that rent do not exist. Her welfare worker tells her this is probably correct. She is told to get enrolled for public housing. Her
neighbor across the hall tells her about the waiting list for public housing.

A person given an absurd task, but obliged to go about it
with a pretense of persistent diligence, is drawn into a kingdom
of futility that would merely seem surreal if she were not si-
multaneously surrounded by 400 rapidly deteriorating adults
who are falling into drugs, depression, prostitution and disease
before her eyes. Soon enough, futility grows into panic, aimless-
ness, disintegration of her sense that she can understand and
grapple with the world. The venturi of the physics lab shreds
bits of paper. A social venturi shred the souls of human beings.

After evenings like the one I spent talking with Susan at
the EAU, I try to anesthetize myself. One way of doing this is
by denial. At a distance, it is easy to distrust my memory. Perhaps a morbid disposition has exaggerated something or has
willfully misunderstood the details. Maybe I got it wrong. Did I
read the sign correctly? If I didn't get it wrong, I tell myself, then
the situation probably has been corrected since.

I'm writing this in January 1987. In the *New York Times* I
read these words: "The Legal Aid Society charged yesterday that
a city shelter for the homeless had violated a pledge made in
court that it [would] not admit pregnant women and young children because of the threat posed by the presence of lead paint.
. . . One of the lawyers . . . said the society had learned of the
situation last week from a pregnant woman who complained
she had been allowed to stay at the shelter without being notified of any possible health threat. . . .

"The shelter, at 78 Catherine Street, near the Manhattan
Bridge on the Lower East Side, has been the focus of a ten-month
dispute between the city and the Legal Aid Society. . . . The society contended in a suit that asbestos and lead levels in the
shelter were 10 to 100 times [the] legal limits." The HRA responded to the suit "by covering lead-painted surfaces with several coats of lead-free paint. . . ." The city also said it had
removed asbestos and it promised the continuous removal of
the lead-paint chips. Medical experts for the city testified, how-

ever, that even with these measures, residents were still at risk. "The city agreed in court not to send pregnant women or small children to the shelter."

Last March, the *Times* reports, "a child was found to be suffering from lead poisoning. Other residents suffered from high blood levels of the toxic metal. . . . Complaints of diarrhea among residents were traced by experts to asbestos contamination."

A Legal Aid attorney later tells me that, despite the city's promise not to send a pregnant woman or small child to this shelter, there was a loophole in the prohibition: The city had set aside one part of Catherine Street (perhaps what Susan calls "some kind of office") as an "overflow" facility for families that came to an EAU as late as midnight. The area was lead free, so the law allowed its use in an emergency—but not more than once for any family. "Assigning her there at all was questionable," he says. "Assigning her a second time was patently illegal."

Susan, of course, would have no way to know that there might be a lead-free section in the building. The sign on the wall was ominous enough to frighten anyone. Nor would legal technicalities of which she could not be aware have been of any help in lessening her sense of fear. If we extricate ourselves from the legalities and place outselves in the position of a woman fighting nausea in the eighth month of her pregnancy, homeless at midnight, bewildered by the regulations, and already frightened by her previous experiences here, we may gain some faint idea of what innumerable homeless women undergo routinely in New York.

Treating any person this way is intolerable. Treating a pregnant woman this way is unspeakable.

2

The Long March

In time of war, civilians sometimes are obliged to join a forced march with invading or retreating armies. Many people die along the way. Children and women are often the first victims.

The forced march undertaken by unsheltered children and their parents in New York is not often made on foot, more often by the public-transit system. Most survive; few without incurring an incalculable damage. At journey's end lies little comfort but a modernized internment.

At every step along the road they face the eyes of an impatient populace. Their transit papers will be subway tokens. Their rations will be food stamps, restaurant allowances, meal tickets to soup kitchens. Instead of visas they will be provided with referral slips that indicate to an anonymous and overburdened welfare system whether or not they meet requirements for sanctuary. Not orchestrated human love but punishment for having failed to navigate the economic mine field of America will be awarded to them as they pass the gates of every relocation center. Like displaced persons, each will be assigned a number.

References to prisons and to camps for displaced persons appear repeatedly in language used by homeless people. The theme is one of being under siege. "There is a sense of terror," says a man whose family has lived at the Martinique for several years. "But the physical fears are not the worst. There is this sense of darkness and foreboding. Doors are always banging late at night. They're made of metal and it echoes through the halls. It's hard to sleep. You feel like you're in jail."

The feeling of internment may be reinforced by rituals of lining up, of having one's room number written down, of receiving one serving—and one serving only—of a desperately needed meal. People who, one month before, may have been strong and full of pride are humbled rapidly. You see it in the corridor outside the ballroom of the Martinique at noon, when adults with their children wait to file past a table to receive a plate of food. "You can always tell the family . . . that's new," observes a priest who works with homeless families in Wisconsin. "Their heads are always down. . . . They're very grateful for everything. They eat very quickly, and then they quickly disappear."

A mother of three children in the Hotel Carter tells me this: She was a teacher's aide, had worked for three years with retarded children, and was living doubled up with relatives when the death of one and marriage of another forced her to the streets. She's been living in the Carter for two years.

"My rent allowance is $270. Places that I see start at $350. Even if you could pay it, landlords do not want you if you're homeless. 'Where do you live?' I say the Carter. That's the end of it. It's hard to do it. You psyche yourself. They want to check you out. You feel ashamed.

"It's the same with public school. The teacher asks: 'Where do you live?' You say the Carter. Right away they put you in a slot. Jennifer is in the fourth grade. She has had four teachers in one year. Teachers keep quitting. Too many kids for them to handle. They can't teach. So I have to see my kids losing their years. Do they put the homeless children into categories? 'Course they do! They know which ones they are."

Food is short: "By the eighteenth of the month I'm running out. I have to borrow. They have got to eat. When we're low we live on macaroni and french fries. I can make a lot from two potatoes. When you're running low you learn to stretch. I don't have the money to buy meat. Even if I did, there's no refrigerator. It won't keep.

"Christmas last year, we stayed in our room. Christmas

this year, we'll be here again. It's a lonely time for everybody. I do what I can to keep the other women up. There are adults here who come to me. They think I'm stronger than I am. They're under stress. I'll talk them down. Do you know what scares them most? It's when the rent is due. You go to your welfare office. You're afraid there's a mistake. It happens for no reason. I can write but I cannot write all the things that come out of my heart."

The city pays the Hotel Carter $63 a night to keep her family in this room. Tourists who stay in newly renovated rooms on higher floors of the hotel pay $35 for a room of comparable size. The renovated rooms are clean and neat, with color television sets and air conditioners and new quilts and linens. The rooms for homeless families have roaches, water seeping through the ceilings, missing window panes, holes in the floor. The homeless families are restricted to three floors where they will not be seen by tourists.

"In the morning I'm up at six. The children go to school at eight. Some mornings there's no food. I give them a quarter if I have a quarter. They can buy a bag of chips. After school I give them soup—or bread with peanut butter. Cooking does pose certain dangers in a place like this. You're careful with a fry pan in this room. If you're using oil and it catches fire, it will go right up the wall."

These are the routine concerns of homeless families. Children in this building face an added injury. The management does not want them to be seen in front of the hotel. But they have to be outside to meet their school bus in the morning. They also have to be dropped off when they return. This is the solution: There is a rear exit, used primarily for trash collection. The exit can be reached through a back corridor. It opens on Forty-second Street next to a shop that sells drug paraphernalia in a block of pornographic movie theaters. This is the place the children wait to meet their bus.

"They told my kids: 'You have to use the back. You're not allowed to use the front.' They herd them down that corridor to the rear door. It doesn't hurt so much that they would want *me* to be hidden. It does hurt that they would want my children to be hid."

Do children know that they are viewed as undesirables? Using the same exit that is used by the hotel to throw away the trash is pretty vivid. They leave with the trash. Perhaps they carry some of its stench with them to school. "We aren't going to get away with this," said Daniel Moynihan. "We are *not* going to get away with this." The twenty-first century, he said, "is going to punish us. . . ." Perhaps he's right. The time of punishment may not be deferred so long.

A woman living on the tenth floor of the Martinique is told that she has cancer. She calls me late at night in Boston. It is, of course, the kind of news that terrifies all people, even in the best of economic situations. Most of us at least have systems of support. We live near neighbors. Some of us have family members near at hand; sometimes they are close enough to drive to our homes, sit up and talk with us, pack our clothes, our children's clothes, and take us back with them into their safer world. They can bring us to the hospital. If the information is unclear, they can bring us to another doctor to confirm the diagnosis, to be sure.

When you are homeless there are no supports.

Mrs. Andrews is forty-two. The first time that we met, before Thanksgiving, she told me she had worked for seventeen years as a secretary and bookkeeper—nine of those years for one firm. She'd lived in the same house for seven years.

How did she end up in the Martinique?

Like many people in this situation, she had been hit with two catastrophes in sequence. First, she had learned that she had cancer in her large intestine. Hospitalized for removal of a part of her intestine, she had to have a hysterectomy as well. Three successive operations coincided with a time in which the man to whom she had been married thirteen years fell into depression, caused by difficulties of his own. He had had a prior drinking problem and it now became much worse. Debilitated by her medical concerns, she had no strength to offer him support. He, in turn, became destructive and disorganized. She had to leave their home.

She had three children: two daughters and one son. With the breakup of her household and her inability to work for several months, she found her economic status dropping very fast. She turned to welfare. One night, six months after her third and final operation, she was sitting with her children in the office of the Church Street EAU.

For several nights the city is unable to assign her to a shelter. When a place is found, it is the Hotel Carter. Bad as it is, she never gets beyond the door. When she arrives at 1:00 A.M., the manager says he can't accommodate a family of four. Why was she sent here? She is too dazed to ask. At 2:00 A.M., she gets back on the subway and returns to the same EAU she has just left. On her return, a social worker seems annoyed. He asks: "Then you refuse this placement?" Although she explains what has transpired, she is forced to sign a paper formally refusing placement at the hotel which has just refused her.

I have asked her about this several times. "I had to *sign* the paper."

Mrs. Andrews is articulate, well organized, and neatly dressed. If this woman could be savaged with so little hesitation, how much more savage is the treatment meted out to women who don't have her middle-class appearance and do not display the style and articulation with which social workers might identify?

"We spent another seven days sitting in the welfare center, 9:00 to 5:00, and every evening 6:00 to 8:00 A.M., trying to sleep there at the EAU. All we had to eat that week was peanut butter, jelly, and cheese sandwiches." Not wanting to exaggerate, she adds: "They gave my children juice and little packages of milk."

After seven days she's given a week's placement at the Holland Hotel on West Forty-second Street, a few blocks from the Carter. This hotel, which has been likened by the *New York Times* to " a kiddie park designed by Hogarth and the Marquis de Sade," was cited in 1985 for nearly 1,000 health and building violations. The owner was later found to have been taking in $6 million yearly, half of which was profit.

At the time that Mrs. Andrews was sent by the city to the Holland, part of the building housed nonhomeless tenants. Only certain deteriorated floors were used to house the homeless. The fourteenth floor, to which the Andrews were assigned for their first night of sleep in thirteen days, had no running water. "Even the toilet had no water," Mrs. Andrews says. "We had to carry buckets to a bar across the street. There was a line of homeless families waiting to bring water back to the hotel. Only one elevator worked. You had to wait an hour."

Two days later, unable to face this any longer, she goes with her children to the EAU. There she is asked to sign another form refusing placement. " 'We gave you a room. You turned it down,' they said." She's given a referral slip and told that she must bring this to her welfare center. At the welfare center she presents the paper to her welfare worker, sits in a chair and waits until the office closes, then is sent back to the EAU to sit up in another chair until the morning. In this way, she and her children pass the next twenty-seven days.

During this time, Mrs. Andrews's fourteen-year-old daughter, Carol, becomes ill. She develops pain and swelling in her abdomen. Examination leads to the discovery of a tumor on her kidney. The kidney has to be removed. Also removed in the same operation are the ovary and fallopian tube on her right side. Carol's doctor tells her mother that she must not be allowed to sit up in a welfare office. Armed with a letter to this effect signed by the physician, the family goes back to the welfare center, then—after another day of waiting—to the EAU, only to repeat this ritual for three more days.

After forty-five days of homelessness, the Andrews are sent at 6:00 A.M., on a day in late September 1984, to a small room without a closet but with four beds in the Martinique Hotel. Seven months later they are moved into a slightly larger room two floors below. It is in this room that we first meet in 1986.

The room has the smell of fresh paint on the day I visit. Also, a new door has been installed. These changes, she believes, were made throughout the building and were prompted by some pressure from the Office of the Mayor. Unfortunately, the keys distributed to residents to match the locks on the new doors were incorrectly made. They are interchangeable in many cases. Mrs. Andrews has been robbed four times.

When we meet, she talks for hours of her fears. Fear is plainly written in her eyes. Forty-five days of destitution, sickness, subway travel, waiting lines, followed by two years of residence in the Martinique, have worn away much of her confidence.

"My mother and father are deceased. Except for the children I have only my grandparents. My grandmother is in a wheelchair. My grandfather is ninety-four years old. I pray for them. When they are gone I have nobody but the kids. I was not religious when I came here. People become religious here," she says, "because each day that you survive seems like a miracle."

Mrs. Andrews' husband has been in and out of psychiatric wards throughout the past two years. Her former boss has told her that he wants her back. She's reluctant to accept the job until she saves some money. If she returns to work she loses welfare and can't stay in the hotel. But welfare rules forbid her to save money. Any significant savings pose the risk of being cut from all support. So she cannot start a bank account in order to prepare for the unlikely chance of moving into an apartment. Even if she had her old job back, she couldn't pay a month's rent and deposit and security, buy furniture, or pay for health insurance. The city is said to have a program that sometimes assists with some of these expenses; few families have been given this assistance. Mrs. Andrews has not heard of such a program.

"I don't eat. I'd stopped smoking back in 1983. Now I smoke three packs a day."

Only in state prisons have I seen so many people craving cigarettes. She lights one cigarette after another, presses it out, looks for a match, hunts for another pack.

"Food is very scarce right now, worse than any time since I've been here." She had received $185 a month in food stamps on June 1. That was cut to $63 in August. It will be cut again to $44 in January. "I have trouble sleeping when we're short of food. I cannot sleep if I don't know that I can feed them breakfast."

Food-stamp cuts have forced her for the first time to accept free bags of food from local charities. "On Saturdays I go to St. Francis Church on Thrity-first Street. Tuesdays, I go to St. John's." In compensation for her loss of food stamps—a net loss of $122 each month—she receives an increase of $8.75 in restaurant allowance every two weeks from the city. Her room rent at the Martinique is about $2,000. Her rent allowance for a permanent apartment, if she were to find one, is $270.

She forces herself to eat one meal a day. Her children, knowing of her cancer history, have tried to get her to stop smoking. She wants to know: "How will I get them out of this?" I want to know: Why do we do this to her?

Her phone call brings me back to talk with her when cancer is again suspected, this time on her skin, just under her left eye. At the hospital, the spot in question has been tested. The results are positive. The doctor, she says, is also concerned about a lump that has developed on her throat. She has to go into the hospital but puts it off two weeks.

On New Year's Eve she phones again. She's going to go into the hospital. She'll have to leave her kids alone. She needs some cash so they can buy necessities until she's home. I send a postal money order for $250. The post office tells me: "It's as good as cash. Any postal clerk will honor it."

The money order is not honored. Even with identification, she is told that she needs someone else to "vouch" for her.

A friend in Manhattan helps me. He calls someone he knows at the post office and she finally gets the cash. She is embarrassed by the trouble she believes she's caused me. On the telephone she tells me that conditions in the building have grown worse. "There's been no light in the elevator for a month. People use cigarette lighters. Or you ride up in the dark. I can't face it. I walk up ten floors."

When she gets out of the hospital, she has good news. The spot on her face and lump on her throat turned out to be benign. By now, however, sleeplessness and fear have left her drained. She's also feeling the results of the last round of food-stamp cuts. Everyone in the hotel she says, is short of food. The president this month requests a billion-dollar cut in food stamps and in child-nutrition funds for 1987.

The city, meanwhile, has run into shortages of shelter space. The shortage has been so acute that twenty-nine families have been sent to a hotel in Newark. The *Times* reports, however, that an HRA spokesperson "said the situation is by no means critical. . . ."

Government is not to blame for Mrs. Andrews' illnesses, her cancer surgery, her panic, her compulsive smoking. Government is certainly to blame for leaving a sick woman homeless more than forty days. It is to blame for sending her at 1:00 A.M. to a hotel from which she will be turned away. It is to blame for making any human being in New York City carry buckets from the fourteenth floor of an unsafe hotel in order to fetch water at a tavern.

The president, too, is certainly to blame for terrorizing women with the fear of hunger. He is no less to blame for the complacent ignorance that he displays when asked to comment on these matters. "If even one American child is forced to go to bed hungry at night . . . ," he says, "that is a national tragedy. We are too generous a people to allow this. . . ."

We are not too generous. The president is wrong. We have been willing to see hundreds of thousands of children go to bed, if they have any beds at all, too hungry to sleep and sometimes too weak to rise on the next morning to await the bus for school.

"Now you're hearing all kinds of horror stories," the president said on an earlier occasion, this time in Minnesota "about the people that are going to be thrown out in the snow to hunger and [to] die of cold and so forth. . . . We haven't cut a single budget. . . ."

Hunger, cold and snow apart, what of this presidential reference to the budget? Dorothy Wickenden, in a *New Republic* article published in 1985, summarizes administration cuts affecting children of poor families in the previous four years: housing assistance ($1.8 billion); AFDC ($4.8 billion); child nutrition ($5.2 billion); food stamps ($6.8 billion); low-income energy assistance ($700 million). In housing, she writes, the Reagan administration "appears to have decided to renounce once and for all any meaningful federal support." HUD's budget authority to help additional low-income families "was cut from $30 billion to $11 billion" in the first Reagan term. "In his fiscal 1986 budget, he proposes to chop that by an additional 95 percent, to $499 million."

The president's first budget director, David Stockman, was noted for his straightforward speech: "I don't think people are entitled to services. I don't believe that there is any entitlement, any basic right to legal services or any other kind of services. . . . I don't accept that equality is a moral principle."

Will future generations read these words with pride?

"When men confront each other as men, as abstract universals," writes Ignatieff, "one with power, the other with none, then man is certain to behave as a wolf to his own kind." The claim of the less powerful—that because they are human they deserve to live—"is the weakest claim that people can make to each other: It is the claim addressed to anyone, and therefore to no one. When there is no family, no tribe, no state, no city to hear, . . . only the storm hears it."

For thousands of homeless people in New York, as in most cities of America during this era of acceptable abstraction, it is probably not true that only the storm can hear their pleas, but it is frequently the case that only the storm answers.

Stockman's theme—no rights, no services—finds application on the grand scale in withholding of essential funds for life support by government; but the idea, once established, finds expression in a multitude of small indignities that homeless people undergo day after day in places where one person exercises power over hundreds who have none.

The guards assigned to offer shelter residents some safety, for example, are frequently only a trifle better off than they; but, as in a prison where a favored inmate often brutalizes those from whom he can dissociate himself only by an overzealous application of the regulations set by his superiors, these are often the most vicious faces of authority that homeless people must confront.

November 27, 1986: On holidays like Thanksgiving, people in a homeless shelter face unusual depression. Those who are most fortunate may be invited elsewhere—some to have dinner with their family, if they have a family with the means to share a meal. Others may eat in one of those huge armories in which a charitable group, under the eyes of TV cameras, offers them a dinner with something the press invariably describes in a November formula as "all the fixings."

Many, however, never get the "fixings"—neither from their families nor from charitable groups. They spend the day alone within their rooms. Sometimes a mother or grandmother who could not provide a meal at home brings something she has cooked and packaged carefully. Sometimes a friend appears.

Waiting here with about a dozen other people, most of them family members, I watch the guards hunched over at their guard post with their squawking intercoms hooked to their belts. I wonder why they seem so much more threatening today than usual. Generally their distaste for the job, or for the residents, is conveyed with lassitude; today it's energized. Is it because there are so few officials, volunteers or crisis workers to observe them? Do they, who have to work on holidays, regret the fact that others might enjoy an hour's respite from the colorless routine?

A woman sitting next to me has come from Brooklyn with a dinner wrapped in foil for her daughter and grandchildren. She arrived at 2:00 P.M. At three, she is still waiting.

"We're short of men," a guard remarks to no one in particular. "Holidays, we send up messages once every hour."

As the minute tick away and people wait for recognition from the guards, she presses the corners of the foil together in a futile effort to preserve the warmth.

A well-dressed woman—middle-aged, soft-spoken—enters the lobby from the street and asks one of the guards to tell her sister that she's here.

"Fifteen-seven gets no visitors," the guard replies.

The woman begins a complicated explanation. She's here to take her sister to their mother's bed. Their mother is in the hospital. Her sister doesn't know. Their mother was taken ill last night.

"Fifteen-seven's on restriction," says the guard. Fixed in his meager station of authority, he seems reluctant to give up an opportunity to heighten panic, to create a needless little patch of pain.

She tells the guard she doesn't need to visit, only to send up a message. But the guard appears unmoved. "You cause us trouble," he says, "you got no rights."

"Would you tell her that her mother's ill?"

The guard replies: "She don't get no messages. Not until she gets her check."

I'm not sure those are the rules; but how is she to know and, even if she does, what can be done? She is about to speak again but he anticipates her words: "Don't block the desk. The waiting area is over there."

She looks confused. Does this mean he's relented? Will he send up the message? Why does he direct her to the waiting area? She's a black woman wearing an old-fashioned net around her hair. The guards are here presumably to keep out prostitutes and people who sell drugs. She doesn't look like either.

Another woman, white and elderly, comes in, make her request, and is instructed to sit down. A Puerto Rican man gets up and offers her his chair. It has a jagged plastic edge; the back has been torn off. There are, in all, six chairs, one broken stool.

Across the lobby on the wall beside the elevator alcove is a poster about crack. Next to it, a crudely penciled sign I saw a year ago: "ABSOLUTELY NO GRAFFITI WILL BE TOLERATED." A young woman, heavily made up, walks past the desk on red stiletto heels. When she doesn't answer an obscene joke from a guard who seems to know her, he runs after her, pulls out his nightstick, and jams it between her legs. She pushes him away and heads off to the stairway in the rear.

All around me: tired, tired faces. The silence drips like water from the rainspout on the back porch of a house that someone left ten years before. Time stops. A damp and dreary afternoon.

"You cause us trouble, you got no rights." But even if you cause no trouble, you do not have many rights. The right to talk to a reporter is effectively denied. The publication of essential legal information, even in a casual newsletter, is prevented. I write in my notebook: "If we want to be sadistic, if we want to do it right, why not also take away their citizenship—withhold their right to vote?" Then I recall that this too was attempted but did not succeed. Court action finally restored the franchise for the homeless families of New York. But the idea remains attractive and is still proposed by policy advisors as another means of rendering dependent status undesirable.

"For adults, the stigma would be institutionalized," in Charles Murray's words, "by taking away the right to vote from anyone who had no source of income except welfare. . . ." Denial of the franchise, Murray has proposed, "would be an official stamp" of second-class status. While recognizing that "the balance" of this and other suggestions he has made to stigmatize poor single mothers "would probably be negative," Murray argues nonetheless that denial of the right to vote make sense in that recipients of public funds should have no role in their disbursement. Notions like these, no matter how whimsically or speculatively offered, don't remain inert. Uncivilized contemplation is contagious.

"Fifteen-seven's got no rights."

The guard transmits the values of a decade that has brutalized him too. He doesn't even say the woman's name. For him, as for New York, she's been reduced to something that can be abstracted and computerized—a disobedient but expensive number.

I have not been in the Martinique for several months. The circumstances that brought me here today are rather special. Mrs. Allesandro knows I live alone and am unmarried and do not have children. She invited me to join her family for Thanksgiving dinner. I have been anticipating this for several days. As I learn later, she has done to a great deal of trouble. It isn't easy to prepare a good Thanksgiving dinner on a hot plate. But a woman who's survived for over seventy years has had a lot of time to figure out some ways to make the best of hopeless situations. The guards have simply managed to destroy her happiness a little.

By the time they send the message up it's after four. The food is cold. The kids are hungry. While she warms the dinner, I go with her son to tell the woman in room 1507 that her mother's in the hospital and that her sister's waiting for her in the lobby.

3

Untouchables

On some nights, after a visit to the Martinique, I have returned to a hotel and steamed myself in a hot shower. Part of the reason is sheer physical exhaustion after walking up long flights of stairs, sitting cross-legged for several hours on a floor within a room in which there are no chairs, remaining sometimes until 3:00 or 4:00 A.M. in order to untangle complicated stories and to be quite sure I have the details right.

But another reason, which I feel some hesitation to confess, is the recognition of so much pathology, so much infection and contagious illness in the homeless population. The little girl that I call Raisin likes to put her fingers on my mouth to win herself a chance to talk. When she's in a thoughtful mood, she puts her fingers in her own mouth and she rests her head against my chest. When I get up to leave she holds her arms around my legs. It is impossible to wish to keep her at a distance. I feel ashamed when, later the same night, I scrub myself with a determination I associate with doctors in a Third-World clinic.

So, in an undeniable and awful sense, even the children do become untouchables. Michael Ignatieff reflects on the reponsibilities that bind us to the outcasts of a social order: "What are our obligations to those stranger at our gates? Take one step outside our zone of safety. . . . There they are, hands outstretched. . . ." He is too generous to note that even our most natural inclinations may be thwarted by a practical consideration like the fear of illness.

The nightmare of the powerless, he writes, "is that one day they will make their claim and the powerful will demand a reason, one day the look of entreaty will be met with the un-knowing stare of force." That nightmare exists already in our nation. We do demand a reason for the claims made by the homeless families of our cities, and the reasons that they give do not always convince us. Ignatieff cites King Lear upon the heath: "O, reason not the need! . . . Allow not nature more than nature needs, man's life is cheap as beasts." We will return to this because it runs precisely counter to a currently held view that "basic needs"—food, roof or burial ditch—are all the poor have any right to ask and all they may expect. It may be enough for now to note that in the cases we have just observed, even nature's minimal needs have not been met.

I think of a mother in the Allerton Hotel, twelve blocks from the Martinique, who is forced to choose, when she goes shopping, between food or diapers for her children. Documentation gathered by David Beseda of the Coalition for the Homeless identifies the subtitution of newspapers for diapers by the mothers of small children who must spend all of their allocated funds for concentrated formula and food for other children. Ignatieff's nightmare is made real each day within Manhattan's zone of danger. Once we escape that zone, the wish to wash ourselves—to scrub away the filth—may be more than a health precaution.

Richard Lazarus, an educated, thirty-six-year-old Vietnam veteran I met two days after Thanksgiving in Grand Central Station, tells me he had never been without a job until the recent summer. In July he underwent the loss of job, children and wife, all in a single stroke. As in almost all these situations, it was the simultaneous occurrence of a number of emergencies, any one of which he might sustain alone but not all at the same time, that suddenly removed him from his home.

"Always, up until last summer, I have found a job that paid at least $300. Now I couldn't find a job that paid $200. When I found an opening at a department store they said that I was overqualified. If someone had asked me a year ago who are the homeless, I would not have known what to reply. Now I know the answer. They are people lilke myself. I went to Catholic elementary school. I had my secondary education in a private military school. I joined the service and was sent to Thailand as an airman." He has a trade. It's known as "inventory data processing." He had held a single job in data processing for seven years until last summer when the company shut down, without a warning, and moved out of state.

"When the company left I could find nothing. I looked everywhere. I got one job for two months in the summer. Part-time, as a security guard in one of the hotels for homeless families."

When I ask which one it was, he says the Martinique. "I clocked the floors for fire check. From the top floor to the lobby I swore to myself: rat infested, roach infested, drug infested, filth infested, garbage everywhere, and little children playing in the stairs. Innocent people, women, children, boxed in by their misery. Most people are permitted to make more than one mistake. Not when you're poor."

In September he was sick. "I was guarding homeless people and I didn't have a home. I slept in Washington Square and Central Park." He's living now in a run-down hotel operated in conjunction with the Third Street Shelter on the Bowery. "When you come in at night the guards wear gloves. They check you with a metal detector. They're afraid to touch me."

While we talk we watch an old man nearby who is standing flat and motionless against the wall, surrounded by two dozen bright-red shopping bags from Macy's. Every so often, someone stops to put a coin into his hand. I notice the care with which the people drop their coins, in order that their hands do not touch his. When I pass that spot some hours later he will still be there. I'll do the same. I'll look at his hand—the fingers worn and swollen and the nails curled in like claws—and I will drop a quarter and extract my hand and move off quickly.

After standing with Lazarus for two hours before a hot-dog stand, I ask him if he'd like to leave the station to sit down with me and get a decent meal. He's awkward about accepting this. When I press him, he explains he had only one subway token and has no more money. If he leaves the station he will need a dollar to get back inside. He agrees to leave when I assure him I can spare a dollar. Outside on Forty-second Street, we're facing the Grand Hyatt. He looks at it with fear.

"The first thing that you see when you come out of there is power."

At a delicatessen next to the Grand Hyatt he explains about the subway tokens. Each morning at the shelter you get in a line in order to receive two subway tokens. This is to enable you to look for jobs; the job search is required. But in order to get the tokens, you have got to prove that you already have a job appointment. "It's a long line. By the time you get the tokens you have missed the job appointment. You wait in line for everything. I get the feeling that the point is not to find a job but to teach us something about who we are. Getting us in line is the idea."

In the resataurant he orders a chicken sandwich and, although he's nervous and his hands are shaking, he eats fast; he's almost done before I've put a paper napkin in my lap. He apologizes but he tells me that this is the first thing he has had to eat since 8:00 A.M. It's now about 8:30 in the evening.

"Before I got into this place I was sleeping in the parks. When it got colder I would sleep all night in an X-rated movie or the subway or the Port Authority. I'd spend most of my time just walking. I would try to bathe each day in public toilets. I'd wash my clothes and lay them outside in the sun to dry. I didn't want to feel like a pariah that nobody would get near. I used to talk with people like yourself so that I would not begin to feel cut off. I invested all my strength in fighting off depression. I was scared that I would fall apart.

"During this time I tried to reunite with my old lady. For me, the loss of work and loss of wife had left me rocking. Then the welfare regulations hit me. I began to feel that I would be reduced to trash. You're never prepared for this. It's like there isn't any bottom. It's not like cracks in a safety net. It's like a black hole sucking you inside. Half the people that I know are suffering from chest infections and sleep deprivation. The lack of sleep leaves you debilitated, shaky. You exaggerate your fears. If a psychiatrist came along he'd say that I was crazy. But I was an ordinary man. There was nothing wrong with me. I lost my wife. I lost my kids. I lost my home. Now would you say that I was crazy if I told you I was feeling sad?

"I was a pretty stable man. Now I tremble when I meet somebody in the ordinary world. I'm trembling right now. One reason that I didn't want to leave the subway was that I feel safer underground. When you asked if I would come outside and get something to eat, my first thought was that you would see me shaking if we sat down for a meal and you'd think I was an alcoholic.

"I've had a bad cold for two weeks. When you're sick there's no way to get better. You cannot sleep in at the shelter. You have *got* to go outside and show that you are looking for a job. I had asthma as a kid. It was gone for twenty years. Now it's back. I'm always swallowing for air. Before I got into the shelter, I did not have Medicaid or welfare. If you don't have an address it's very hard. I scrambled to get into the computer.

"Asthma's common at the shelter. There's a lot of dust. That may be why. Edema [swollen feet]—you get it from sitting up so much and walking all day long. If you're very hungry and you want a meal you can get it at St. Francis. You can get a sandwich at Grand Central every night at ten o'clock. So if you want to keep from starving you are always on the move. If you have no subway tokens then you jump the stile. So you're always breaking rules and so you start to have this sense of premonition: 'Sooner or later I'll be caught.' You live in constant fear.

"The welfare workers are imperious and punctual. No matter how desperate you are, they're short of time. I ask them: 'Will my records go upstairs?' They snap at me: 'Can't you see that we're about to close?' All I asked them was a simple question.

"A year ago I never thought that somebody like me would end up in a shelter. Nothing you've ever undergone prepares you. You walk into the place—the smell of sweat and urine hits you like a wall. Unwashed bodies and the look of absolute despair on many, many faces there would make you think you were in Dante's hell. Abandon hope. I read a lot. I'm not a lazy man.

"I slept with my clothes on the first night that I was there. I was given a cot but they were out of sheets. I lay awake. I heard men crying in their sleep. They're sound asleep and they are *crying.* What you fear is that you will be here forever. You do not know if it's ever going to end. You think to yourself: It is a dream and I will wake. Sometimes I think: It's an experiment. They are watching you to find out how much you can take. Someone will come someday and say: 'Okay, this guy has suffered long enough. Now we'll take him back into our world.' then you wake up and get in line . . .

"Listen to me: I've always worked. I need to work! I'm not a lazy man." His voice rises and the people at the other tables stare. "If I thought that I could never work again I'd want to die."

He explains to me that you can work inside the shelter for a token salary. For twenty hours' work they pay $12.50. He has done this. "Even sixty cents an hour makes you feel that you are not completely dead. It may be slave labor but it gets you certain privileges, like being first in line for meals. I'm one of the residents they like because I follow all the rules. Those rules are very important. If you make a single error you are out. More than that, you lose your benefits. You put your welfare card in the machine. 'NO BENEFITS. YOUR CASE IS CLOSED.' You're dead. It's thirty days before your case can be reopened.

"When I'm very scared I go into the public library to read. You have to stay awake. They throw you out the minute that you close your eyes. When I was at rockbottom I went to a priest. It was the first time I had asked to be confessed in twenty years. Alone in that big beautiful church, it occurred to me that the Creator had been teaching me a message that I'd never learned. 'I've given you a couple of gifts. Now share them with your brothers.' I would ask if there could be a God. Then I'd say: 'We have free will. God did not do this to me.' That's all. That's my theology.

"My only relatives alive in New York City are my father and my children and my wife. My father's in the Hebrew Home for the Aged. He's eighty-three. He's had several strokes. So I can't tell him what has happened. When I go there I put on the cleanest clothes I have. He asks about the children and I tell him everything is fine.

"The worst thing I have ever undergone was when I lost

my wife. She was my guidance system. If I can ever get a job I'll save up money for a while. I'll stay in the shelter so that I can save enough to put down money for a home."

I ask him if he can save money.

"Not officially. You do it off the books."

He tells me his wife is doubled up for now in somebody's apartment with his children. At ten o'clock he says he has to get back to the shelter. "Curfew's at eleven. If you miss it, then you sleep outside." I ask for his address. He writes it out: Kenton Hotel, 8 East Third Street. Bed number 135.

"I'm a number. When I was evicted I was given a court docket number. When I got on welfare I received another number. Now I'm in the shelter I have a bed number. If my wife and I can get our kids in a hotel someday, we'll have another number, a room number. I have to keep repeating to myself: I have a name. I was born. I have a mother and a father. I am not a number.

"When you go to welfare the first thing you have to do is show them that you have a birth certificate. Many people lost their birth certificate when they were dispossessed. Or you lose it in the streets or in the shelter if somebody steals your clothes. But you have to prove that you were born in order to receive a check. Why do they do this? How much can you stand?"

We say good-bye outside the subway ramp on Forty-second Street. I give him the dollar—he refuses to take more—and we shake hands. I write to him later but I've never gotten a response. It's possible that, in my haste, I got the wrong bed number. Back in the zone of safety in my clean hotel I wash my hands.

Many homeless people, unable to get into shelters, frightened of disease or violence, or else intimidated by the regulations, look for refuge in such public places as train stations and church doorways.

Scores of people sleep in the active subway tunnels of Manhattan, inches from 600-volt live rails. Many more sleep on the ramps and station platforms. Go into the subway station under Herald Square on a December night at twelve o'clock and you will see what scarce accommodations mean at the rockbottom.

Emerging from the subway, walk on Thirty-second Street to Penn Station. There you will see another form of scarce accommodations: Hot-air grates in the area are highly prized. Homeless people who arrive late often find there is no vacancy, even in a cardboard box over a grate.

A man who's taken shelter from the wind that sweeps Fifth Avenue by sleeping beneath the outstretched arms of Jesus on the bronze doors of St. Patrick's Cathedral tells a reporter he can't sleep there anymore because shopkeepers feel that he is hurting business. He moves to the south side of the church where he will be less visible.

Stories like these are heard in every state and city of the nation. A twenty-year-old man in Florida tells me that he ran away when he was nine years old from a juvenile detention home in Michigan. He found that he was small enough to slip his body through the deposit slot of a Good Will box. Getting in was easy, he explains, and it was warm because of the clothes and quilts and other gifts that people dropped into the box. "Getting out," he says, "was not so easy. I had to reach my arms above my head, grab hold of the metal edge, twist my body into an *S*, and pull myself out slowly through the slot. When I was fourteen I was too big to fit into the slot. I believe I am the only person in America who has lived for five years in a Good Will box."

Thousands of American people live in dumpsters behind restaurants, hotels, and groceries. A woman describes the unimaginable experience of being awakened in the middle of a winter's night by several late-arriving garbage trucks. She nearly drowned beneath two tons of rotting vegetables and fruit.

A thirty-four-year-old man in Chicago found his sanctuary in a broken trash compactor. This offered perhaps the ultimate concealment, and the rotting food which generated heat may have protected him against the freezing weather of Chicago. One night, not knowing that the trash compactor had in his absence been repaired, he fell asleep. When the engine was turned on, he was compressed into a cube of refuse.

People in many cities speak of spending nights in phone booths. I have seen this only in New York. Public telephones in Grand Central Station are aligned in recessed areas outside the main concourse. On almost any night before one-thirty, visitors will see a score of people stuffed into these booths with their belongings. Even phone-booth vacancies are scarce in New York City. As in public housing, people are sometimess obliged to double up. One night I stood for an hour and observed three people—man, woman, and child—jammed into a single booth. All three were asleep.

Officials have tried a number of times to drive the homeless from Grand Central Station. In order to make conditions less attractive, benches have been removed throughout the terminal. One set of bench has been left there, I am told, because they have been judged "historic landmarks." The terminal's 300 lockers, used in former times by homeless people to secure their few belongings, were removed in 1986. Authorities were forced to justify this action by declaring them, in the words of the city council, "a threat to public safety." Shaving, cleaning of clothes, and other forms of hygiene are prohibited in the men's room of Grand Central. A fast-food chain that wanted to distribute un-sold donuts in the terminal was denied the right to do so on the grounds that this would draw more hungry people.

At one-thirty every morning, homeless people are ejected from Grand Central. Many have attempted to take refuge on the ramp that leads to Forty-second Street. The ramp initially pro-vided a degree of warmth beause it was protected from the street by wooden doors. The station management responded to this challenge in two ways. First, the ramp was mopped with a strong mixture of ammonia to produce a noxious smell. When the people sleeping there brought cardboard boxes and news-papers to protect them from the fumes, the entrance doors were chained wide open. Temperatures dropped some nights to ten degrees.

In a case that won brief press attention in December 1985, an elderly woman who had been living in Grand Central on one of the few remaining benches was removed night after night during the weeks preceding Christmas. On Christmas Eve she became ill. No ambulance was called. At one-thirty the police compelled her to move to the ramp outside. At dawn she came inside, climbed back on bench number 9 to sleep, and died that morning of pneumonia.

At Penn Station, fifteen blocks away, homeless women are denied use of the bathroom. Amtrak police come by and herd them off each hour on the hour. In June of 1985, Amtrak officials issued this directive to police: "It is the policy of Amtrak to not allow the homeless and undesirables to remain. . . . Officers are encouraged to eject all undesirables. . . . Now is the time to train and educate them that their presence will not be tolerated as cold weather sets in." In an internal memo, according to CBS, an Amtrak official later went beyond this language and asked flatly: "Can't we get rid of this trash?"

In a surprising action, the union representing the police resisted this directive and brought suit against Penn Station's managment in 1986. Nonetheless, as temperatures plunged during the nights after Thanksgiving, homeless men and women were ejected from the station. At 2:00 A.M. I watched a man about my age carry his cardboard box outside the station and try to construct a barricade against the wind that tore across Eighth Avenue. The man was so cold his fingers shook and, when I spoke to him, he tried but could not answer.

Driving women from the toilets in a railroad station raises questions that go far beyond the issue of "deterrence." It may surprise the reader to be told that many of these women are quite young. Few are dressed in the familiar rags that are suggested by the term "bag ladies." Some are dressed so neatly and conceal their packages and bags so skillfully that one finds it hard to differentiate them from commuters waiting for a train. Given the denial of hygienic opportunities, it is difficult to know how they are able to remain presentable. The sight of clusters of police officials, mostly male, guarding a women's toilet from its use by homeless females does not speak well for the public conscience of New York.

Where do these women defecate? How do they bathe? What will we do when, in her physical distress, a woman finally disrobes in public and begins to urinate right on the floor? We may regard her as an animal. She may by then begin to view herself in the same way.

Several cities have devised unusual measures to assure that homeless people will learn quickly that they are not welcome. In Laramie Wyoming, they are given one night's shelter. On the next morning, an organization called "The Good Samaritan Fund" gives them one-way tickets to another town. The college town of Lancaster, Ohio, offers homeless families one-way tickets to Columbus.

In a number of states and cities, homeless people have been murdered, knifed, or set on fire. Two high-school students in California have been tried for the knife murder of a homeless man whom they found sleeping in a park. The man, an unemployed house painter was stabbed seventeen times before his throat was slashed.

In Chicago a man was set ablaze while sleeping on a bench in early morning, opposite a popular restaurant. Rush-hour commuters passed him and his charred possessions for four hours before someone called police at noon. A man who watched him burning from a third-floor room above the bench refused to notify police. The purpose was "to get him out," according to a local record-store employee. A resident told reporters that the problem of the homeless was akin to that of "nuclear waste."

In Tucson, where police use German shepherds to hunt for the homeless in the skid-row neighborhoods, a mayor was recently elected on the promise that he'd drive the homeless out of town. "We're tired of it. Tired of feeling guilty about these people," said an anti-homeless activist in Phoenix.

In several cities it is a crime to sleep in public; in some, armrests have been inserted in the middle of park benches to make it impossible for homeless people to lie down. In others, trash has been defined as "public property," making it a felony to forage in the rotted food.

Grocers in Santa Barbara sprinkled bleach on food discarded in their dumpsters. In Portland, Oregon, owners of some shops in redeveloped Old Town have designed slow-dripping gutters (they are known as "drip lines") to prevent the homeless from attempting to take shelter underneath their awnings.

Harsher tactics have been recommended in Fort Lauderdale. A city council member offered a proposal to spray trash containers with rat poison to discourage foraging by homeless families. The way to "get rid of vermin," he observed, is to cut their food supply. Some of these policies have been defeated but the inclination to sequester, punish and conceal the homeless has attracted wide support.

"We are the rejected waste of the society," said Lazarus. "They use us, if they think we have some use, maybe for sweeping leaves or scrubbing off graffiti in the subway stations. They don't object if we donate our blood. I've given plasma. That's one way that even worthless people can do something for democracy. We may serve another function too. Perhaps we help to scare the people who still have a home—even a place that's got no heat, that's rat infested, filthy. If they see us in the streets, maybe they are scared enough so they will learn not to complain. If they were thinking about asking for a better heater or a better stove, they're going to think twice. It's like farmers posting scarecrows in the fields. People see these terrifying figures in Penn Station and they know, with one false step, that they could be here too. They think: 'I better not complain.'

"The problem comes, however, when they try to find a place to hide us. So it comes to be an engineering question: waste disposal. Store owners certainly regard us in that way. We ruin business and lower the value of good buildings. People fear that we are carriers of illness. Many times we are. So they wear those plastic gloves if they are forced to touch us. It reminds me of the workers in the nuclear reactors. They have to wear protective clothing if they come in contact with the waste. Then you have state governors all over the United States refusing to allow this stuff to be deposited within their borders. Now you hear them talking about dumping toxic waste into the ocean in steel cans. Could they find an island someplace for the homeless?"

His question brings back a strange memory for me. In Boston, for years before the homeless were identified as a distinguishable category of the dispossessed, a de facto caste of homeless people dwelt in a vast public-housing project built on a virtual island made, in part, of landfill and linked only by one access road to the United States. Columbia Point, adjacent to a camp for prisoners of war in World War II, was so crowded, violent and ugly that social workers were reluctant to pay visits there, few shop owners would operate a business, and even activists and organizers were afraid to venture there at night. From the highway to Cape Cod, one could see the distant profile of those high-rise structures. A friend from California asked me if it was a prison. He told me that it looked like Alcatraz. I answered that it was a housing project. The notion of shoving these people as far out into the ocean as we can does bring to mind the way that waste-disposal problems sometimes are resolved.

New York has many habitable islands. One of those islands has already earned a place in history as the initial stopping point for millions of European refugees who came to the United States in search of freedom. One reason for their temporary isolation was the fear that they might carry dangerous infection. New York's permanent refugees are carriers of every possible infection; most, moreover, have no prospering relatives to vouch for them, as earlier generations sometimes did in order to assure that they will not become a burden to the state. They are already regarded as a burden. An island that served once as quarantine for aliens who crowded to our shore might serve this time as quarantine for those who huddle in train stations and in Herald Square.

Lazarus may not be paranoid in speaking of himself as human waste; he may simply read the headlines in the press. "I just can't accommodate them," says the owner of a building in midtown Manhattan. The mayor of Newark, where a number of homeless families have been sent from New York City, speaks of his fear that displaced families from New York might be "permanently dumped in Newark." He announces a deadline after which they will presumably be dumped back in New York.

New Yorkers, according to the *New York Times*, "are increasingly opposing [city] attempts to open jails, shelters for the homeless, garbage incinerators" in their neighborhoods. The *Times* reports the city has begun to "compensate communities" that will accept "homeless shelters and garbage-burning generating plants.

Do homeless children have some sense of this equation?

"Be not forgetful to entertain strangers," wrote Saint Paul, "for thereby some have entertained angels unawares." But the demonology that now accrues to homeless people, and the filth with which their bodies soon become encrusted, seem to reassure us that few of these strangers will turn out to have been angels in disguise.

When homeless infants die in New York City, some are buried not in New York itself but on an island in an unmarked grave. Homeless mothers therefore live with realistic fears that they may lose their infants to anonymous interment. Another fear is that their child may be taken from them at the hour of birth if they should be homeless at the time. Hundreds of babies taken by the state for this and other reasons—often they are very ill and sometimes drug addicted—remain in hospitals, sometimes for months or even years, before a foster home is found. Some of these "boarder babies," as they are described, have been kept so long that they have learned to walk and, for this reason, must be tethered in their cribs. Infants held in hospitals so long, physicians tell us, are likely to grow retarded. Some, even after many months, have not been given names. Like their homeless parents in the city's shelters, they remain bed numbers.

Many of these children do in time find homes, though most end up in dismal institutions where conditions are no better and often a great deal worse than those they would have faced had they been left with their own parents. Mayor Koch attempted in 1986 to establish a group home for six or seven of these babies in a small house on a quiet street in Queens. Unknown vandals set the house on fire. "Afraid of Babies in Queens," the *New York Times* headlined its editorial response.

It seems we *are* afraid of homeless children, not only in Queens but everywhere in the United States. It is hard to know exactly what it is we fear (the children themselves, the sickness they may carry, the adolescents they will soon become if they survive, or the goad to our own conscience that they represent when they are visible, nearby); but the fear is very real. Our treatment of these children reaffirms the distancing that now has taken place. They are not of us. They are "the Other."

What startles most observers is not simply that such tragedies persist in the United States, but that almost all have been well documented and that even the most solid documentation does not bring about corrective action. Instead of action, a common response in New York, as elsewhere, is the forming of a "task force" to investigate. This is frequently the last we hear of it. Another substitute for action is a press event at which a city official seems to overleap immediate concerns by the unveiling of a plan to build a thousand, or a hundred thousand, homes over the course of ten or twenty years at an expense of several billion dollars. The sweep of these announcements tends to dwarf the urgency of the initial issue. When, after a year or so, we learn that little has been done and that the problem has grown worse, we tend to feel not outrage but exhaustion. Exhaustion, however, as we have seen, turns easily to a less generous reaction.

"I am about to be heartless," wrote a columnist in *Newsweek* in December 1986. "There are people living on the streets ... turning sidewalks into dormitories. They are called the homeless. ... Often they are called worse. They are America's living nightmare. ... They have got to go."

The author notes that it is his taxes which pay for the paving and the cleaning of the streets they call their home. "That makes me their landlord. I want to evict them."

A senior at Boston University sees homeless people on the streets not far from where he goes to class. He complains that measures taken recently to drive them from the area have not been sufficiently aggressive: "I would very much like to see actions more severe. . . ." Perhaps, he admits, it isn't possible to have them all arrested, though this notion seems to hold appeal for him; perhaps "a more suitable middle ground" may be arrived at to prevent this "nauseating . . . element" from being permitted to "run free so close to my home."

"Our response," says one Bostonian, "has gone from indifference to pitying . . . to hatred." I think this is coming to be true and that it marks an incremental stage in our capacity to view the frail, the ill, the dispossessed, the unsuccessful not as people who have certain human qualities we share but as an outcaste entity. From harsh deterrence to punitive incarceration to the willful cutting off of life supports is an increasingly short journey. "I am proposing triage of a sort, triage by self-selection," writes Charles Murray. "The patient always has the right to fail. Society always has the right to let him."

Why is it that writings which present these hardened attitudes seem to prevail so easily in public policy? It may be that kindly voices are more easily derided. Callous attitudes are never subject to the charge of being sentimental. It is a recurrent theme in *King Lear*, writes Ignatieff, that "there is a truth in the brutal simplicities of the merciless which the more complicated truth of the merciful is helpless to refute." A rich man, he observes, "never lacks for arguments to deny the poor his charity. 'Basest beggars' can always be found to be 'in the poorest things superfluous.' "

"They are a nightmare. I evict them. They will have to go."

So from pity we graduate to weariness; from weariness to impatience; from impatience to annoyance; from annoyance to dislike and sometimes to contempt.

"No excuses are good enough," the *New York Times* observed in reference to the Holland Hotel in 1985, a year before I spoke wth Mrs. Andrews of her stay in that hotel. But, in the event, excuses did suffice. The city did, and does, continue to send children to the Holland and to many similar hotels. Nearly 200 families, with 450 children, are still living in the Holland as I write.

Can it be these children have by now become not simply noxious or unclean in our imagination but something like an ulcer to society, a cancer, a malignant growth?

"If the point is to dispose of us most economically," said Lazarus, "why do they need to go to all this trouble and expense? Why not end this misery efficiently? Why not a lethal injection?"

This question, voiced in panic and despair, is one perhaps that he would not have posed if he were in a less tormented state of mind. There is an answer. I believe it should be stated here because the rhetoric of desperation may be taken, otherwise, for a realistic vision of America as it exists today. The answer is that we have failed in many ways to do what conscience and American ideals demand but have yet to fall so far as to wish anyone's demise. Despite the grave injustices that we allow, or lack the power to confront, we do not in fact want to "dispose" of *any* people—or "compact" them into concentration camps or any other institutions of internment. The truth is: We do not know what we want to do with these poor people.

We leave them, therefore, in a limbo and, while waiting in that limbo, many who are very young do cease to be a burden to society.

But the question of this shaken man emerging from the underground of New York's subway system to gaze up at the Grand Hyatt may suggest a slightly different question: Might a day come in the not-too-distant future when a notion of this sort may be advanced and not regarded as abhorrent? It has happened in other advanced societies. We know this, and we also know that no society is totally exempt from entertaining "rational" solutions of this kind.

State terrorism as social welfare policy—which is, I think, a fair description of what Lazarus, a credible witness of life at the bottom in Manhattan, has perceived—has not yet achieved acceptance in our social order; but it may no longer be regarded as beyond imagination. When we speak the unspeakable, think the unthinkable, and permit the impermissible, we are not far from a final darkness.

4

One Childhood: No Second Chance

Someday there will be no Martinique Hotel on Thirty-second Street in New York City. Someday there will be no "pigpen" for the children of our nation's capital. Someday there may be no children living in the streets and subways of America. Someday, but not yet. Not for children who are living now and will have no chance to live their childhood again.

For now, these sad realities exist. The purpose of this book is to attest to their existence, to give witness to the toll they take upon the children of the dispossessed, and to pay tribute to the dignity, the courage, and the strength with which so many parents manage to hold up beneath the truly terrifying problems they confront.

I have been cautioned by some of the shelter organizers in New York not to romaticize these people. Have I observed this warning? Not enough perhaps. It is very hard to strike a balance.

I end up with a crazy quilt of details that have stirred me. Annie Harrington pictures the "parquet floor" within the house she does not own and never did and probably never will. She pictures where that house would be: "The neighborhood was nice. The neighbors liked me. And the landlord liked me. . . . We bought a grill to barbecue outside on summer nights."

Doby's answer to the TV camera: "I would make cheeseburgers!" His answer made his mother laugh. They were still there, all of them, a full year later.

Holly's idea of heaven: "Peaceful . . . glorious . . . paradise . . . No welfare, EAU . . . No nothin' . . . He's in peace." Benjamin is free from suffering now. I don't know where Holly went or whether she and David stayed together.

Mr. Allesandro's midnight watch over his strange and watchful son. His reliance on his mother: What if she died? Seeing his need for her, I feared it too.

Gwen: to whom the priest had said that she was suffering beause she loved her mother more than God. For that love, he said, she had to pay a price. It was a rather high price. She is, I think, still living in a shelter.

Most vividly, most frequently, I think of Rachel in her robe and gown. "If there was a place where you could sell part of your body . . . I would do it." And I asked her, when she spoke of women who would sell their bodies: "Would you do it?" And she told me: "Ain't no 'would I?' I would do it. . . . Yes. I *did*."

Women like Rachel haven't had much chance to make their voices heard in the United States in recent years.

"Mister, it ain't easy to be beggin'. . . . Can you get the government to know that we exist?" And when her welfare worker asked, "You had another baby?"—"Yeah!" she said. "I had another baby. What about it? Are you goin' to kill that baby?"

As of now, we do not have an answer to that question.

If you would like to help, these organizations will be grateful for your support:

Burnside Community Council (direct services to homeless and advocacy in the Northwest): 313 East Burnside Street, Portland, Oregon 97214. (Donations tax-exempt.)

Camillus House (direct services to homeless): P.O. Box 1829, 728 N.E. First Avenue, Miami, Florida 33101. (Donations tax-exempt.)

Central Arizona Shelter Services (advocacy and direct services): 1209 West Madison Street, Phoenix, Arizona 85007. (Donations tax-exempt.)

Community for Creative Non-violence (advocacy and direct services to homeless in Washington): 1347 Euclid Street, N.W., Washington, D.C. 20009.

Education Action Fund, Inc. (direct assistance to families in the Martinique Hotel, and to other families in urgent need known to the author of this book): P.O. Box 145, Byfield, Massachusetts 01922. (Donations tax-exempt.)

National Coalition for the Homeless (advocacy and direct services, national and New York City): 105 East 22nd Street, New York, NY 10010. (Donations tax-exempt.)

National Union of the Homeless (organizing homeless people, job training, advocacy): 2001 Spring Garden, Philadelphia, Pennsylvania 19130. (Donations tax-exempt.)

Appendices,
Notes,
Bibliography

Appendix A
Economies of Scale

When they die, where are the children of the homeless laid to rest?

A remarkable study, written by Judith Berck for the Coalition for the Homeless, provides some information. At the time of Benjamin's death, an average funeral in New York City cost $2,500. Burial costs averaged $1,000 more. The sole public assistance available for both expenses was $250. This sum, however, known as a "death benefit," was granted only if the bereaved family could find a funeral home willing to attend to the deceased for $600 or less. The death benefit, moreover, could not be given to the parents at the time of burial. The city first had to investigate their assets to determine whether they were eligible. Families were required to fill out extensive forms in order to receive the benefit. They would then be forced to wait three to six months before the payment could be processed.

The least expensive burial plots in New York City start at $200 for an unmarked and nontitled grave. A family therefore was required to come up with $600 for a minimum-rate funeral, if a funeral home could be located to perform a simple ceremony at this price, and an additional $200 for a grave. This money, if it could not be borrowed from friends or contributed by a charitable group, had to be taken from the family's living stipend. Eight hundred dollars is far in excess of the cash benefits provided monthly to an AFDC family of four people in New York. Even in normal circumstances, therefore, necessary funds would not be available. A homeless family whose child has been desperately ill is probably in debt to many people at the time the child dies.

"The alternative," writes the coalition, "is the terminal disgrace of a pauper's grave in Potter's Field."

Potter's Field, located on Hart's Island in Long Island Sound, is New York City's public burial ground. Burials are performed by prison inmates who live on the island. As a prison facility, the island is a restricted area, inaccessible except by ferry. Parents cannot attend their child's burial.

"Logistics alone," according to the coalition, "probably do not account for the no-visit rule. The economies of scale yielded by mass burials do not allow for much in the way of individual funeral amenities. Burial rites would, in all likelihood, prove disturbing to those attending."

The unembalmed bodies are taken in rough wooden boxes by the truckload from the hospital morgues. Twenty to thirty boxes, costing $37 each, are buried at a time in trenches. "The boxes are stacked three deep and two across. . . ." There are no grave markers. After thirty or forty years, the graves are bulldozed to make room for more.

Potter's Field, the coalition writes, is "a site for disposal . . . never a locus of remembrance. It serves to diminish, not memorialize, the existence of those who died poor. No traces are left behind which indicate that they had ever lived. . . ."

Between 1981 and 1984, nearly half the children who died in New York City before their second year of life were buried at Potter's Field. Almost a third of all persons buried at Potter's Field during those years were infants.

Even parents who somehow find the funds for private burial may discover that they are too late. If a funeral director does not contact the morgue to "hold" the child's body, or if he does this but then fails to claim it in two days, the body is technically unclaimed. If still unclaimed after another two days, the body can be shipped to Potter's Field or used for research purposes, though generally the body is held longer. After a body is used for research, it must then be sent to Potter's Field. "The exception is infants," reports the coalition, "in which case the hospital may itself incinerate the remains."

Not all homeless mothers can expect to be assisted by the Coalition for the Homeless. The coalition, with its limited resources, has been able to pay for only six burials over the past two years. Occasionally, a generous crisis worker in a hotel like the Martinique, moved by a sense of personal obligation, will contribute money or will help the mother to track down a funeral director who will conduct an inexpensive ceremony. This action, however, may constitute a violation of the city's rules, as it necessitates the favoring of one funeral director over another. City employees, the coalition writes, "are forced to jeopardize their jobs" in order to provide this help.

It is unclear where Benjamin is buried. Funds raised by the coalition to pay for his funeral may not have been adequate to pay for private burial. Holly refers to "an island." It is possible that she is speaking of Hart's Island. Another possibility is that Benjamin is buried in a grave on Staten Island where, because the water table is so high, the graves cannot be deep and, partly for this reason, are the least expensive in the city.

The sum of $250, established in 1966, was not adjusted for inflation for two decades. In 1986, after the fire at the Brooklyn Arms in which four children died, the city raised this allocation to $900. The death benefit is now in keeping with the market prices for a no-frills funeral, plain coffin, and interment. Of all benefits allowed the poor in New York City, burial is the only one that bears some true connection to prevailing costs. Cost-of-living benefits lag far behind the cost of death in this respect.

The forty-five acres of Hart's Island used for burying the poor are, according to the author of the coalition's study, tended with dignity by the thirty-five prison inmates who reside there. "The currently used sections," she reports, "resemble a park." Except for an abandoned missile site nearby, the area is pastoral. "Grass and underbrush," she writes, "cover the burial ground. A noisy band of geese keep year-round watch."

Prospects: Facing the Year 2000

I am not a specialist in housing policy. It would be misleading to present this book as anything more than the description of a journey that began for me a few days before Christmas 1985 and has continued to the present time. It would, however, seem a waste of learned experience not to add here certain recommendations made by those who know this problem best: the homeless men and women who have told their stories in these pages and the advocates who work beside them.

Two challenges present two simultaneous and separate tasks. The first is emergency relief for those who are now homeless. The second is an answer to conditions that have forced them to the streets.

EMERGENCY SOLUTIONS

In specific reference to New York: It seems reprehensible to leave the shelter of a homeless family to the profit-seeking portion of the private sector that now owns and manages these ruinous hotels. Ethically, it is unacceptable that people should profit from the suffering of those whose anguish they cannot alleviate but to whom they presently bring only added grief and a proliferation of health hazards.

Ethics apart, it is self-evident that, in this situation, the familiar code words of the decade—namely that "the private sector handles things like this with the least waste"—will not surivive examination. For less than three fourths of what is spent to house a family in the Holland, Brooklyn Arms or Martinique, charitable organizations have created healthier conditions and returned poor people far more rapidly to a productive life and to a stable housing situation.

Whether by use of eminent domain based on a declaration of

municipal emergency, or by expropriation through the courts in cases where code violations or an owner's tax arrears can justify such action, buildings like those we have described—if they must continue to be used at all—ought to be placed within the governance of organizations like the Red Cross or of groups derived from public/private partnerships.

Even if the present owners of these buildings must be reimbursed at the prevailing market values, long-term savings to the public justify the costs. The land value of a property like the Martinique is very high. But the hotel's value has also been inflated by emergency conditions. It has been suggested that the city might selectively devalue certain buildings by refusing to make use of them, one at a time, in order to reduce them to their actual worth. Suppose, however, that this proves unrealistic. Even a one-time purchase price of $35 million for the Martinique Hotel is less than what the city pays its owners in five years. After purchase, the city would be in possession of a building which it might, in later years, convert to permanent housing. The city could also later sell the building for substantial profit and employ the revenues to build low-income housing elsewhere.

Members of the New York City Council have expressed some reservations in regard to purchase of hotels. Their arguments, summarized in the notes to this book, are worth examination. Both political and policy considerations may make this plan unworkable. In such a case, it has been suggested that the city might at the very least employ the process of "net leasing" to obtain the use, if not the ownership, of these hotels for operation by nonprofit groups that have already proven their success in housing homeless families in humane conditions.

We may recapitulate some numbers here: The Red Cross, at the present time, leases a tourist hotel in New York City. In that building it houses ninety families. It charges the city $41 nightly for a family, provides all families with refrigerators, phones and air conditioning, and returns half of its residents to permanent housing in about four months. The Henry Street Settlement's Urban Family Center, in which Holly and her kids were housed after the death of Benjamin, charges the city $34 nightly for each family. It returns most of its guests to permanent housing in eight months. The Samaritan House in Brooklyn, in which one of the families I first came to know within the Martinique was subsequently placed, gives shelter to twenty-five or thirty families in a year and finds permanent housing for the average family in four months. (The citywide average, we have seen, is thirteen months.) Samaritan House provides a kitchenette on every floor, arranges day care in the neighborhood, provides job training, parenting help and adult education, and is able to finance much of this through a substantial loan from Citibank—a good example of the private sector's role in partnership with a nonprofit organization whose rental costs are paid with public funds.

Although these institutions are unusual in that they are run by dedicated organizers, there is no scarcity of dedication in New York or elsewhere in America; the scarcity is in supply of buildings. The buildings exist; we know who owns them. Ethics and municipal self-interest coincide in pointing the direction we should take.

The entire apparatus of "deterrence"—EAUs and barracks and short-term hotels—should be dismantled in New York and should be taken as a cautionary lesson by municipal leaders elsewhere. It doesn't work in humane terms; nor does it function as deterrence. On this subject, the important study carried out in autumn 1986 by a committee of the New York City Council made an observation cited above only in summary. The full statement is this: "Present policy bases its programs on the theory that if homelessness is made comfortable, more people will allow themselves to remain or to become homeless. The Committee found no evidence to support this. . . . On the contrary, the programs providing the best conditions with the best social services have the best placement record. Programs with the worst conditions usually have the longest average length of stay."

The mayor of New York has recently reversed his thinking on the matter of deterrence—at least to the extent that he no longer advocates the building of more congregate shelters and has proposed instead that twenty "transitional shelters" be established, with a certain degree of privacy afforded to each resident. Progress on this plan has been painfully slow. The plan has been cut back already to eleven shelters as a consequence of neighborhood resistance. Only seven of these shelters are for families. If they are at length constructed, they will be available at earliest by 1989 and will offer only 700 families temporary shelter. The mayor's new policy, however, is regarded by observers as a hopeful sign.

Granting implementation of the changes recommended here, what are the ingredients that we may look for in a family shelter?

A dignified and healthy shelter ought to offer every family a safe room or suite of rooms, with space appropriate for family size; refrigerators in every room or suite; kitchens or kitchenettes for every family, or for every group of three to seven families; phones available on every floor; a reliable bell system and an intercom arrangement so that families are not cut off from the outside world—nor denied the means to call for help in an emergency; on-site therapy for those with histories of drug abuse; replacement of the often untrained and manipulative guards by competent security; day care, preschool and prenatal programs operating on site; adult literacy and job training programs, libraries, space for meetings, films, and other entertainment, areas for children's play, and separate areas where parents may relax in civilized surroundings; a simplified system for payment of benefits and the direct payment of all rents by city agencies, in order to spare residents the make-work rituals that now prevail; nurses or doctors present in the shelters; a limit of 100 families in a single building.

Even 100 is quite high. A compromise between the ideal and the realistic might suggest a range of 25 to 80 families: a maximum of 100 to 300 people in one building, large enough to make it possible to offer necessary services, small enough to fend off the inevitable siege mentality that comes with larger numbers. Equally important are a rapid system for enrolling kids in school and a prescribed arrangement for communication between school and shelter residents; an end to policies that penalize two parents who wish to reside together with their children; an end to disincentives for part-time employment and, more to the point, a system of rewards to make such work appealing.

One recommendation made by several shelter operators runs counter to the thinking of some of the homeless families I have met. Certain shelter operators think it best to sort out families in diverse degrees of need (emotional or otherwise) and assign them to distinctly separate quarters. While some separation seems essential in the case of those with truly dangerous disorders, it would seem unwise if the same policy should be applied to those at the reverse side of the spectrum—those who are most stable, organized and undefeated. To remove such adults (Gwen or Kim or Annie, for example) from the mainstream of the sheltered population undermines all possibility of building a self-help community: one in which those with greatest strengths and highest education levels may assist those with the least. Such separation also makes impossible a sensible approach to the entire issue of "work ethic" that has been suggested by some of the homeless people I have met.

That approach, briefly, is this: Many people in the shelters have good histories of work sustained over long periods of time. Such people might be put to work right in the shelter. Mrs. Andrews, who has typed numerous memos for my use in preparation of this book, would be an ideal secretary or bookkeeper in a shelter run by a nonprofit group. Mr. Allesandro, with more than a decade of experience in maintenance of residential buildings, might be given work within a shelter which would dignify his competence and ingenuity. Several women, we have seen, have had experience in nursing or as teachers' aides or preschool teachers. A health-care center or a preschool in a homeless shelter might provide such women with the kind of work that can prepare them for authentic jobs once they have homes. A woman like Kim would be a natural teacher in an adult education program. "They look at us to see what isn't there," said Kim, "and not what *is*." Finding what skills exist within the homeless population, then finding ways to use those skills in the creation of a healthier community within the shelter walls, would demonstrate some true respect for the work ethic.

In reference to work, these final points may warrant some consideration:

1. People do not learn respect for work by having their noses rubbed in "the work ethic" as if they were stable boys being given a respect for horsemanship by having their faces shoved into manure. Manufactured business (scrubbing graffiti in the subway, raking leaves, decoding welfare regulations) does not teach us a work ethic. People with limited education need job training that includes something a great deal more sophisticated than what is called "job readiness." They need delivery of education that provides them with both analytic and specific skills. Even those skills, however, will be worthless if the jobs do not exist. Jobs that can support someone with modest education in a city like New York are, as we know, in short supply. One way to begin creation of these jobs is in the rehabilitation of low-income housing and the evolution of a network of related services in health care, child care and office management.

2. Even for those like Lazarus who already have employment skills, it is unrealistic to expect that jobs can be pursued, obtained and competently filled so long as homelessness remains a sword above their heads. Prolonged anxiety renders return to work, no matter how appealing, very hard. Dignified shelters of the sort that we propose heightens the dignity of those we shelter; in so doing, it restores the energy and the stability required to reenter the job market. A permanent home need not always be the precondition of employment. A decent shelter system makes it possible for housing and employment to be seen as twin goals, either of which renders the other more attainable.

3. Caring for children under conditions we have seen within this book is a demanding job. Even in an excellent shelter, raising a preschool child may be almost full-time work. In a healthy shelter, parenting can be a form of active education in itself, while the provision

of good day care will accelerate transition to the mainstream of employment.

To go any further with these tentative suggestions would exceed the scope of what has been suggested to me by the people cited in this work and would distort the purpose of this book. A substantial literature, published by organizations like the Coalition for the Homeless, by individuals like Chester Hartman and Kim Hopper, and by governmental agencies (the Massachusetts Committee for Children and Youth, for instance), offers details to expand and sometimes to correct the statements offered here.

All of the above, however, presupposes our preparedness no longer to perceive a shelter system as a penalty for failure but to see it as an invitation to the homeless to regain a useful place within society. It also calls for a redoubled sense of urgency—a willingness to move with ingenuity and speed—that is not present in New York or any other city I have seen.

A painful example of resistance to enlightened action was described in early 1987 in an editorial in the *New York Times*. "It's been 18 months," the *Times* observed, since a philanthropist named Leonard Stern "offered a $1 million challenge grant" to build a shelter for some of the families now consigned to places like the Martinique. The challenge was accepted by Andrew Cuomo, son of New York's governor. "Yet only now," according to the *Times*, "is the project starting to move. . . . It will take an additional year before the first occupants arrive. . . ." Why, asked the *Times*, "will it take 30 months" to build "200 tiny temporary housing units in New York? It took only 20 months during World War II to plan and build Oak Ridge, Tennessee" —a city of 75,000 residents, on what had been empty land. Perhaps, concluded the *Times*, the answer lies precisely in the fact that New York City is *not* empty land. It is "a human cauldron, bubbling with conflicting aims and interests." Among those interests are construction unions which reject cost-saving plans and neighborhood groups objecting to an influx of a large number of children in a settled area. The *Times* goes on to warn that, even now, "without remarkable cooperation," the 30-month delay could be extended to five years. All this for construction of a mere 200 units to address the needs of what will be almost 6,000 homeless families by the time this tiny shelter, even by most optimistic estimates, is ready to be used.

This reference to the speed with which Oak Ridge was planned, completed and occupied in World War II reminds us that in time of an accepted crisis we can do both well and rapidly what we believe it in our national self-interest to achieve. Is it unrealistic to believe that we might duplicate that dedication here?

LONG-TERM SUGGESTIONS

All discussion of emergency shelter carries the risk of drawing our attention from the cause of homelessness and turning it instead to questions of "the way to operate a better poorhouse" for the dispossessed. There are those who are prepared to live with the idea that homeless people have deserved, and shall be offered, nothing more. Most Americans don't share this view. We therefore need to ask what it will take to end the need for institutions of this nature altogether.

Any long-term answer calls for sweeping changes at both national and local levels. Changes at either level presuppose a clarification of the status housing holds within our national imagination. Is it "a gift"—a kindliness, a favor—or is it more properly perceived as an inalienable right? If it were the former, private charity and the occasional largesse of government would be an adequate response. But shelter is not a gift; it is among the first of all rights civilized societies owe to their citizens. How may fulfillment of this right be furthered at the national and local levels?

At the municipal level there should be stiff penalties attached to the warehousing of low-income living units (i.e., leaving them unoccupied to free them for conversion) and a moratorium on all conversions, until such a time as every citizen is housed. This is a policy few urban politicians can espouse without the alienation of those interests whose support appears essential for their reelection; courageous politicians ought to do so anyway and brave the risks.*

Other practical actions are less controversial. Among these are the following: municipal intervention, prior to eviction, to enable city agencies to meet back rent for tenants on the verge of dispossession—a policy which, while it is costly, could not possibly approach the cost imposed upon a city once a family is displaced; rehabilitation of all vacant city-owned apartments (over 100,000 units in New York in 1986, as we have seen) and foreclosure on those other rental units owned by landlords who refuse to meet tax obligations to the city (an additional 100,000 units in New York, according to the city council); restoration of semivacant and deteriorating public housing; construc-

---

* This issue might be set aside for good if realtors were not permitted to contribute to municipal election funds. Recommendations to this effect are offered perennially in Boston and New York. Politicians are often challenged to refuse such gifts; legislation could settle the matter by making receipt of gifts like these—and those of other seeking favors from municipalities—illegal.

tion of new housing, not in massive clusters isolated in the least attractive neighborhoods (a policy that guarantees reconstitution of the
dangerous conditions that exist already in such places as the Martinique) but, wherever possible, as "in-fill" housing—units spotted here
and there in normal residential areas, that pose no specter of invasion
to a stable neighborhood but will simply add a modest number of low-
income homes; finally, a policy of "linkage" to assure that proceeds
from construction undertaken by developers on property, often of
great value, sold by city agencies be directly tied to funding for low-
income housing.

"Linkage" is a familiar term in mayoralty campaigns. Mayor Ray
Flynn of Boston has attempted to apply the concept in a conscientious
way. The opposition posed by realtors have been formidable. Even
Flynn may soon be forced to step back from his former promises by
pressure from developers. In New York, the promise of linkage has
been raised at times when an expensive parcel of desired property was
granted to developers in face of protests from low-income-housing
advocates. In one recent case, a piece of land (the parcel on which New
York's Coliseum stands) was sold to a developer for $455 million. The
city's rebuttal to its critics was that this large sum of money could be
used to build a house for every homeless family in New York. In fact,
however, the revenue received has been applied not to low-income
housing but to "general funds"—which means that only a small portion will be used for the relief of homelessness.

The concept, then, is easily neutralized. Even where funds derived from luxury development are directly tied to the provision of
specific housing units, we often find, after the dust has cleared, that
the projected housing will be "mixed"—by which the city means a
mix of "low" and "moderate" and "middle-income" units, and more
of the last than the first. Even those units defined as "low" are generally assigned to families with an income of as much as $15,000. As
Annie Harrington observed: "That isn't nowhere near where I am at.
What good will that do for somebody like me?"

Linkage is little more, for now, than an attractive plank for an
electoral campaign. What it would take to make it something more is
a transformed political agenda at the local level that cannot be opti-
mistically expected.

Even if cities should determine to pursue some of these goals, it
is apparent that they cannot be achieved without a vast influx of
federal funds. Without a national housing policy that renders possible
the same or parallel efforts in all geographical areas at once, cities that
evolve a policy of expeditious action might in fact become attractive

magnets to the dispossessed. Boston, New York, Newark, Philadelphia, and Washington, D.C., are separated by short distances that even an indigent family can traverse if its survival is at stake. Any city in this area that does what should be done may soon become enticing to the homeless families in those other nearby cities that do less, and may therefore face a self-repeating challenge that it cannot meet alone. Only a national housing policy can meet the need described within this book.

What might such a federal policy include?

Among a number of elements proposed by homeless advocates, some of the most sensible are these: immediate allocations to restore existing public housing and to rehabilitate substandard city-owned apartments; revision of rules that now restrict emergency shelter funds to self-repeating waste in payments to such institutions as the Martinique; the redirection of such funds to meeting rents for ordinary housing when and where it still exists; a vast expansion of federal subsidies to bridge the gap between prevailing market rents and 25 percent of monthly income for all families in need of homes.

Subsidies, however, are of no use if a landlord won't accept them. In Washington, D.C., 10,000 people were qualified for housing subsidies in January 1987; $15 million had been allocated for this purpose by the District. In the four months preceding January, certificates for such subsidies had been awarded to nearly 500 families; but only 99 had found apartments. Over 100 certificates expired before landlords had been found who would accept them. About 260 families with still-current subsidies were, according to the *Washington Post*, "still looking."

There have been some more alarming revelations in regard to subsidies in recent months. Officials, according to the *New York Times*, note that "over the next decade more than half-a-million low- and moderate-income families may be ousted from federally subsidized apartments built in the 1960s and 1970s," because the law permits owners to forego further subsidies after a number of years and return their units to the private market. A California assemblyman estimates that 70,000 apartments in California may be subject to conversion for this reason.

The Congressional Budget Office says that 57 percent of low-income units subsidized under two federal programs are "potentially eligible" for conversion in the next ten years. With over half of subsidized housing units subject to conversion at the same time that the number of homeless families is increasing 20 to 25 percent each year, an intensification of the housing crisis seems almost inevitable.

Even the long lists for subsidized housing, according to the *Sacramento Bee,* mask the true dimensions of the problem: "The lists are closed to new names, says HUD. New HUD construction was halted under the Reagan administration in 1983. Reagan wanted the government out of the housing business." When asked about welfare families faced with high rent, Wayne A. Stanton, who oversees welfare benefits to families for the federal government, offers this advice: "My only reaction to that would be that they ought to look for different places to live."

If this policy is not reversed, the only places that low-income families will have left to look are going to be bridges, tents and shelters.

Even if conversion can be stopped, however, and subsidies expanded, the heart of the problem will remain unchanged. That problem—voiced repeatedly by Columbia University professor Peter Marcuse, Robert Hayes, and others—is that the construction of low-income housing has ceased to be profitable while local and federal regulations offer strong incentives for development of upscale dwellings and commercial office space. The federal government, while stating its wish to "get out of the housing business," remains very much in the housing business by the tax incentives it provides developers.

Subsidies and linkage, even at their best, are stopgap measures. The ultimate problem is that there is not enough low-income housing, public or private, subsidized or not, to meet the needs of poor Americans. Only a multi-billion-dollar federal program can create the millions of new units that are needed, and only a sense of national emergency can render allocations on this scale politically conceivable.

The climate, however, may be growing more auspicious. An unexpected national phenomenon, the evolution of a number of local "unions" of the homeless, places a new pressure on some urban politicians. While many observers look with dread, others with skepticism, on such bootstrap operations, they have been able to enroll some competent organizers. In the fall of 1986, over 1,000 homeless people in New York gathered at Riverside Church to form a union. Many previous skeptics were astonished by the turnout and the skill with which the meeting was conducted. All of this suggests a future role for people such as Kim and Mrs. Andrews as spokespersons of, not simply for, the dispossessed.

At the national level, Senators Albert Gore and Daniel Moynihan introduced in autumn 1986 a bill ("The Homeless Persons' Survival Act") initiated by the National Coalition for the Homeless. Although the bill was not enacted, the One-hundredth Congress has since implemented several measures it contained.

In late January 1987, the Senate voted overwhelmingly to add an immediate $50 million to existing federal funds to build more shelters and provide food for the homeless. One week later, House Democratic Whip Tom Foley introduced a bill to add $500 million more. In March the House approved this allocation, to be used immediately, and added $225 million more for food and nutrition programs for the homeless to be spent over the next three years. Other congressional leaders— Henry Gonzalez, Mickey Leland, and Jim Wright of Texas, William Gray of Pennsylvania, Ted Weiss of New York—pushed for more ambitious actions.

In July of 1987, a bill authorizing slightly more than $1 billion in emergency assistance to the nation's homeless in the next two years finally reached the president's desk. The president signed the bill on the evening of July 22. "A White House official," according to the *New York Times*, conceded that "it was unusual for the president to sign the bill in the evening." He said that the timing was intended to demonstrate the president's "lack of enthusiasm" for the legislation. The signing of this bill at evening in the twilight of the Reagan presidency lent a sad, embittered and reluctant note to its enactment.

The number of homeless families meanwhile is increasing. That increase far exceeds most earlier projections. New York City's Commission on the Year 2000 predicts a shortfall of 372,000 housing units in the city within thirteen years. This estimate, which the commission calls "conservative," tells us that one million family members— one in every seven residents of New York City—will be doubled up or homeless in this century.

Nationwide, nearly 19 million Americans will be homeless by the year 2003, according to a recent study funded by the Congress and carried out by M.I.T. professor Phillip Clay. Low-income housing advocates believe this estimate is very cautious.

Whether the apparent increase in political momentum will be able to keep pace with the increase in need cannot be known; but on the answer to this question rest the lives of several hundred thousand newborn infants and small children in all cities of America.

None of the suggestions offered here is going to eradicate the fact of child poverty in the United States. What they can do, however, is to take the harsh edge from the most extreme form that such poverty assumes. And, while they will not resolve the questions that surround the presence of an underclass in our society, they will help us to prevent a massive increase in that underclass by salvaging the health and hopes of many children such as Christopher and Doby. There are many things we *don't* know how to do. One thing we know how to do, if we have the will to do it, is to use our wealth and our technology to guarantee that every citizen, above all every child, will be housed in safe and dignified conditions. On this point, therefore, this brief collection of ideas drawn largely from the words of homeless people properly concludes.

Page **ORDINARY PEOPLE**

0 to 000   Conversation in Martinique Hotel, December 1985; follow-up conversations, March, November 1986.

Peter and Megan were interviewed in a television documentary, "Down and Out in America," first shown on HBO in 1986. I saw the film 12 months after my first meeting with this couple. Certain background information and some dialogue are adapted from the film. Some details are disguised. Information on this superb documentary: Joseph Feury Productions, Inc., 610 West End Avenue, New York, NY 10024.

Hotel rental of $3,000: Peter's estimate. See notes for pp. 00, 00.

Number of homeless children in America: Robert Hayes, counsel to the National Coalition for the Homeless. (Telephone interview, August 7, 1987.)

The population of Atlanta is 452,000; Denver, 493,000; St. Louis, 453,000. (1980 census.)

OVERVIEW: A CAPTIVE STATE

0   "This is a new population. . . ." All quotations not attributed to documented sources are from author's interviews, 1985 to 1987.

Fifty percent of individuals served by city shelters were seeking shelter for first time (New York City and national): *The Growth of Hunger, Homelessness and Poverty in America's Cities in 1985*, U.S. Conference of Mayors, January 1986; *Hardship in the Heartland: Homelessness in Eight U.S. Cities*, by Dan Salerno, Kim

Hopper, and Ellen Baxter, Community Service Society of New York, June 1984; *The Making of America's Homeless: From Skid Row to New Poor, 1945–1984,* by Kim Hopper and Jill Hamberg, Community Service Society of New York, December 1984.

0   Increase in numbers of homeless children: *A Status Report on Homeless Families in America's Cities,* U.S. Conference of Mayors, Washington, D.C., May 1987; *Safety Network,* National Coalition for the Homeless, October/November 1986.

Newsweek (January 6, 1986) reports that two thirds of the children of homeless families surveyed in Boston, in a study conducted in 1985, were under five years of age. According to the U.S. Conference of Mayors (January 1986), "Families with children comprise 80 percent of the homeless population in Yonkers. Sixty-six percent of New York City's homeless are families. In both Chicago and Boston, 40 percent of the homeless population are parents and their children."

Numbers of homeless individuals and families, New York City: Conversations with Robert Hayes and David Beseda, National Coalition for the Homeless, 1987. According to the New York City Human Resources Administration, 18,219 family members, including 11,972 children and 6,247 parents in 4,962 families, were given shelter by New York City in June 1987. ("Monthly Report," New York City Temporary Housing Program for Families with Children, Crisis Intervention Services, HRA, June 1987.) Crisis Intervention Services identified below as "CIS."

Average age, homeless children and parents, New York City: *A Shelter Is Not a Home,* Report of the Manhattan Borough President's Task Force on Housing for Homeless Families, March 1987. (Identified below by name of Manhattan Borough President David Dinkins.) See also press release by Mr. Dinkins, March 24, 1987.

Massachusetts statistics: *Streetlife,* Massachusetts Coalition for the Homeless, September/October 1986; *Safety Network,* December 1985; *Newsweek,* January 6, 1986.

Children, 40 percent of poor, 26.8 percent of population: *New York Times,* May 23, 1985. See also Daniel P. Moynihan, *Family and Nation,* San Diego: Harcourt Brace Jovanovich, 1986.

Children in poverty, increase in numbers, decline in welfare benefits: *New York Times,* November 20, 1985.

700,000 children in New York City live in poverty: "Children of Poverty," by Andrew Stein, *New York Times Magazine,* June 8, 1986.

100,000 New York City children have no health insurance: *Newsday*, September 26, 1986.

Increase in percentages of New York City children in poverty: *The Changing Face of Poverty: Trends in New York City's Population in Poverty: 1960–1990*, by Emanuel Tobier, Community Service Society of New York, November 1984.

0   Denver and Cleveland: *Hardship in the Heartland*, cited above.

Milwaukee Journal, December 29, 1982.

Governor Milliken declares "state of human emergency": *Hardship in the Heartland*, above.

0   Take-home pay of $450 a month: At minimum wage of $3.35 for 160 hours (four weeks), gross income before deductions is $536.

0   Homeless people living in caves: Many instances are cited in cities as diverse as Pittsburgh and Atlanta and, most recently, even in New York City. See *Homelessness in America, A Forced March to Nowhere*, by Mary Ellen Hombs and Mitch Snyder, Community for Creative Non-violence, Washington, D.C., 1982.

Increase in homeless families, Washington, D.C.: *Washington Post*, January 8, 1987.

0, 0   Numbers of homeless in America: *The Faces of Homelessness*, By Marjorie Hope and James Young, D.C. Heath and Company, Lexington, Massachusetts, 1986; *National Neglect/National Shame: America's Homeless: Outlook—Winter 1986–87*, National Coalition for the Homeless, September 1986; *Homelessness: A Complex Problem and the Federal Response*, U.S. General Accounting Office, Washington, D.C., April 1985; *HUD Report on Homelessness, II*, Subcommittee on Housing and Community Development of the Committee on Banking, Finance and Urban Affairs, House of Representatives, Ninety-ninth Congress, Washington, D.C., December 4, 1985.

In discussion of HUD's number count, according to the National Coalition for the Homeless, "Chairman Gonzalez said that the HUD report was intended to squelch outcries by advocates for the homeless and certain members of Congress. . . . Gonzalez concluded that the report was not only 'sloppy' but intentionally deceptive and prepared with 'malice aforethought.' " (*Safety Network*, January 1986.)

HUD's pressure on consultants: "The Housing Part of Homelessness," by Chester Hartman, in *The Mental Health Needs of Homeless Persons*, ed. by Ellen Bassuk, Jossey-Bass, San Francisco, 1986.

Dorothy Wickenden, in the *New Republic* (March 18, 1985), states: "Most studies judge the correct number to be two or three million." The *New York Times* (March 5, 1987) estimates "three million homeless in the United States." Additional discussion of numbers' debate: *Boston Globe*, September 6, 1986; *Newsweek*, December 16, 1985.

0   17,000 families doubled up, New York City, 1983: *New York Times*, April 21, 1983.

35,000 families doubled up, New York City, 1986: According to David Dinkins, "approximately 20 percent" of the New York City Housing Authority's 175,000 units "are home to more than one family." The *New York Times* (June 22, 1986) reports that "at least 35,000 families are living doubled up illegally" in city-owned apartments.

According to estimates cited by the New York City Council, between 100,000 and 150,000 families were doubled up in public and private housing in New York City in 1986. See *Report of the Select Committee on the Homeless*, chaired by Abraham Gerges and researched by committee council Robert Altman, prepared in November 1986, released January 22, 1987.

0   Number of persons doubled up in New York City: According to Cathy Bezozo, Office for Policy and Economic Research, HRA, the average family on welfare in New York City includes 2.9 persons. The average homeless family includes 3.7 persons. (Telephone interview, August 17, 1987.) The average size of families doubled up falls between these figures.

0   According to *Newsweek* (January 2, 1984), "the number of American families sharing quarters in 1982 was up 58 percent—the first such increase since 1950."

0   Doubling up: In 1978, 1.3 million families were doubled up in the United States; the number rose to 2.6 million by 1983. *(The Making of America's Homeless*, cited above.) By 1985, the National Coalition for the Homeless estimated as many as 10 to 20 million persons (approximately 3 to 6 million families) doubled up in the United States. (*The Search for Shelter*, by Nora Richter Greer, American Institute of Architects, Washington, D.C., 1986.)

According to David Dinkins, 50 to 60 percent of families entering New York City shelters were previously doubled up. The New York City council study estimates 57 percent of homeless families in New York City were previously doubled up.

Number of people in danger of eviction: "Seattle's Mayor Charles Royer noted in May 1985, 'For every homeless person in Seattle, there are ten others who are at risk. . . .' " (*The Search for Shelter*, cited above.)

Rentals and mortgage payments compared to family income: Chester Hartman, cited above.

0   Loss of rental units, increase in rents, persons paying nearly three quarters of income for rent: *Hardship in the Heartland; The Making of America's Homeless.*

0   Statistics for Boston: *Boston Globe Magazine*, December 15, 1985.

Vacancy rates for San Francisco, Boston, New York City: *The Making of America's Homeless;* U.S. Conference of Mayors, May 1987; *The Nation,* April 4, 1987; *Christianity Today,* October 4, 1985.

Evictions and welfare rent ceilings in New York City: *The Making of America's Homeless* and David Dinkins.

Decline in federal support for low-income housing: New York City Council study, above.

HUD official: quoted by Hartman, above.

0, 0   Hartman: See above.

0   The U.S. Conference of Mayors (January 1986) cites statement on dying industries from officials in Chicago.

0   Job-market transformation: "MacNeil/Lehrer Newshour," PBS, April 7, 1987; *Sacramento Bee*, March 15, 1987; *The Nation*, April 4, 1987. The American Institute of Architects' study, cited above, reports that New York City lost 80,000 blue-collar jobs between 1980 and 1985. The U.S. Conference of Mayors (April 1987) predicts a loss of 36,000 jobs in auto manufacturing plants in the Detroit area: "Only about a quarter of [these jobs] will be replaced by the end of this decade."

Jim Hightower, commissioner of the Texas Department of Agriculture, observes: "Nearly half of the new jobs created from 1979 to 1985 pay less than a poverty-level wage—$180 a week." (*New York Times*, June 21, 1987.)

John D. Kasarda, chairman of the sociology department at the University of South Carolina, states that, in the 14 years preceding 1986, New York City "lost almost 500,000 jobs in those industries where the average job holder has not completed high school." (*New York Times*, October 22, 1986.)

"If anything," officials in Boston told the U.S. conference of Mayors, "the recovery has exacerbated the situation as the increased attractiveness of the city has tightened the housing market." Officials in San Francisco added this: "The 'national economic recovery' has not addressed the causes of homelessness. In fact, the so-called 'recovery' denies the existence of such problems." (U.S. Conference of Mayors, January 1986.)

0 *The Federal Response to the Homeless Crisis, Third Report,* House Committee on Government Operations, Ninety-ninth Congress, Washington, D.C., April 1985.

Homeless crisis will increase: "Unless major new initiatives are begun, New York City by the year 2000 is likely to need 372,000 housing units more than it will have," according to a study by a mayoral commission. ("Housing Needs Will Get Worse, Study Predicts," *New York Times,* July 20, 1987.) Relatively affluent Westchester County spent $750,000 for emergency housing in 1983, has budgeted $32 million for 1987, and predicts that this expense will rise to $90 million by 1988. (*New York Times,* July 19, 1987.)

New York City spends $274 million in 1987 (projection): *New York Times,* January 10, 1987. About $150 million for homeless families: See notes for p. 00.

0 Growth in numbers of families sheltered in New York City: Episcopal Bishop Paul Moore, lecture to Federation of Protestant Welfare Workers, New York City, April 24, 1985; *Struggling to Survive in a Welfare Hotel,* by John H. Simpson, Margaret Kilduff, and C. Douglass Blewett, Community Service Society of New York, 1984; *New York Times,* December 4, 1985; *Newsday,* November 28, 1986. See also notes for p. 0.

0 Prediction of 6,000 families sheltered in New York City by summer 1988: *New York Times,* October 30, 1986.

2.3 children in each homeless family in New York: New York City Council and David Dinkins. The average homeless family sheltered in New York City contains 1.4 adults and 2.3 children, for a total of 3.7 persons. See notes for p. 0.

Nationally, according to the U.S. Conference of Mayors (April 1987), 30 percent of homeless families are headed by two parents. In New York City, according to the same report, the official figure is 15 percent. An additional 15 to 20 percent in New York City probably have two parents present, with the man officially unrecorded because he is living with his family off the books. (See part one, chapter 2, "Grieving for a Lost Home" for discussion of concealed cohabitation.)

The population of Laramie, Wyoming, is 24,410. The population of Key West is 24,292.

The population of New York City is 7,086,096: U.S. Conference of Mayors, April 1987.

0, 0, 0, 0, 0 The route taken by a homeless family is described in the New York City Council study.

New York City's deterrence policy: See "Koch Limits Using Welfare Hotels—Homeless to Be Sent First to Dormitory Shelters," *New York Times,* December 17, 1985. For update on mayor's policy, see p. 000, Appendix.

0, 0, 0, 00 Data on Roberto Clemente shelter: New York City Council and author's interview with Robert Hayes, May 1987.

Kim Hopper, coauthor of several of the Community Service Society reports cited in this book, emphasizes an additional reason why families in a barracks shelter are likely to seek placement in a long-term hotel: Only after hotel placement does a family qualify for city help in finding permanent housing.

Families with children forced to sleep overnight at EAUs: See part two, chapter 5, "Distancing Ourselves from Pain and Tears." Both policy and practice seem to have changed since 1986. Robert Hayes reports (1987) that families no longer remain overnight at EAUs.

According to the New York Human Resources Administration, 3,423 homeless families were residing in hotels in autumn 1986. ("Monthly Report," CIS, November 1986.)

The rest remained in barracks, short-term hotels, or model shelters: A smaller number, according to Kim Hopper (correspondence, June 1987), remained for very brief periods of time in "overflow shelters" run by EAUs.

Numbers of families in particular hotels and average length of stay: "Monthly Report," CIS, October and November 1986; June 1987. The 16-month length of stay at the Martinique Hotel was recorded in October 1986. The Hotel Carter, where average length of stay was 4–6 months in June of 1987, now holds very few homeless families. On December 31, 1985, there were 444 families in the Prince George Hotel, 389 in the Martinique, 240 in the Holland.

Over 1,400 children in Martinique Hotel at Christmas 1985: *New York Daily News,* December 24, 1985; interview with Tom Styron, National Coalition for the Homeless, December 20, 1985; "Monthly Report," CIS, June 1987.

Public-housing units in New York City, waiting list, and length of wait: David Dinkins. According to *Newsweek* (January 2, 1984), waiting time for applicants for public housing in Miami is 20 years.

Robert Altman, counsel to the New York City Council Select Committee on the Homeless, notes that the 200,000 names on the public-housing waiting list include some families that have since found housing. Even if we discount for these families, the ratio of applicants to units and the very low turn-over rate among the occupants of public housing seem to justify the estimate of 18 years presented in the Dinkins study.

00, 00   Comparative costs in New York City shelters: New York City Council; *New York Daily News*, August 18, 1986; *New York Times*, March 7, 1986. Kim Hopper and Robert Altman emphasize that the figure provided for nightly rents at the nonprofit shelters do not include provision of social services. See also notes for p. 000.

Monthly rents in Martinique Hotel and numbers of persons per room are contained in a "rate chart" prepared by the hotel and obtained by the author from researchers in New York City. The rent for a family of four persons is established in this manner: $53.00 (basic charge), $4.38 ("sales tax"), $2.00 ("city tax"), $2.65 ("new city tax"), $1.08 ("fridge"), for a total of $63.11 nightly. A monthly rental (31 days) would, by the rate chart, total $1,956. A family of six in two rooms, again according to the rate chart, pays $97.95 per night; $3,036 for a 31-day month. These rates include hotel taxes. After residence of three months, the taxes cease to apply. Annual rent for a famly of four in its first year at the Martinique, therefore, might be broken down as follows: First three months, $1,956 × three months = $5,868. Next nine months, $53 per day (no tax) + $1.08 (refrigerator) × 31 = $1,676 × nine months = $15,084. Total for twelve months, family of four: $20,952. According to the study commissioned by David Dinkins, a year's rent at the Martinique for a family of four, excluding all taxes (for example, a second or third year of residence), totals $19,716. Whether with or without taxes, a year's rent is approximately $20,000.

Rent receipts I have examined, however, sometimes vary inexplicably from rents established on the chart. In the case of one large family I have met—14 people packed into three rooms—monthly rent is $5,700: $68,400 a year.

00   Cost of barracks shelters about $200 nightly including administration and social services: The *New York Times* (March 7, 1987)

estimated the monthly cost for a family of four at the Roberto Clemente shelter at nearly $6,000 a month. Robert Altman, counsel to the New York City Council, indicates that cost for most congregate shelters are comparable to those for Clemente. (Telephone interviews, June and July 1987.)

Welfare support to families is known in most states and in federal legislation as AFDC (Aid to Families with Dependent Children). In New York State, it is known as ADC (Aid to Dependent Children). I use the federal designation in this book.

Restaurant allowance of 71 cents per person per meal: Author's interview with Robert Hayes in January 1986. The restaurant allowance granted to a homeless family in New York City was increased in 1987 to compensate for a sharp decrease in food-stamp allocations by the federal government. In the second half of 1986, however, families in New York City shelters saw their food-stamp allocations drastically diminished but were forced to wait for several months before a commensurate increase in the restaurant allowance went into effect. During this period, many families underwent severe and extended periods of hunger. (See notes for p. 00.)

More than half those eligible for WIC in New York City don't receive it: According to Arthur Young, Health Program administrator, Department of Health (New York State), 374,000 women and children in New York City are eligible for WIC. Of these, about 204,000 (55 percent) do not receive it. (Telephone interview, August 17, 1987.)

Other statistics on WIC: *Faces of Homelessness,* (cited above); *Washington Post,* February 3, 1987. See also notes for p. 00 ff. and p. 000.

At the time of my initial visits, families received all benefits except their hotel rental check by mail. Since the spring of 1986, the process has been computerized. All benefits but rent are now obtained at cash-dispensing institutions.

00   A woman travels three hours twice a month to obtain her rental check: this is a familiar situation. The requirement sustains the myth that hotel residence is temporary. Even those in residence at the Martinique three years must make this time-consuming journey twice a month. Irrationality in the shelter system is heightened by the very high turn-over in the city's welfare staff. The division of the HRA with specific governance of children in life-threatening situations ("Special Services for Children") has a 60-percent turn-over rate among case workers, according to the *New York Daily News* (June 5, 1986).

AFDC rental limits in New York City: provided by HRA employees.

"If the government were to raise these limits by $100 . . ." Kim Hopper observes, however, that the government could not raise these rental limits for a homeless family without raising limits for all families on welfare.

New York City rental allocations for AFDC families, while insufficient to meet local rents, are very high compared to those in many other sections of the nation. In Indiana, a family—no matter of what size—was granted $100 a month for rent in 1984. In New Mexico, a family of four was granted $66 a month. (*Newsweek*, January 2, 1984.)

PART ONE

Epigraph: *Uprooted Children: The Early Life of Migrant Farm Workers*, by Robert Coles, New York: Harper and Row, 1970.

1. A MOOD OF RESIGNATION

00, 00 Historical data on the Martinique Hotel: George B. Corsa Hotel Collection, New-York Historical Society.

00, 00 New York City Council information on Martinique Hotel is included in its report of January 1987.

00 "The City Council tells us that the owners of the building are Bernard and Robert Sillins. . . ." According to Suzanne Daley, who has covered homeless stories for the *New York Times*, the manager of the Martinique, Mr. Tucelli, has identified himself as one of the hotel's owners. (Phone conversation with Suzanne Daley, June 22, 1987.)

00 Mr. Tucelli is also consultant to Prince George Hotel: *New York Daily News*, March 20, 1986.

Fifteen occupied floors above the lobby: The Martinique Hotel has a "sixteenth" and "seventeenth" floor above the lobby, but there is no "thirteenth" floor and the top floor is unoccupied.

00 "Two of the men who work here . . ." Social workers in the Martinique have scrupulously respected clients' privacy. Information on residents was obtained directly from those residents and, where possible, was corroborated independently.

00 Infant mortality statistics: *New York Daily News*, March 18, 1986; *Washington Post*, February 3, 1987; *New York Times*, May 6, 1986; telephone interview with Children's Defense Fund, June 1987.

One nurse: At the time of writing, there is an expanded health team in the Martinique, financed in part by the government, in part by the Children's Aid Society.

"The Empire State Building is two blocks away. . . ." The Empire States Building extends from West 33rd to West 34th Street. The Martinique Hotel extends from West 32nd Street to West 33rd Street. The buildings are separated at one point only by 33rd Street.

00 ff.   Interviews at Martinique Hotel, December 1985; follow-up interviews, 1986.

00   "This room is costing $1,500. . . ." According to the rate chart of the Martinique Hotel, a family of three pays $49.51 per night—or $1,535 for a 31-day month. After three months, if taxes are subtracted, the family pays $42.08 per night—or $1.304 a month.

Gwen's day-long wait at her welfare center for her hotel check is repeated in stories told by many hotel residents. More knowledgeable residents learn after a time that checks are not prepared until 4:00 P.M. on the day that they are due. Even with this knowledge, many homeless parents go to their welfare centers early in the day out of fear that last-minute problems may develop.

00, 00   Waiting list for public housing: David Dinkins, above.

2. GRIEVING FOR A LOST HOME

00–00   Approximately $150 million, cost for sheltering homeless families in New York City in 1986: The *New York Times* (August 15, 1987) places the figure at $156 million (fiscal year 1986.) The New York City Council projects $158 million for 1987.

$72 million spent to house over 3,000 families in welfare hotels, $14 million to Horn partnership, Mayor Koch's words ("a question of supply and demand"), political contributions by hotel owners: "Who Owns the Welfare Hotels?" by William Bastone, *Village Voice*, April 1, 1986.

Hotels owned by Mr. Horn and his partners; data on Martinique Hotel, Holland Hotel, and Prince George Hotel: *Village Voice* (above) and rate chart of Martinique Hotel.

In regard to political contributions by hotel owners, the *Voice* makes this exception for the Sillins family: "Unlike the Horn partnership, the Sillins group does not make political contributions."

The *Voice* says this of the manager of the Martinique: "Three residents told the *Voice* that they have seen Tucelli carrying a gun in the hotel."

Further discussions of political contributions by realtors and others in New York City: *New York Times*, Editorial, March 30, 1986.

Statements by Mayor Koch as congressman in 1970, number of homeless families sheltered in hotels and cost to city at the time: *Village Voice* (above) and "Transcript: 60 Minutes," CBS News, February 2, 1986.

Universities pay average of $355 a month: New York City Council member Ruth Messinger, in reference to New York University and Fordham University, cited in *Village Voice*, above.

00, 00   American Psychiatric Association and Reverend Tom Nees: *New Republic*, March 18, 1985.

Kim Hopper and Jill Hamberg: *The Making of America's Homeless*, cited above.

00 ff.   Interviews in Martinique Hotel, December 1985; follow-up interviews, 1986.

00   *Everything in Its Path; Destruction of Community in the Buffalo Creek Flood*, by Kai T. Erikson, New York: Simon and Schuster, 1976.

00   Rent of $1,900 monthly: See notes for pp. 00 and 00.

00   "There's no fire escape outside this window. . . ." There are fire escapes at the two stairwells of the Martinique Hotel; rooms facing the inside courtyard also have fire escapes. Many rooms in other locations do not.

00   No elevator working: After a certain hour in the evening, residents explain, all but one of the four elevators are turned off. See notes for p. 000.

00   *Wealth and Poverty*, by George Gilder, New York: Basic Books, 1981. Gilder appears aware of the danger that his words may be construed as racist. "The problem," he says, "is neither race nor matriarchy in any meaningful sense." He adds, however: "It is familial anarchy among the concentrated poor of the inner city, in which flamboyant and impulsive youths rather than responsible men provide the themes of aspiration. The result is that the male sexual rhythms tends to prevail. . . . 'If she wants me, *she'll* pay,' one young stud assured me. . . ."

00, 00   Rules on cohabitation: Interviews with HRA employees, May 1987.

00   "The father becomes extinct. . . ." The same pattern, according to

the U.S. Conference of Mayors (April 1985), may be seen throughout the nation: "In two thirds of cities surveyed, families must break up" in order to be given shelter. Officials from Denver, Nashville, and Portland (Oregon) cite the fact that "AFDC is not available to two-parent families" in those cities.

According to Dr. Larry Brown, of the Harvard School of Public Health, "in over half the states in the nation," children "don't qualify for AFDC, as long as the father's in the home. In other words, the father's forced to abandon the family. . . ." (*The Media and Children's Issues*, Children's Express, report of a symposium held November 25 and 26, 1985. Transcript available: Children's Express, 20 Charles Street, New York, NY 10014.)

"About half the states currently deny assistance to children in two-parent families." (*New York Times*, July 19, 1987.) A bill introduced in 1987 by Senator Daniel Moynihan is intended to remove this restriction.

Hotel Carter, a $12.40 and $16.70 fees for visitors: Interview with resident of Hotel Carter, January 1986. The *Village Voice* (April 1, 1986) states: "A $16.50 fee for each visitor is demanded from welfare tenants [at Carter] while no such pressure is placed on other guests." The Carter has sharply reduced the number of homeless families in residence over the past year.

The comparison between government support for a child living with her mother on AFDC and government support for a child in foster care requires some explanation. Research by Jacqueline Pitts of the Community Service Society of New York provides a breakdown of three categories of those placed in foster care, and the funds assigned to each, in the period in which this narrative takes place. (1) Children without special problems: $267 monthly for a child through the age of five; $315 monthly for a child six to eleven, $363 monthly for a child twelve or over. (2) Children with "special needs" (boarder babies and "Article 10" placements—a category that refers to children taken from their parents for "abuse or neglect"): $584 monthly, not variable by age. (3) "Exceptional" children (e.g., those with severe handicaps, including AIDS): $886 monthly, not variable by age. In addition, foster children in all three categories receive a clothing allowance based on age: $261 yearly through age of five; $365 yearly, six to eleven; $566, twelve through fifteen; $692, sixteen and older. These clothing allowances are lump-sum payments made at time of placement. The same sum is then paid each year in quarterly installments. Children under four also receive $40 monthly for diapers.

All foster children receive Medicaid through the agency that places them. Placement agencies sometimes offer certain extras: music lessons, summer camp, etc. No food stamps are allocated for the foster children, since the fees above include room and meals.

It is difficult to say which of the allocations identified with the three categories listed above is the proper one for a comparison to the support provided to a welfare child living with his or her parents. It will be come evident that allocations for all three categories are much higher than the funds available to children with their families.

A child of twelve, Angelina's age (see part one, chapter 4), receives $363 monthly, basic grant, in foster care; plus $566, lump-sum payment for clothes on placement; plus $141.50 quarterly thereafter (also for clothes); plus Medicaid; plus whatever extras the placement agency may offer. If we exempt the initial lump-sum clothing payment, which is granted one time only, it appears she would receive $363 monthly, plus $47.17 monthly for clothes ($566 divided by 12) for a total of *$410.17 per month*, plus Medicaid, and whatever "extras."

If a child of Angelina's age were to be taken from her mother against her mother's wish—not at a time of homelessness but simply while they lived in substandard conditions—the reason would likely be "abuse or neglect" and she would therefore qualify as a child with "special needs." In that case, the foster parents would receive $584 monthly plus the $47.17 monthly clothing allocation, for a total of *$631.17 monthly*, plus Medicaid and "extras."

What would this child receive if she remained with her mother—not in the Martinique Hotel, but in an ordinary AFDC situation? AFDC benefits do not vary by age. They do vary by numbers of people in a family. The increase in an AFDC grant grows progressively less for each child in a family. Thus, the allocation for a family of four persons, divided by four, yields a much smaller sum per person than the same calculation for a family of two persons. To make the comparison as conversative as possible, Ms. Pitts calculates the AFDC grant to a child in a family of two (e.g., mother a one child)—a calculation which will give the highest possible sum per child. The basic AFDC grant for such a family is $189.50 monthly for "living expenses" and "home energy allowance," plus $108 monthly for food stamps, plus $227 monthly for rent allowance: a total of $524.50. Divided by two, this yields *$262.25 monthly* for all food, housing, clothing, other costs; plus Medicaid.

To summarize: a nonhomeless 12-year-old in an AFDC family in New York City at the time this narrative takes place receives *$262.25* monthly and Medicaid. If she were in foster care under ordinary placement, she would receive *$410.17* monthly and Medicaid. If she were taken from her mother for "abuse or neglect," she would receive *$631.17* monthly and Medicaid.

As the AFDC calculation in this case is based on the smallest possible family, and therefore the largest possible allocation per child, it is conservative to state that a nonhomeless AFDC child without severe handicaps living in New York City with her mother receives, at most, 42 percent of what she would receive if taken from her mother for "abuse or neglect" and 64 percent of what she would receive if placed in foster care for other reasons. Although AFDC rent allowances will rise an average of 13 percent (about $35) in 1988, foster-care payments will rise a great deal more. A child of Angelina's age taken from her mother for "abuse or neglect" after 1987 will bring a foster parent $795.17 monthly, including clothes allowance. The disproportion, then, is going to be more extreme. The government's provision of much larger sums for foster care is prompted by the difficulty in attracting foster parents.

00   Family break-up described by Los Angeles attorney: *The Federal Response to the Homeless Crisis*, U.S. Congress, April 1985, cited above. See also "The Feminization of Homelessness: Homeless Families in Boston Shelters," by Dr. Ellen Bassuk, lecture given in Cambridge, Massachusetts, June 11, 1985.

In November 1985, the Legal Aid Society sued New York City, according to the *New York Times* (November 8, 1985), because it had "routinely placed hundreds of children in foster care because their parents were homeless or living in sub-standard housing." These are poor people, said Legal Aid, "who can't afford a decent place to live. . . . The city is taking their children away." The suit, according to the *Times*, described homeless parents who were "threatened with the loss of custody" of children when they asked for shelter. In general, it is not New York City policy to separate a family solely on the basis of a lack of housing. For further discussion, see part two, chapter 5, "Distancing Ourselves from Pain and Tears."

00, 00   A description of the difficulty of preparing meals under crowded hotel conditions is provided in *Struggling to Survive in a Welfare Hotel*, cited above.

Conditions for meal preparation in the Martinique Hotel have improved somewhat as a consequence of the willingness of the hotel to permit illicit use of broiler ovens, crock pots, and other cooking utensils in addition to hot plates; but residents place themselves at physical and legal risk by use of such utensils. Cooking in a hotel room in New York City is illegal; food budgets for homeless families in hotels, however, are determined on the assumption that such cooking will take place.

3. THREE GENERATIONS

00–00   Interviews in the Martinique Hotel, December 1985; follow-up interviews, 1986.

"I measure it: nine feet by twelve . . ." The *New York Daily News* (February 28, 1986) quotes the words of New York State Assembly member Clarence Norman: "At the Martinique, one adult and three children are living in an apartment no larger than ten by twelve feet. It was so small, we had to back in and back out."

00 ff.   Interview in Martinique Hotel, December 1985; follow-up interviews, 1986.

Details on the background and present welfare status of Mr. Allesandro's mother are unclear to me, as are the reasons for the city's initial refusal to place him with his mother and its apparent willingness to let her reside with him in the Martinique Hotel. Some biographical details, here as in most interviews, are disguised.

00   President Reagan: *New York Daily News*, May 22, 1986.

00   Edwin Meese: *New York Times*, December 10, 1983; also quoted in *Hardship in the Heartland*, cited above.

Marian Wright Edelman: *Homelessness in America*, Community for Creative Non-violence, cited above.

Limestone caves and surplus food: *Sacramento Bee*, February 25, 1987.

"President Reagan illegally deferred $265 million that Congress appropriated for other programs in order to fund government pay raises, the General Accounting Office says. . . . On January 28, Reagan sent up a special program to Congress, announcing 26 deferrals. . . . The second and most controversial [deferral] involved $28 million for the transportation of food for the homeless." (*Washington Post, National Weekly Edition*, April 20, 1987.)

00   "Food-stamp benefits have been cut in half for welfare families living in New York City hotels under a recently implemented federal policy that counts hotel rent as part of the families' public assistance income." (*Newsday*, October 22, 1986.) The policy, in-

stituted by the U.S. Department of Agriculture, had been in effect for three years but its implementation had been resisted by New York State and City officials until August 1986. On November 7, 1986, the *New York Times* reported that local officials would make up for some of the cuts by an emergency increase in the $64-a-month restaurant allowance homeless families were receiving. By the spring of 1987, social workers told me that the food-stamp decrease had been equalized by the increase in the restaurant allowance.

4. RACHEL AND HER CHILDREN

00 *The Needs of Strangers: An Essay on Privacy, Solidarity, and the Politics of Being Human,* by Michael Ignatieff, New York: Penguin Books, 1984.

00 ff. Interview in Martinique Hotel, December 1985; follow-up interview, January 1986.

00 "$3,000 every month . . ." According to the Martinique Hotel rate chart, a family of five persons in two rooms pays $2,584 for a 31-day month. Without taxes, the rent becomes $2,203. It is possible that Erica is in error, that my notes are in error, or that the rental cost is capriciously determined.

00 Congregate shelter on Forbell Street in Brooklyn: Between 90 and 100 families sleep in one large divided room. (Telephone interview with shelter personnel, July 1987; CIS "Monthly Report," October 1986, June 1987.)

   "I was forced to sign a paper. . . ." I believe she is in error. The prohibition on cooking is shown to residents in writing upon arrival at the Martinique. No other resident has spoken of signing such a statement.

00 Reference to mail delay in receipt of welfare check: At time of interview, her case had not yet been shifted to the computerized system that enables welfare clients to obtain their benefits from cash-machines.

5. THE BIG STREET

00 *The Road Not Taken, A Selection of Robert Frost's Poems,* ed. by Louis Untermeyer, New York: Holt, Rinehart and Winston, 1971.

00 ff. Interview in Martinique Hotel, January 1986.

00 Stephen has no subway token to get to school: Homeless families in welfare hotels, according to Kim Hopper, receive a school transportation allowance for each child who is not transported by a

school bus. Rachel's benefits were often cut, however; she may also have used transportation funds for food or other needs, or may have misused these funds.

PART TWO

00   Epigraph: *American Notes: A Journey,* by Charles Dickens, New York: Fromm International Publishing Corporation, 1985.

1. CONCEALMENT

00   Child poverty rate, decline in federal support, cancellation of White House Conference on Children: Children's Express Symposium, November 1985, cited above. See especially: Judith Weitz, Children's Defense Fund, quoted in symposium transcript. "On average," according to the *New York Times* (July 30, 1987), "the inflation-adjusted value of welfare payments has fallen 35 percent since 1970."

Housing discrimination against children: *New York Times,* Editorial, June 2, 1986. See also *Youth Law News,* March/April 1987.

00 ff.   *New England Journal of Medicine,* Vol. 313, No. 1, July 4, 1985. "Relentless efforts" to reduce health services to "low-income persons . . ." Specific reference is to Medicaid.

According to the *Boston Globe* (February 8, 1987), "Boston's infant mortality rate rose to 15.5 deaths per 1,000 live births in 1985 from 11.8 in 1984, said [Mayor Ray Flynn's] adviser on human services." In a press release of January 2, 1986, Mayor Flynn, chairman of the U.S. Conference of Mayors' Task Force on Hunger and Homelessness, stated: "When it comes to poverty in America, those Americans most asked to bear the brunt of the federal deficit reduction effort are women and children." See also *Women and Children Last,* by Ruth Sidel, New York: Viking Penguin, 1986.

"The cumulative effect of legislative changes enacted in 1981 will amount to a reduction of . . . $5.2 billion from child nutrition programs from 1982 to 1985 (Congressional Budget Office, 1983.)" Cited in *The Making of America's Homeless,* above.

00   Dr. Ellen Sassuk: "The overall depression scores were higher than [for] those who were comparably poor and those registered in a psychiatric clinic." (Lecture of June 11, 1985, cited above.)

00, 00   Information on New York's Family Court, "status offenders," and costs of placement: "The Court of Tears and Misery: Inside New York City's Family Court," by Jody Adams Weisbrod and Bruce Cory, Vera Institute, New York, 1985, unpublished manuscript distributed at Tarrytown conference, December 1985; *Trends: A*

Statistical Bulletin on the Status of Children and Families in New York State, New York State Council on Children and Families, Vol. 1, No. 3, November 1983; telephone interviews with New York University Law School professor Martin Guggenheim, May 1987. "The more secure or extreme environments cost, easily, $80,000," according to Professor Guggenheim. John Billenson, Department of Juvenile Justice, New York City, corroborates Mr. Guggenheim's estimate of $25,000 to $50,000. He believes the $80,000 figures would represent an infrequent maximum for secure detention. (Telephone interview, August 1987.)

Placement of homeless children in state custody: *New York Times*, November 8, 1985; *Safety Network*, December 1985.

000 Cost per adult prison inmate, New York City: The New York State Commissioner of Corrections cited the figure of $113 a day—$41,245 if projected for a year—in the *New York Times*, April 26, 1987.

000 Letter from women in Martinique describes death of guard: February 16, 1987. Such incidents are reported often in the press. See, for example, "Sleep of the Just for Welfare Girl," column by Jimmy Breslin, *New York Daily News*, February 15, 1987.

The victims of these altercations are less often guards than residents: "A resident of a welfare hotel was stabbed to death yesterday. . . . A guard at the hotel was charged with the murder. The victim's ten-year-old son was also injured. . . ." The boy, "stabbed in the chest," is "at Bellevue Hospital with a collapsed lung. The police were called after the boy had stumbled, bleeding and dazed, to the lobby." (*New York Times*, January 15, 1987.)

000 New York prison population approaching 15,000: The *New York Times* (March 25, 1987) estimated the city's current jail population at "about 14,700." The figure was expected to reach 16,000 by autumn 1987(*New York Times*, April 25, 1987.)

Converted ferry boat used as prison: *New York Times*, April 25, 1987. Prison space is so scarce in New York that the head of the state's prison system now contemplates the purchase of "a decommissioned British troop barge," formerly used in the Falkland Islands, for use as a "floating prison." (*New York Times*, June 5, 1987.)

Plans for new prison and reaction of Staten Island borough president: *New York Times*, March 25, 1987.

000, 000 "The Mugger and His Genes," review by Mayor Edward Koch of *Crime and Human Nature* by James Q. Wilson and Richard Herrnstein, in *Policy Review*, winter 1986. Excerpt from review:

"Through their painstaking and comprehensive analysis of a massive amount of scientific research conducted within the past ten years, Wilson and Herrnstein effectively destroy the shibboleth that poverty causes crime. This notion has been used to justify a list of rapes and broken heads in the past. The authors demonstrate that 'as income rises so does crime,' and that 'chronically criminal biological parents are likely to produce criminal sons,' irrespective of economic conditions."

000, 000   Information on P.S. 64 in New York City: "New York's Homeless Children: In the System's Clutches," a long and very powerful reportage by Suzanne Daley, *New York Times*, Febaruary 3, 1987. See also "Strangers in Their Own Schools," Editorial, *Newsday*, March 24, 1986.

000   New York Board of Education, lack of information on homeless children: *New York Times*, February 3, 1987.

           "One-room schoolhouse" in barracks shelters: *New York Times*, December 3, 1985.

000–000   Long commutes for homeless children in Westchester County: *New York Times*, November 2, 1986.

           Ten-year-old commutes to school in Yonkers 60 miles twice a day: *New York Times*, April 23, 1987.

           Motels in other counties offer cheaper rooms: *Reporter Dispatch* (Gannett Westchester Newspapers), May 30, 1987.

           "Is there a reason she must ride to Yonkers every day?" A state law, according to the *New York Times* (July 19, 1987) mandates that "children must return to their former school district in [Westchester] County to attend school." Half the transportation cost, the *Times* reports, is paid with federal funds.

000   On weekends, homeless families in New York City compete for space with prostitutes: *Perchance to Sleep: Homeless Children Without Shelter in New York City*, National Coalition for the Homeless, December 1984. Certain hotels in New York City, termed "hot-sheet hotels" because they rent rooms by the hour to prostitutes, are also used to house homeless families when there are no other options, according to Kim Hopper.

000, 000   Increase of 500 percent in families seeking shelter in Washington, D.C., data on the Annex, city's reaction: *Washington Post*, January 8, 9, 24, 1987.

000   The Pitts Hotel: *New Republic*, March 18, 1985.

000   U.S. Congressmen Ted Weiss: *Time*, October 15, 1984.

New York City's high school drop-out rate is placed by New York City Council member Andrew Stein at "40 percent overall, 70 percent among minority groups." ("Children of Poverty," *New York Times Magazine,* June 8, 1986.) The latter are statistically the poorest children in New York City. According to the Urban League, "72 percent of black children do not complete high school in New York City." (*Status of Black New York Report,* New York Urban League, 1984.) Another *New York Times* report (February 26, 1987) places the city-wide drop-out rate, between ninth and twelfth grades, at 54 percent: considerably higher than official figures indicate.

Homeless children out of school: "In Los Angeles, 'regarding school attendance, the Travelers Aid study determined that, of the children in their study old enough to attend school, 43 percent were not currently attending.' " U.S. Conference of Mayors, April 1987.

000   "Concealment is apparently important. . . ." Concealment takes place on a national scale also. When the United Nations proclaimed 1987 "The Year of Shelter for the Homeless," it prepared a film on homeless people in Brazil, Sri Lanka and New York City. The U.S. Mission to the U.N. intervened. In the words of a former U.S. diplomat, "We just gave them what we thought was political advice for their own good." The political advice hinted that the U.S. Congress, which was currently withholding $110 million owed the U.N. for 1986, might find fault with the film because it did not emphasize what the diplomat termed "the individual-rights element"—i.e., "the fact that these are people who in some cases wish to stay on the streets. . . ." (*The Progressive,* March 1987.)

2. STEREOTYPES

000 ff.   Interviews in Martinique Hotel, December 1985; follow-up interviews, 1986.

Disguise of persons in this book is proportionate to the degree of jeopardy in which they stand or in which their words may place them. Kim's words and certain other factors leave her vulnerable to retaliation. Her background, if accurately described, would identify her readily. Biographical data therefore is more heavily disguised in this case than in any other chapter.

000   Tuberculosis in homeless shelters: According to the *New York Times* (March 30, 1987), tuberculosis "is a rapidly growing problem among the homeless in New York City," but is found "almost entirely among men. . . ."

000   Number of vacant city-owned units in New York and estimates for costs of rehabilitation: New York City Council, study completed November 1986, published January 1987, cited above; former HRA Commissioner James P. Dumpson, in study commissioned by David Dinkins, 1987, cited above; interviews with Robert Hayes and others at National Coalition for the Homeless, 1987; *Village Voice*, April 1, 1986; *Newsday*, November 28, 1986; *New York Times*, January 21, 1987; *New York Post*, April 23, 1987. See also *Room to Spare But Nowhere to Go*, a report by New York City Comptroller Harrison J. Goldin, April 23, 1987.

"The cost of rehabilitating a unit varies. The first apartment viewed by [Committee members] cost over $30,000 to renovate, yet other apartments on the tour cost as little as $4,500 to renovate. 'Gut' rehabilitation can cost from $20,000 to $30,000. . . ." (City Council.)

"Rehabilitation costs on city-owned property have risen to more than $30,000 a unit and they continue to rise." (*New York Times*, January 21, 1987.)

"The city . . . cites the $50,000 to $60,000 rehab cost per unit as prohibitively expensive." (*Village Voice*, April 1, 1986.)

In a 145-page report (April 23, 1987), City Comptroller Harrison Goldin claimed the city could house 4,000 homeless families in vacant units of partially unoccupied city-owned buldings within a year or 18 months. Of these 4,000 units, he noted, over 1,700 could be readied for occupancy at a cost of "perhaps $14 to $15 million" —at most, $9,000 each. The issue has become heavily politicized, but it appears to be agreed that thousands of units could have been made habitable up to 1987 for $30,000 or less; almost exactly what is paid each year to house a family of five persons at the Martinique Hotel. (Family of five in two rooms at the Martinique pays $27,000 to $31,000 per year, depending on whether taxes are subtracted after first three months.)

000, 000   "*No* heat and *no* hot water" at the Brooklyn Arms: According to the city council study, "Heat and hot water can be scarce, particularly in the winter."

Welfare workers fearful to visit rooms: "The CIS workers try to contact residents once every month, but cannot visit residents in their rooms, due to an HRA determination that it is too dangerous. . . ." (City Council.)

The Brooklyn Arms Hotel, according to the *New York Daily News* (July 14, 1986), is "owned by Bertram Fields" and "leased to independent operators." William Bastone of the *Village Voice* states that it is leased from Mr. Fields by Morris Horn and his partners.

Alleged involvement of guards in drug trade at Brooklyn Arms: *New York Daily News*, July 23, 1986.

Fire, garbage, alleged lack of fire alarm, etc., at Brooklyn Arms: *New York Daily News*, July 12, 1986.

Political contributions by operators of Brooklyn Arms: *New York Daily News*, July 15, 1986.

Newsday (November 7, 1986) reports that, prior to the fire, three people had died in elevator accidents in the hotel and that the hotel had "about 500 housing code violations" at the time of the fire.

Parents charged with endangerment, arrested and jailed prior to burial of children: *New York Daily News*, July 14 and 18, 1986.

Hotel not criticized by city: "Officials said there was no indication that neglect by the landlord had led to the fire." (*New York Times*, July 13, 1986.)

Burial funds increased: "The city is considering raising the funeral benefits it provides welfare recipients, Mayor Koch said yesterday after meeting with a Brooklyn minister in connection with the deaths of four young children in a welfare hotel." (*New York Daily News*, July 15, 1986.) "City officials yesterday moved up by nine months the effective date of higher burial benefits authorized for welfare recipients. . . . The move, prompted by the deaths of four children in a Brooklyn welfare hotel, will immediately increase burial benefits from $250 to $900." (*Newsday*, July 18, 1986.)

In June of 1987, the Brooklyn Arms was again the subject of brief news attention. Senator Daniel Moynihan, denouncing conditions in New York's welfare hotels as "a scandal, an outrage, an ulcer," according to the *New York Times* (June 2, 1987), "singled out one hotel in Brooklyn, the Brooklyn Arms, as filthy and as a fire hazard. . . . 'It is a place where—unless God spares them—children are going to die.' "

Details on Allerton Hotel: New York City Council.

Details on Bayview Hotel: "A convicted loan shark who owes the city more than $40,000 in back taxes admits to pulling down $600,000-a-year in profits from housing the homeless in the city's most expensive welfare hotel." The figure of $100 per night is also cited. (*New York Daily News*, December 8, 1985.)

Holland Hotel: See part three, chapter 2, "The Long March."

City Council on deterrence policy: study cited above.

Mayor Koch: *New York Times,* December 17, 1985; *New York Daily News,* December 8, 1985.

000   Congressional testimony of ten-year-old boy and the reaction of Mayor Koch: *Newsday,* March 20, 1986; *New York Daily News,* March 17, 18, 19, 23, and April 5, 1986.

Newsday, March 20, 1986: "In airing his feelings on the subject . . ., the mayor said that the benefit package received by a family of six—such as [boy's name deleted]—is valued at a total of $20,400 a year. He included in that package the family's government-paid allowance [for potential apartment rental] and potential Medicaid payments. 'Over 75,000 city employees earn less than $20,000,' the mayor wrote. 'Office aides make $14,000 a year; health aides $13,600. And they all work for a living. I wonder why they bother.' "

New York Daily News, March 19, 1986: "In Albany yesterday to lobby for state aid, Koch brushed aside a suggestion from a welfare mother that he live on welfare before concluding that homeless families get enough help. 'Oh please, you live on it,' Koch replied when asked about the suggestion. . . . Asked if $6 a day is enough to feed a child, Koch said, 'You bet it is.' "

000   George Orwell quotes one of his own characters in a semi-fictional story "The Spike," published in *Adelphi,* March 1931; later included in *Down and Out in Paris and London,* San Diego: Harcourt Brace Jovanovich, 1961.

000   "As to conditions at the hotels . . ." Statement of Harvey Robbins, acting commissioner of the HRA, is included in a letter of September 18, 1986, to New York City Council member Abraham Gerges, printed in full in city council study.

Details about concealment of cooking utensils and preannounced inspections: Many residents and city employees familiar with the Martinique Hotel confirm this.

Physical conditions in the Martinique: "The State Court of Appeals, in a unanimous decision," the *New York Times* reports (June 5, 1987), "held that the emergency housing system of New York City must provide and enforce minimum standards of decency for homeless families." While the court did not determine whether the city met such standards, Legal Aid Society attorney Steven Banks observed that "almost everyone in the system is living in conditions that violate these standards." The lead plaintiff in the suit "was placed with her children in the Martinique Hotel near Herald Square." According to court documents, she "found a roach-infested room with a urine-soaked mattress and filthy sheets."

000–000   "other rights go by the board. . ." There is no consistent prohibition on an admission of journalists. It is, however, "an accepted understanding," according to a city employee, that, if a tenant speaks ill of the hotel to a reporter, a way will be found "to get that person out." Since most residents are already breaking several rules (the official prohibitions on cooking or cohabitation with an unregistered person, for example), justification for eviction need not make reference to communication with the press.

Suit to regain the franchise for homeless people: The case, brought shortly before the 1984 presidential election, was won in 1985. Plaintiffs were represented by Robert Hayes and the law firm of Davis Polk and Wardwell. Federal District Judge Mary Johnson Lowe enjoined the city from barring the homeless from the right to vote. The mayor instructed his corporation counsel to appeal. Some months later, the city quietly gave in. (*Safety Network*, January 1986.)

Banned newsletter: *Martinique Monitor*, November 1985. A nonresident familiar with the Martinique Hotel states that "all copies" were removed from residents' mailboxes, either by hotel management or by city officials.

Refrigerators, dispute with hotel management, etc.: Interviews with several residents and others familiar with the Martinique Hotel confirm all details except the estimated price of "less than $200," which is Kim's supposition and seems accurate. The rate chart of the Martinique Hotel lists "$1.08" nightly for "FRIDGE."

Details concerning payment of hotel rent: Kim's words on issuing of checks are confirmed by HRA employees.

000   No day care: A day care program was finally begun in June of 1987. According to a recent visitor, half the ballroom has been walled off to create a preschool area with a new kitchen and new floor. I am told that the hotel cooperated in this effort.

3. THE PENALTIES OF FAILURE

000   *Everything in Its Path*, by Kai Erikson, cited above.

Interviews in Martinique Hotel, 1986.

000   Lead paint in Martinique Hotel: New York City Council, above. I am told that there has been some abatement since. A new danger, however, was discovered in the spring of 1985. According to the *New York Daily News* (June 18, 1987), "A mountain of cancer-causing asbestos—illegally packed in open containers—was un-

covered yesterday in the Martinique Hotel . . . Dangerous asbes-tos-coated pipes were also found in the hotel's lobby and on the sidewalk—within easy reach of the welfare hotel's 1,500 children . . . Sanitation [Department] spokesman Vito Turso said that his office was considering criminal action against the hotel 'for clearly violating the law.' " See also *New York Times*, June 19, 1987.

Danger of exposed metal frames: After the accident described later in this chapter, Kim said: "Now the hotel will get rid of these beds." In fact, as early as December 1985, parents who protested vigorously enough had managed to convince the management to replace these metal frames by wooden bunk beds. Subsequently, all or most such metal beds have been replaced.

000   "Churning . . ." *The Making of America's Homeless*, cited above; *New York Times*, April 24, 1987. An eloquent and detailed de-scription of "churning" by a welfare recipient is included in *Chil-dren's Express Symposium*, cited above.

Let Us Now Praise Famous Men, by James Agee and Walker Evans, Boston: Houghton Mifflin, 1941.

"Spanish is her first language." Her mother, however, speaks En-glish with proficiency. A resident who knows her tells me that she is learning disabled.

000   Filty carpets: Carpets in the hotel have since been replaced by linoleum or tiles.

000   Kai Erikson, see above.

000   Rent notice from Martinique Hotel: These notices now read: "Your rent is due. Please go to your center."

Restaurant allowance and food-stamp allocation for a homeless mother with four children in January 1986: Laura's information confirmed by HRA employees. The cited restaurant allowance was for half the month, food stamps for the full month.

000   Lead poison: See City Council, as cited in part one, chapter 1, "A Mood of Resignation," p. 00.

000   "This is true. I seen it . . ." In *Struggling to Survive in a Welfare Hotel* (cited above), the Community Service Society says this: "Hotel staff ask for sexual favors from women in exchange for provision of services." Reference is specifically to Martinique Hotel.

000     $1,500 rent for two weeks: According to Martinique Hotel rate chart, rent with tax for five persons in two rooms should be $2,584 for a 31-day month, or about $1,290 for each semi-monthly check.

Without taxes, each of these checks should be about $1,100.

000   *Uprooted Children*, by Robert Coles, cited above.

000   Average length of stay: See notes for p. 00 of "Overview."

4. THE ROAD TO POTTER'S FIELD

000 ff.   Interviews at Henry Street Settlement's Urban Family Center, Baruch Place, New York City, January 1986; follow-up interviews in later months.

000   Holly's effort to obtain G.E.D., her mother's eviction, eight months in two Manhattan welfare hotels, residence at Holland, experience at Clemente: Robert Hayes believes the two hotels in which Holly lived prior to the Holland were the Latham and the Carter. Note that I do not distinguish, in this book, between "shelters" and "hotels." I have no way to corroborate the other information she supplies on these matters nor her previous statements on her childhood in foster care, her education and early work experience. Data compiled by the Coalition for the Homeless and some of my later conversations with Holly indicate that her mother had lived for some time in homeless shelters and that she was in the Martinique while Holly lived there. Certain details on Holly's background, and on David's, are disguised to guard their privacy.

000 ff.   Date of child's birth, life, sickness and death are contained in a press release and chronology released by the HRA on December 19, 1985. Additional data is provided in a confidential 33-page chronology compiled by David Beseda and Mark Bullock of the Coalition for the Homeless, made available to me with Holly's permission by Robert Hayes. See also "Blind and Deaf Infant's Short Life on the Rolls of New York's Homeless," *New York Times*, December 20, 1985; *New York Daily News*, November 27, December 18 and 20, 1985.

000   Incubator, oxygen, IV, Holly's need to solicit blood donations: I have no corroboration for these statements.

"Seizure disorder . . ." *New York Times*, December 20, 1985.

000   Eviction from Mayfair: The HRA and Coalition for the Homeless both refer to a physical quarrel involving David and/or the father of Holly's older children. It appears that police were called. Holly tells me that an employee of the Mayfair had made sexual advances to her, that he saw David's presence as an obstacle, and that this was the immediate reason for her eviction.

000, 000   "I stayed there with him in the hospital . . ." The HRA reports that Benjamin was readmitted to the hospital on March 27 and released on May 1. During this period, according to the HRA, Holly received at least four one-night placements, spent some nights with her mother, and an unspecified amount of time on Long Island. The Coalition for the Homeless indicates that, wearied by short-term placements, she stayed for a time with David's mother. It appears that she could not have stayed with Benjamin for the entire five-week period. She was there, it seems, during the final weeks. Records indicate that a physician contacted her on April 18 to tell her of the need for surgery. The Coalition for the Homeless reports that she went to the hospital immediately.

The coalition notes that Holly was not a good manager of her affairs, that she seems to have resisted acceptance of the extreme seriousness of Benjamin's illness, and may even have seen his condition as a means by which to improve her family's opportunity to be granted permanent housing. But the coalition also notes that Holly was "religious" in keeping clinic appointments for Benjamin, was with him at the hospital as much as possible in view of the difficult logistics with which she was faced, and was regarded by many observers as an affectionate mother.

Letter from hospital: See notes for p. 000.

000   "I told my social worker . . ." It is unclear if she means her Income Maintenance (welfare) worker or a social worker at Beth Israel.

000   Benjamin released from hospital: Records indicate the hour was 5:30 P.M.

"It was rainin' as a matter of fact. Not a warm night . . ." On May 1, 1985, the evening was cool and cloudy but there was no rain. The next two days, May 2 and 3, however, were unseasonably cold. It rained on both days. On May 6, the last night before Holly brought her son back to the hospital, the weather in New York was cool and it was raining.

"I had that letter . . ." The letter from Benjamin's doctor (New York Times, December 20, 1985) asked that he be given "suitable housing to support his condition."

"For seven days . . ." As her later words make clear, she was not on the street all seven days.

"I would sit from nine to five, the welfare center . . . and from five to eight o'clock at EAU." The Brooklyn Emergency Assistant Unit is open from 4:00 P.M. to 8:00 A.M., seven days a week. See p. 000 for details on Holly's placements during this week. HRA records do not indicate that she was at her welfare office during this time but they confirm that she was repeatedly at the EAU. I believe she is referring here to the general procedure she had undergone for many months, not to these specific days. According to Scott Rosenberg (Legal Aid Society), the procedure she describes, including "a referral" by the I.M. center to an EAU, is not unusual.

000, 000   "A nice hotel in Queens . . ." On May 1 and 2, according to the HRA, she was placed at the Turf Club Hotel in Queens. On the next night (May 3), the HRA reports that she was sent to the Martinique Hotel but returned with her children to the EAU on May 4 at 4:30 P.M., saying she had been denied a room by the Martinique. After a wait of ten hours and 15 minutes, she was sent with her children to the Hotel Carter at 2:45 A.M. (morning of May 5) but returned after midnight (12:50 A.M. of May 6), terming the Carter "unlivable." The HRA reports it had "no vacancies available" that night and that Holly and Benjamin remained at the EAU until 9:50 A.M. on May 6. The following evening, Benjamin was readmitted to Beth Israel for the final time. See also notes for pp. 000, 000.

000   "So we was goin' in the cold and rain. . . ." See notes for p. 000.

000   "The baby looks like it is dyin'. . . ." It's unclear whether Holly is attributing these words to a welfare worker at her Income Maintenance Center or at the EAU. According to the Coalition for the Homeless, Holly spent May 6 at her welfare center and went to the Brooklyn EAU at night. At 3:00 A.M. on May 7, the coalition states, David left the EAU to take Benjamin to Beth Israel. The HRA places Benjamin's admission to the hospital much earlier that night, at 5:15 P.M.

000   Holly beaten by father of her other children: See notes for p. 000.

000, 000   HRA records indicate that Holly was offered placement at the highly reputable Red Cross Family Center on the night of May 6 but refused this. The Coalition for the Homeless, citing Legal Aid Society records, confirms this. Holly tells me that she asked, when told of this placement, whether there was someone there who could care for Benjamin when she left to go to welfare or the store. (She says she asked specifically whether there was a nurse or doctor present.) When she was told that she could leave her children with one of the other women in the shelter, she became alarmed. It seemed unsafe to her, she said, and this is why she wanted David with her. In retrospect it is easy enough to view this as poor judgment. Any shelter, but especially that offered by the Red Cross, would have been safer for Benjamin than the itinerant existence that she had been leading. The HRA states that, at midnight, it placed her at the Turf and that, the next night—after Benjamin had been readmitted to Beth Israel—it found her a week's placement at a hotel called the Le Marquis. One week later, the HRA reports, it offered to send her to the Clemente shelter, which she refused, and finally placed her at the Carter. Whatever the real reason for Holly's refusal to accept the offer of the Red Cross shelter, it is important to note that truly safe and reputable shelter was offered to her only at the intervention of the Legal Aid Society. It is remarkable that the city would have tried—twice in the preceding week—to place a child in Benjamin's condition in places like the Martinique and Carter. After months of exposure to dangerous conditions in so many unsafe shelters, it is believable that Holly no longer had sufficient faith in any authority figures (even those at Legal Aid) to recognize a good place for her child when it finally was made available.

The behavior of the HRA throughout these months seems characterized, not by a lack of kindness, but by asphyxiating chaos. The HRA commissioner later observed that, during Benjamin's entire life, "there was never a complaint filed" with the proper agency. The city did, in one respect, accept responsibility. The HRA commissioner conceded that "the primary weakness illustrated by this tragic story" was a "lack of concentrated and focused services." His assistant, however, told the *New York Times* that, based on her review of the case, "everyone did his or her job conscientiously." Both people, according to the *Times*, "conceded a need for improvements. . . ." (HRA report and *New York Times*, December 20, 1985.)

000   The Hotel Carter: See notes for pp. 000, 000. Benjamin's life seems to have been cursed from start to end by three of the best known and most hated shelters in New York in 1984 and 1985. Conceived at the Holland, born while his mother lived at the Martinique, he lived out his last days while she struggled to survive conditions in the Carter. For documentation on the Carter, see part three, chapter 1, " The Long March."

000   "Evicted from the Carter . . ." The Coalition for the Homeless indicates that Holly was still living at the Carter and was telephoned there by the hospital, at the time that Benjamin died. Other than on this detail, the report assembled by the coalition seems to support the sequence she describes. It adds that she was next assigned (May 29) to the Martinique but did not go there. By June 1, she was living in the Hamilton Place Hotel.

000   Benjamin's death: The HRA says it was told by the hospital that the cause was "brain infection" or "infection of the shunt," but cites Holly's statement that she had been told the baby choked to death. The Coalition for the Homeless says that Benjamin died at 6:55 A.M. on May 21, 1985.

000, 000   "Welfare gave $250 . . ." Death benefits have since been raised to $900. (See Appendix A, "Economies of Scale."

HRA employee called the Coalition for the Homeless, requesting funds for burial: confirmed by Robert Hayes and David Beseda.

Holly still homeless: According to the Coalition for the Homeless, she had been placed at the Hamilton Hotel by the time of Benjamin's funeral.

"Some place on an island . . ." See Appendix A, "Economies of Scale."

Holly's reference to a nervous breakdown: Coalition records suggest a suicide attempt shortly after Benjamin's burial.

5. DISTANCING OURSELVES FROM PAIN AND TEARS

000   Fears shared with psychologist: *New York Times*, May 12, 1986. See also "The 39th Witness," by A. M. Rosenthal, *New York Times*, February 12, 1987.

"Some 800 families . . ." *A Crying Shame: Official Abuse and Neglect of Homeless Infants*, National Coalition for the Homeless, New York, November 1985.

000, 000   Letter of Carol Bellamy: cited in *A Crying Shame*.

000   Mothers and children sleeping in city welfare offices: *New York Times*, November 20, 1984, December 12 and 16, 1985; *New York Daily News*, March 14, 1986.

On November 20, 1984, the *New York Times* stated: "Some homeless families, mostly mothers and young children, have been sleeping on chairs, counters and floors of the city's emergency welfare offices." Reacting to an earlier *Times* report to the same effect, the mayor said: "This woman is sitting on a chair or on a floor. It is not because we didn't offer her a bed. We provide a shelter for every single person who knocks on our door." On the same day, the HRA reported that, in the previous eleven weeks, it had been unable to give shelter to 153 families.

In the subsequent year (1985), the city later reported, about 2,000 children slept in welfare offices during a three-month period because of a lack of shelter space for families. (*New York Daily News*, May 14, 1986.)

Legal Aid Suit: *New York Times*, September 7, 1986.

000   Thomas J. Main, op/ed essay, *New York Times*, November 27, 1986. Research is not Mr. Main's only suggestion. "But what may

we do positively," he asks, "to solve the homeless families problem?" He answers by restating his initial point: "The sad fact is that there is probably no short-term answer." In his closing words he concedes the need for low-income housing—a need, however, which is now denied its urgency.

000   William Raspberry: *Washington Post*, January 9, 1987.

000   Andrew Stein: op/ed essay, *New York Times*, January 17, 1987.

000   David Dinkins: cited above.

Comparative figures on subsidized housing construction: U.S. Senator John Kerry, newsletter to constituents, February 1987.

Housing allocations compared to defense expenditures: *The Faces of Homelessness*, by Hope and Young, cited above.

Andrew Stein: "Children of Poverty," *New York Times Magazine*, June 8, 1986.

000   Herbert Spencer is quoted in *Blaming the Victim*, by William Ryan, New York: Pantheon Books, 1971.

30-month wait to use public van: See notes for "Overview."

000, 000   *Losing Ground: American Social Policy, 1950–1980*, by Charles Murray, New York: Basic Books, 1984; *Commentary*, May 1985. Murray proposes that the government might "commission advertising campaigns whose mission would be . . . to ruin the image of the single woman with a baby." He proposes the "stigma" might be "reinforced" by intensifying the unpleasantness of welfare procedures: "Instead of trying to reduce the rudeness of welfare workers and eliminating eligibility investigations . . ., such practices would be encouraged."

"The natural system . . ." Murray explains that by a "natural state" he means one which "produces very few children born into single-parent families." But the juxtaposition of his terms—"natural state," "natural system," "natural results"—resonates with the social Darwinism ("natural selection") of his nineteenth-century antecedents. It has been observed that Mr. Murray does not always ask that he be taken literally. It is his manner to set forth an idea, elaborate on it for a time, then step away as if he were not serious. Increasing public opprobrium for single women already on welfare, he concedes, "seems patently unfair." (He goes still further and concedes that it would be "contemptible.") Having thus distanced himself from his own suggestions, he adds that, no matter how frivolous they seem, "they represent just about the only strategies available." The *Commentary* essay in which most of these statements appear is titled: "Helping the Poor: A Few

Modest Proposals."

6. ABOUT PRAYER

000   Conversation in Boston, January 1986.

PART THREE

Epigraph: *The Making of America's Homeless,* cited above.

1. SEASONAL CONCERNS

000 ff.   Interview and author's observation at Church Street EAU: November 1986. The Emergency Assistance Unit on Church Street has since been closed and replaced by an EAU on Catherine Street.

000–000   Lead-paint problem, other complaints, and litigation re Catherine Street shelter: *New York Times,* December 14, 1985, March 8 and 11, May 9, 1986; *New York Daily News,* April 22, June 25, August 30, 1986.

Statement of Dr. Saundra Shepherd, pediatrician at Montefiore Hospital, and results of testing by independent agency: *New York Times,* March 11, 1986.

Covering lead-based paint with lead-free paint: The New York City Council (cited above) stated that the city "renovated the Shelter, but only painted over the lead paint. A City expert testified that to contain any lead poisoning the City would need to hire 38 workers to mop the floors constantly." Advocacy groups report that the implications of the term "abatement" (removal of dangers constituted by lead-based paint) have been much disputed in New York; the same dispute has prevailed for over 20 years in Boston. Real abatement, according to David Beseda (National Coalition for the Homeless), calls for stripping a wall down to its surface, or covering the original wall with sheetrock, prior to repainting.

Dr. Laurence Finberg, chairman of the Department of Pediatrics, State University of Health Science Center at Brooklyn, is cited from a letter of September 8, 1986: *New York Times,* September 25, 1986

000   "They let me stay there in some kind of office. . . ." See notes for pp. 000 and 000.

000   Handcuffs: I have no confirmation of this.

000   *Childhood and Society,* by Erik Erikson, New York: Norton, 1963.

000, 000   *New York Times,* January 10, 1987.

000, 000

Background information on lead-free area at Catherine Street and apparent illegality of placement: Scott Rosenberg, Legal Aid Society, Homeless Family Rights Project, telephone interview, June 1987; correspondence with Kim Hopper, June 1987.

2. THE LONG MARCH

000   *Everything in Its Path*, Kai Erikson, cited above.

000, 000   Priest in Wisconsin: *Homelessness in America*, Community for Creative Non-violence, cited above.

000–000   Interview in Hotel Carter, January 1986; follow-up visit to Carter, November 1986.

                     Data on Hotel Carter: *New York Times*, December 29, 1985; "Sixty Minutes," CBS, February 2, 1986; *Village Voice*, April 1, 1986. Use of rear entrance by school children was discontinued in early 1986.

                     Senator Daniel Moynihan: "Sixty Minutes," above.

000 ff.   Interviews in Martinique Hotel and by telephone, November and December, 1986; follow-up interviews, 1987.

000–000   Waiting at welfare office during day, EAU at night: The EAUs do not open until late afternoon.

                     Woman at EAU given a "referral slip" to her welfare center: This procedure, according to Scott Rosenberg (Legal Aid Society), does take place, but very rarely.

                     Daughter's illness and number of days before family is placed in Martinique Hotel: Exact sequence remains unclear.

000   Data on Holland Hotel: *New York Times*, November 4, 23, 26, December 11, 1985; March 10, 1986; July 15, 1987.

                     "A kiddie park designed by Hogarth and Marquis de Sade . . ." See "Children in Sordid Sea," Editorial, *New York Times*, December 5, 1985.

                     Two categories of tenants at Holland, lack of water, etc.: Mrs. Andrews has repeated these details several times. David Beseda confirms her general portrayal of the Holland. According to the HRA, a Crisis Intervention center was first established at the Holland in November 1983; the winter of 1983–1984 seems to have marked the turning-point in the hotel's transition to a homeless shelter.

000   Rules on savings permitted or prohibited by welfare regulations: interviews with several residents and with HRA employees. According to Michael Hoyer, director of the Central Resources Sec-

tion, HRA, AFDC and General Assistance ("Home Relief") recipients in New York were allowed to save a maximum of $1,000 before it interferes with benefits. (Telephone interview, August 11, 1987.)

000   Increase of $8.75 in restaurant allowance in November 1986: This is the period in which New York had announced but not yet fully implemented plans to equalize food-stamp cuts. (See note for p. 000.) It is possible she means $8.75 for each person, rather than for her entire family.

Rent about $2,000 monthly: One of her rent receipts, apparently for half of January 1987, reads "$1,134.55"—which appears to indicate a monthly rent of $2,269.10. According to the rate chart of the Martinique Hotel, a four-member family pays $946.65 (including tax) for 15 days—or $1,956.41 for a 31-day month. Without tax, the monthly rent should be $1,676.48. Inconsistencies between rate chart and the rents residents claim to pay are common.

000   Reference to a single elevator with no light: "After 9:00 P.M.," Mrs. Andrews tells me, "the back elevators are turned off. Only one elevator in front is left in operation."

$1 billion cut in foot stamps and child-nutrition programs announced for 1987: *New York Times*, January 2 and 6, 1987.

29 families housed at Newark Hotel: *New York Times*, November 3, 1986.

HRA says situation is not critical: *New York Times*, November 3, 1986; January 27, 1987.

000   President Reagan: *Philadelphia Inquirer*, August 3, 1983 (first citation); speech in Bloomington, Michigan, February 8, 1982 (second citation), cited in *Homelessness in America*, Community for Creative Non-violence, above.

000, 000   Budget cuts: The *New Republic*, March 18, 1985. See also *Washington Post*, September 26, 1986.

000   David Stockman: *Homelessness in America*, above.

The Needs of Strangers, Michael Ignatieff, above.

000   Shelter guards in New York City are frequently untrained and their qualifications are checked only on a random basis. (*New York Daily News*, February 28, 1987.) See also "City Criticized for Way It Selects Shelter Guards," *New York Times*, November 1, 1986.

000   Charles Murray: *Commentary*, May 1985. Murray credits William F. Buckley with this suggestion.

3. UNTOUCHABLES

000   Michael Ignatieff's specific reference is to people in underdeveloped nations. (*The Needs of Strangers*, above.)

000   Newspapers substituted for diapers: *A Crying Shame*, cited above.

000 ff.   Interview: November 29, 1986.

000   "When you come in at night . . ." Similar procedures exist at Third Street Shelter and nearby Kenton Hotel in which Lazarus sleeps, according to Keith Summa, National Coalition for the Homeless. (Telephone interviews, June 1987.)

000   Job search, line, subway tokens: The regimen of life in the men's shelter is confirmed by Keith Summa, National Coalition for the Homeless.

000   Difficulty in obtaining welfare benefits if homeless and unsheltered: Robert Hayes, Kim Hopper, and others confirm this. In speaking of panhandlers, the *New York Times* (July 31, 1987) reports: "Most receive no public assistance, and cannot, unless they have an address where payments can be mailed." Those who have a shelter address, however, according to the *Times* (July 16, 1987), "receive no cash on the theory the shelters provide their basic needs." In practice, according to Keith Summa, it is difficult but possible for an unsheltered individual to obtain General Assistance (known as "Home Relief" in New York State) if he or she can obtain a post office box or provide a friend's address. In a place like the Third Street Shelter or Kenton Hotel, social workers help to expedite the application process. Sheltered individuals do receive some benefits and may soon receive more. A recent New York State Supreme Court ruling has established that homeless men and women in city shelters are entitled to Medicaid and cash welfare grants. (*New York Times*, July 31, 1987).

000, 000 Work program for homeless men, curfew at Kenton Hotel, etc.: confirmed by Keith Summa, Coalition for the Homeless, and by New York City Council, cited above. In *Hardship in the Heartland*, cited above, the Community Service Society of New York makes this observation: "Men and women in the city's pilot work program work 20 hours a week for which they are paid $12.50. Can anyone honestly argue that paying people 63 cents an hour for makework will transform the allegedly 'shiftless' into models of industry? When shorn of its rhetoric, it is plain that such a program does nothing to prepare people for gainful employment or self-determination. Rather, it would appear to perpetuate dependency because the only work it offers is the forced product of an artificial market. Further, by making labor mandatory but valuing it so meanly, it compounds the shame of those desperate enough to seek shelter in the first place. Thus shelters would revert to nineteenth-century workhouses, and the poor would be penalized for their poverty."

30 days before case can be reopened: HRA employees and Robert Hayes confirm this. See also *New York Times,* May 14, 1987.

Prohibition on savings: The limit is $1,000. See note for p. 000.

000   Sleeping in the active subway tunnels: *Newsday,* January 29, 1987.

St. Patrick's Cathedral, homeless man driven from "outstretched arms of Jesus . . ." *New York Times,* November 17, 1986.

000   Man dies in trash compactor in Chicago: *The Faces of Homelessness,* by Hope and Young, above.

000, 000   Driving the homeless from Grand Central Station: Virtually all details, including death of elderly woman Christmas morning, 1985, are contained in the New York City Council study; other details confirmed by George McDonald, America's Homeless Political Action Committee, New York City, in interviews November 1986 and June 1987, and by the author in several visits during November and December 1986. Metro North police, not New York City police, have responsibility for Grand Central Station.

000, 000   Pennsylvania Station, women driven from bathroom: New York City Council.

Amtrak directives: The document from which these words are cited is an Amtrak "interoffice memo" signed by S.L. Nickerson and dated June 13, 1985. The memo concludes: "Immediate removal on a continuous basis . . . will eventually produce the desired effect." The *New York Times* (November 29, 1986) reports another memo containing similar instructions, issued August 29, 1986, and describes the legal action taken by the American Federation of Railroad Police to resist such orders. Television station WCBS, on November 29, 1986, cited by name an Amtrak official who asked: "Can't we get rid of this trash?"

000   Laramie, Wyoming: *The Faces of Homelessness,* cited above. Columbus, Ohio: *Columbus Dispatch,* November 16, 1986, and *Lancaster Eagle-Gazette,* November 14, 1986. Stabbing in California took place in Santa Barbara: *Time,* March 31, 1986.

000, 000   Man set ablaze in Chicago: *Wall Street Journal,* December 1, 1986. The man survived, according to the *Journal,* "because the flames didn't eat through his many layers of clothing."

000   German shepherds in Tucson, election platform of mayor of Tucson, words of anti-homeless organizer in Phoenix: *Newsweek*, January 2, 1984. Measures to prevent homeless people from sleeping in public: *New York Times*, March 31, 1986; *Time*, March 31, 1986; *USA/Today*, August 20, 1986; *Times-Picayune/States Item*, May 13, 1986. Bleach on discarded food in Santa Barbara: *Time*, March 31, 1986. "Drip lines" in Portland, Oregon: These were described to me by Michael Stoops and Beverly Curtis (Burnside Community Council) in October 1986. Fort Lauderdale: *Hardship in the Heartland; The Search for Shelter; The Faces of Homelessness*. (All cited above).

000   Columbia Point: *Boston Globe*, March 19, 1986; June 5, 12, 26, 1987. Additional information on Columbia Point: John Madden, former president of Dorchester Historical Society. (Telephone interview, August 12, 1987.)

In Los Angeles, in 1987, the county commissioner proposed the lease or purchase of a barge dating from World War II to house 400 homeless people. The barge, docked in Puget Sound, was finally rejected for fiscal and other reasons. (*Washington Post*, August 21, 1987.)

000   "I just can't accommodate them. . . ." *New York Times*, September 18, 1986.

New York City's homeless "dumped" in Newark: *New York Times*, October 1, 1986.

Jails, shelters, incinerators: *New York Times*, April 23 and 27, 1987.

000   Epistle of Paul to the Hebrews: 13, 2.

Burial of poor children: See Appendix A, "Economies of Scale."

000   Boarder babies: *New York Daily News*, January 22 and 23, February 24, 1987; *New York Times*, December 12 and 29, 1986, February 8, April 25, May 6, 1987. The *New York Daily News* (February 24, 1987) reported that there were about 300 such infants in city hospitals. See also "Afraid of Babies in Queens," Editorial, *New York Times*, April 23, 1987.

000   Ambitious plans that dwarf immediate concerns: *New York Times*, April 17 and 30, 1986; December 24, 1986.

000, 000   *Newsweek*, December 1, 1986. Early on, the writer says, "I felt pity for those in the streets . . . I'm now deaf to people in the street. I'm not happy about it, but there it is . . . Tell me why they are allowed to make the street their home—day and night, hot and cold—when I can't park a car at the curb without paying a meter.

How is that possible?"

000   Boston University student and response: *Boston Phoenix*, December 30, 1986.

Losing Ground, by Charles Murray, above.

000   *The Needs of Strangers*, by Michael Ignatieff, above.

"No excuses are good enough. . . ." Editorial, *New York Times*, November 6, 1985. According to the "Monthly Report," CIS, June 1987, there were 194 families in the Holland Motel on June 30, 1987.

ECONOMIES OF SCALE

000 ff.   *Remembrance and Poverty: The Road to Potter's Field*, by Judith C. Berck, National Coalition for the Homeless, May 1986. See also *New York Times*, August 8, 1987.

PROSPECTS: FACING THE YEAR 2000

000   "For less than three fourths . . ." The Coalition for the Homeless estimates that the city spends $2.1 million yearly for every 90 families housed in the Martinique Hotel. "According to a variety of not-for-profit agencies, a 90-room hotel can be operated with a full complement of building and social services . . . for approximately $1.5 million." By this calculation, a nonprofit shelter would cost about 71 percent of what is now paid at the Martinique. (*Perchance to Sleep*, cited above.)

Eminent domain: "In September of 1983 the mayor, faced with the prospect of filthy, overpriced hotels, thought the use of eminent domain was 'a good suggestion.' Frederick A.O. Schwarz, Jr., the city's corporation counsel, suggested that this was 'really a pretty simple process' and could begin in a month's time." (*Perchance to Sleep*.)

000   Objections to the seizure and purchase of welfare hotels by the city: Robert Altman, counsel to the New York City Council's Select Committee on the Homeless, argues that the purchase of hotels by eminent domain or other means would be extremely costly. The land value of the Martinique, added to its business value, he believes, might bring its market price to $35 million. This argument, for reasons I have stated, does not seem persuasive. But Altman, voicing what he believes to be the view of many city council members, raises a more important point. The city's ownership of hotels like the Martinique, he feels, would not only divert scarce funds from construction and rehabilitation of permanent housing but would also set an unwise precedent by

placing the city "in the human warehouse [shelter] business." Altman, who has been remarkably patient and helpful in assisting with the preparation of this book, is far more knowlegeable than I about New York. I differ with him cautiously. The counterargument, made frequently by Kim and others, is that the city is already in the human warehouse business. It runs some dreadful shelters of its own. It pays the private sector to run many more. Civil ingenuity, the bootstrap energy of women such as Kim, and the unselfish efforts of nonprofit groups could surely coalesce to operate a "better" warehouse if such institutions must exist at all. By any cost-effective logic, there must be some salutary benefit to be derived from profits that are now lost to South African investors or to owners such as Horn and Sillins. If the Martinique grosses $8 million in a year, at least $3 million (possibly much more) is profit. Part of this money could be used to make this building into a true "regeneration center" for its residents; part could be used to create a fund from which people such as Kim might be awarded loans to rehabilitate some of those boarded buildings that the city owns—many of which, as we have seen, could be rendered habitable very quickly with the rent that keeps a family in the Martinique for just one year. Hostility to this idea may be derived from an unwillingness to see in homeless families the capacity for self-reliant and self-liberating enterprise. My acquaintance with several people such as Kim may bias my opinion; if so, I think the bias is a good one.

The argument that funds should go instead to permanent housing would be more persuasive if such housing were in fact under construction or were going to be built in time to help those who are homeless *now*. Altman observes, in this regard, that New York City's Department of Housing Preservation and Development (HPD), which speaks of rehabilitating 5,000 units every year, "just lacks the capability" to get this done. Last year, says Altman, HPD managed to rehabilitate only 2,900 units. Even the most ambitious plans proposed in New York City do not pretend to meet the housing needs of its poor people for at least two decades. The city's Commission on the Year 2000 expects a shortfall of 372,000 units in 13 years. The 3,000, 4,000 or 5,000 units that the city hopes to build this year, or next, or the year after, offer little hope of housing to poor people in New York within this century.

A real question faces New York City and much of America: Are we going to house our citizens or are we prepared instead to relegate several million people to a permanent existence in an almshouse? The ethical answer to this question is self-evident. But it is barbarous to sacrifice one generation to the notion that we may, perhaps, do something better for the next. To tell Gwen that the city cannot seize the Martinique Hotel to let a decent group of people (like herself) turn it into an enlightened sanctuary—and to add that this cannot be done because the money should be "saved" for building houses that are not now being built, and won't be built in adequate numbers until both her children are adults—is very much like telling someone with still-curable lung cancer that the money for surgery would be more wisely spent in teaching the next generation of the risks of cigarettes. Homeless people need sanctuary now—houses tomorrow.

000      $41 (Red Cross) and $34 (Henry Street Urban Family Center): These figures (the first for a family of three, the second for a family of up to four persons) do not include the costs of social services. The $63 (with tax) charged by the Martinique for a family of four includes no social services either.

Average length of stay shorter in nonprofit shelters: It is fair to note that some of the model shelters exercise a degree of selectivity in their admissions. This factor may increase the speed with which they have been able to find people homes; two more important factors are the social services and partisan support that they provide.

000, 000   Samaritan House holds up to ten families at a time: 25 to 30 in a year. This and other information on Samaritan House: *New York Times*, February 18, 1987.

000   City council study: cited above.

000   Slow progress on transitional shelters: *New York Times*, June 18 and August 20, 1987.

000   The possibilities for building a self-help community within a shelter are limited to some degree by the transient nature of its population. Even in a period of four to six months, however, a good deal of camaraderie develops; former residents, once placed in permanent housing, often retain strong loyalties. Many adults who have left the Martinique since I first visited have returned repeatedly to offer help to those who are still there.

000   For more detailed recommendations, see *Alternatives to the Welfare Hotel*, by Victor Bach and Renee Steinhagen, Community Service Society of New York, 1987.

000, 000   Slow progress on Leonard Stern's initiative: *New York Times*, December 20, 1985; February 11, 1987. See also *New York Times*, Editorial, February 20, 1987. The *Times* reports that "construction unions resisted prefabrication that threatened their traditional allocation of jobs on the site. . . ." The editorial adds that the city charter of New York was also an obstacle to negotiation of a necessary construction loan.

000   Warehousing of low-income units: *New York Daily News*, February 4, 1986. For a comparable situation in Hoboken, New Jersey: *New York Times*, May 1, 1987.

Municipal intervention prior to eviction: New York City has a modest program, which expended $25 million in 1985, to provide such intervention. (*New York Times*, November 14, 1986; January 25, 1987.) Its implementation, according to HRA employees, has not been impressive.

Suggested restrictions on political gifts: Mayor Koch has recently lobbied to restrict those who contribute over $3,000 to the campaign of a member of the city council or the Board of Estimates (of which he is a member) from receiving "discretionary benefits"—e.g., favorable development decisions—for four years after the election to which they have made contributions. "The mayor lobbied very hard, very appropriately," said city council member Ruth Messinger. His efforts were unsuccessful. (*New York Times*, July 13, 1987.)

000, 000   Vacant city-owned apartments and additional units that might be taken by the city for nonpayment of taxes: Extensive discussion of these and related issues are contained in the city council study and report by Harrison Goldin, both cited above.

000   Linkage in Boston: "There is no other city that does parcel-to-parcel linkage. . . . We're going to say if you develop here [downtown], it means you have to develop there [in the neighborhoods]. . . ." (Mayor Ray Flynn, *Boston Globe*, November 7, 1986.) Flynn deserves respect for his persistence on this issue. He has also given strong support to homeless-advocacy groups. The resistance he faces comes not only from developers but also from residents of stable communities fearful of low-income housing and/or homeless shelters. For an example of neighborhood opposition to his efforts: *Boston Globe*, January 30, 1987.

000, 000   Sale of Coliseum site at Columbus Circle in Manhattan and efforts at "linkage" in New York City: *New York Times*, November 30, 1986; February 8 and 23, May 31, 1987.

"If something has extraordinary value, you are losing that value if you don't take advantage of it," said the city's finance commissioner. "Take the Coliseum site. If we put up low-income housing on the site, we probably could have bought every person who would ever live there a mansion out on Long Island and a yacht, and still be ahead of the game. It makes more sense to take the resources being brought into the site to generate low-income housing elsewhere. . . ." (*New York Times,* November 30, 1986.)

Mayor Koch, in February 1987, proposed a somewhat novel linkage plan: The notion was to grant developers permission to build higher residential stuctures than the city's code would ordinarily allow if they would agree to build, preserve or renovate low-income dwellings in the same community or within a half-mile of the luxury tower. A harsh reaction from developers, however, was voiced almost instantly. "Your objectives are admirable," one realtor said. "Unfortunately the market won't allow it." Another developer said the plan might work if the low-income housing could be built a mile from the luxury apartments. (*New York Times,* February 23, 1987.)

000   "That isn't nowhere near where I am at . . ." One recent example: "Families with incomes significantly higher than originally announced, reports the *New York Times* (April 14, 1987), "will be eiligible for apartments under the first phase of the Koch administration's ten-year plan to renovate abandoned city-owned housing. The rule, which was not mentioned when the program was announced, would enable developers to rent most of the first 3,400 apartments under the program to households with incomes up to 20 percent 'in excess of targeted incomes,' according to a city request for proposals from developers." The change in plans, according to critics, makes it "extremely unlikely that low-income families could rent many of the apartments. . . ."

000   Federal policy on public housing, subsidies, Section Eght: *The Faces of Homelessness,* cited above; *Washington Post,* October 9 1986, March 10, 1987.

The Reagan administration has proposed the concept of a "voucher" as a substitute for subsidies. In one version of this plan, vouchers would presumably enable low-income families to purchase units of public housing. The thrust of the proposal is to "privatize" public housing and, in effect, remove the federal government from the issue altogether. In another variation, the administation has proposed the use of vouchers for low-income rentals but would permit them to expire in five years. (Section Eght subsidies generally last for 15 years.) Rental vouchers, as advocated by the Reagan administration, also differ from Section Eight subsidies in that they impose no maximum rent. Tenants may choose housing that rents well above the value of the voucher if they are prepared to pay the supplement themselves. The danger in this is the likelihood that low-income families will attempt to pay the difference from their food and clothing budget and, when this becomes untenable, will be unable to meet rents and face eviction. (See *The Search for Shelter* and *The Faces of Homeless-*

ness, cited above; *Boston Globe*, November 21, 1986; *Washington Post*, October 9, 1986; *New York Times*, May 17, July 19, 1987.)

Obstacles to use of subsidies, Washington, D.C., and elsewhere: *Washington Post*, February 12, 1987; *Hardship in the Heartland*, above.

000   Loss of subsidized units in the next ten years: *New York Times*, April 14, 1987; *Sacramento Bee*, March 29, 1987.

000   Meeting at Riverside Church, November 1986: Author's notes and interview with National Union of the Homeless organizer Chris Sprowal.

Senator Gore announced his sponsorship of "The Homeless Person's Survival Act" at the September 1986 convention of the National Coalition for the Homeless in Washington, D.C.

000   Federal legislation for the homeless, proposed or enacted in 1987: *New York Times*, February 7, March 25, 1987; *Boston Globe*, January 30, 1987; *Washington Post*, March 4 and 24, 1987.

President Reagan's reluctant signing of $1 billion bill for homeless aid: *New York Times*, July 24, 1987.

Toward the Twenty-first Century, Housing in New York City, by Carol Felstein and Michael A. Stegman. The Commission on the Year 2000, New York, 1987.

000   "Over 18.7 million Americans will be unable to find affordable housing by the year 2003, according to a study released by the Neighborhood Reinvestment Corporation, a nonprofit group funded by Congess." The study, titled *At Risk of Loss: The Endangered Future of Low-Income Rental Housing Resources*, was written by Phillip L. Clay, Associate Professor of City Planning at the Massachusetts Institute of Technology. (*Safety Network*, August 1987.)

Books and Documents of Special Relevance

BOOKS

The Unsheltered Woman: Women and Housing in the 80's, ed. by Eugenie Ladner Birch. New Brunswick: Center for Urban Policy Research, 1985.

Families in Peril: An Agenda for Social Change, by Marian Wright Edelman. Cambridge: Harvard University Press, 1987.

Everything in Its Path: Destruction of Community in the Buffalo Creek Flood, by Kai T. Erikson. New York: Simon and Schuster, 1976.

Homelessness in America: A Forced March to Nowhere, by Mary Ellen Hombs, and Mitch Snyder. Washington, D.C.: Community for Creative Non-Violence, 1986.

The Faces of Homelessness, by Marjorie Hope and James Young. Lexington, MA: D.C. Health & Co., 1986.

The Needs of Strangers: An Essay on Privacy, Solidarity, and the Politics of Being Human, by Michael Ignatieff. New York: Penguin Books, 1984.

Family and Nation, by Daniel Patrick Moynihan. San Diego: Harcourt Brace Jovanovich, 1986.

Signal Through the Flames: Mitch Snyder and America's Homeless, by Victoria Rader. Kansas City: Sheed & Ward, 1986.

Blaming the Victim, by William Ryan. New York: Pantheon books, 1971.

Women and Children Last: The Plight of Poor Women in Affluent America, by Ruth Sidel. New York: Viking Penguin, 1986.

DOCUMENTS

Toward the Twenty-first Century, Housing in New York City, by Carol Felstein and Michael A. Stegman, The Commission of the Year 2000, New York, 1987.

Private Lives/Public Spaces: Homeless Adults on the Streets of New York City, by Ellen Baxter and Kim Hopper, Community Service Society of New York, 1981.

One Year Later: The Homeless Poor in New York City, 1982, by Kim Hopper, Ellen Baxter, Stuart Cox, Lawrence Klein, Community Service Society of New York, 1982.

Struggling to Survive in a Welfare Hotel, by John H. Simpson, Margaret Kilduff, C. Douglass Blewett, Community Service Society of New York, 1984.

Hardship in the Heartland: Homelessness in Eight U.S. Cities, by Dan Salerno, Kim Hopper, Ellen Baxter, Community Service Society of New York, 1984.

New York City's Poverty Budget: An Analysis of the Public and Private Expenditures Intended to Benefit the City's Low-Income Population in Fiscal 1983, by David A. Grossman and Geraldine Siolka, Community Service Society of New York, 1984.

The Changing Face of Poverty: Trends in New York City's Population in Poverty: 1960–1990, by Emanuel Tobier, Community Service Society of New York, 1984.

The Making of America's Homeless: From Skid Row to New Poor, 1945–1984, by Kim Hopper and Jill Hamberg, Community Service Society of New York, 1984.

Alternatives to the Welfare Hotel: Using Emergency Assistance to Provide Decent Transitional Housing for Homeless Families, by Victor Bach and Renee Steinhagen, Community Service Society of New York, 1987.

1933/1983—Never Again, by Mario Cuomo, National Governors' Association Task Force on the Homeless, Washington, D.C., 1983.

No Place Like Home: A Report on the Tragedy of Homeless Children and Their Families in Massachusetts, by Ellen Gallagher, Massachusetts Committee for Children and Youth, Boston, 1986.

Room to Spare but Nowhere to Go, by Harrison J. Goldin, Office of the Comptroller, New York, 1987.

The Federal Response to the Homeless Crisis, 3rd Report by the Committee on Government Operations, Ninety-ninth Congress, Washington, D.C., April 1985.

The Search for Shelter, by Nora Richter Greer, The American Institute of Architects, Washington, D.C., 1986.

Increasing Hunger and Declining Help: Barriers to Participation in the Food Stamp Program, Physician Task force on Hunger in America, Harvard School of Public Health, 1986.

HUD Report on Homelessness—II, Subcommittee on Housing and Community Development of the Committee on Banking, Finance and Urban Affairs, House of Representatives, Ninety-ninth Congress, Washington, D.C., December 4, 1985.

A Shelter Is Not a Home, Report of the Manhattan Borough President's Task Force on Housing for Homeless Families, New York, 1987.

Where Do You Go from Nowhere? by the Health and Welfare Council of Central Maryland, Maryland Department of Human Resources, Baltimore, 1986.

Perchance to Sleep: Homeless Children Without Shelter in New York City, National Coalition for the Homeless, New York, 1984.

Single Room Occupancy Hotels: Standing in the Way of the Gentry, National Coalition for the Homeless, New York, 1985.

A Crying Shame: Official Abuse and Neglect of Homeless Infants, National Coalition for the Homeless, New York, 1985.

An Embarrassment of Riches: Homelessness in Connecticut, National Coalition for the Homeless, New York, 1985.

Mid-America in Crisis: Homelessness in Des Moines, National Coalition for the Homeless, New York, 1986.

Remembrance and Poverty: The Road to Potter's Field, National Coalition for the Homeless, New York, 1986.

National Neglect/National Shame: America's Homeless: Outlook Winter 1986–87, National Coalition for the Homeless, New York, 1986.

Stemming the Tide of Displacement: Housing Policies for Preventing Homelessness, Joint Report of the National Coalition for the Homeless, Community Action for Legal Services, New York Lawyers for the Public Interest, New York, 1986.

Cruel Brinkmanship Revisited: The Winter of 1985–86, National Coalition for the Homeless, New York, 1986.

Report of the Committee on General Welfare on the Homeless Crisis, New York City Council, January 22, 1987.

A State of Emergency: Hunger in the Empire State, New York State Committee Against Hunger, New York, 1985.

The Summer Hunger Crisis, New York State Committee Against Hunger, New York, 1985.

Status of Black New York Report, New York Urban League, 1984.

National Growth in Homelessness: Winter 1986 and Beyond: A

Follow-up Report, The Partnership for the Homeless, New York, 1986.

The Homeless: Overview of the Problem and the Federal Response, by Karen Spar and Monique C. Austin, Congressional Research Service, The Library of Congress, September 1984.

Homelessness in America's Cities; Ten Case Studies, U.S. Conference of Mayors, Washington, D.C., 1984.

The Growth of Hunger, Homelessness and Poverty in America's Cities in 1985, U.S. Conference of Mayors, Washington, D.C., 1986.

A Status Report on Homeless Families in America's Cities, U.S. Conference of Mayors, Washington, D.C., 1987.

Homelessness: A Complex Problem and the Federal Response, U.S. General Accounting Office, Washington, D.C., 1985.

The National Health Care for the Homeless Program: The First Year, by James D. Wright, Eleanor Weber-Burdin, Janet W. Knight, Julie A. Lam, Social and Demographic Research Institute, University of Massachusettts, Amherst, 1987.

Acknowledgments

The initial version of this book was written with the help of Debby Stone and its final version with the help of Beth Epstein. Gage Cogswell typed the book in its successive stages, a grueling task for which I cannot offer adequate thanks.

Throughout this process I have relied upon the research skills, good taste and calm advice of Tisha Graham. We have worked together on several books over the past ten years, but never one so painful. For her meticulous attention to questions of accuracy in New York City, I owe her special gratitude.

A generous woman named Carol Porter provided some of the most sensitive insights into the substance of this work at a stage when its completion was uncertain. She died suddenly before the book was finished. I grieve for her and miss her deeply.

The book has been read at various times by Ruth Sidel, Roger Boshes, Kim Hopper, David Beseda, Gretchen Buchenholtz, Sandy Brawders, and Diana Cooper. Robert Altman, legal aide to the New York City Council's Committee on the Homeless, and Scott Rosenberg of the Legal Aid Society have been helpful in the clarification of important details. Keith Summa of the National Coalition for the Homeless, Jacqueline Pitts of the Community Service Society of New York, and several officials of the New York City Human Resources Administration have also been of help in clarifying questions on welfare procedures in New York.

Belle Newton has been my most patient guide and critic since this work began in 1985. I am unusually privileged to have had Jim Wade as my editor.

Most essential were the trust and openness of residents of homeless shelters and some of the health professionals and social workers who are in contact with them daily. For their willingness to share their stories with a stranger, I am grateful.

DATE DUE